D0710686

Pittsburgh Series in Bibliography

Pittsburgh Series in Bibliography

HART CRANE: A DESCRIPTIVE BIBLIOGRAPHY
Joseph Schwartz and Robert C. Schweik

F. SCOTT FITZGERALD: A DESCRIPTIVE BIBLIO-
GRAPHY
Matthew J. Bruccoli

F. SCOTT FITZGERALD

A DESCRIPTIVE BIBLIOGRAPHY

Matthew J. Bruccoli

UNIVERSITY OF
PITTSBURGH PRESS
1972

Library of Congress Catalog Card Number 77–181395
ISBN 0–8229–3239–3
Copyright © 1972, University of Pittsburgh Press
All rights reserved
Henry M. Snyder & Co., Inc., London
Manufactured in the United States of America

Unreservedly

to Scottie

naturally

Contents

x   Contents

These scholars merit my special gratitude:

JENNIFER ATKINSON
FREDSON BOWERS
ALEXANDER CLARK
C. E. FRAZER CLARK, JR.
JOHN COOK WYLLIE

Acknowledgments

I BEGAN this bibliography as a graduate student in 1957 with the encouragement of my cherished friend and teacher, the late John Cook Wyllie. If he were still helping me, this book would be better. I owe another special debt of gratitude to C. E. Frazer Clark, Jr, the best book collector I know. Jennifer Atkinson checked every entry in this bibliography—and did more. My largest debt is to my wife: Arlyn, more than anyone else, made it possible for me to do this bibliography.

I thank the following librarians: William Runge and John Via, Alderman Library, The University of Virginia; T. A. J. Burnett and the superb staff of the British Museum; Roger Stoddard, Houghton Library, Harvard University; Dean Keller and Hyman W. Kritzer, Kent State University Library; Willie Stephenson and the staff of The Library of Congress; J. Q. Bennett, William Cagle, and David Randall, Lilly Library, Indiana University; Mrs. Mary Goolsby and the staff of the McKissick Library, University of South Carolina; W. D. Thorn, National Library of Australia; Richard Olson, Northwestern University Library; Charles Mann, Pennsylvania State University Library; Alexander Clark, Robert S. Fraser, and Mrs. Wanda Randall, Princeton University Library; Donald Gallup (my first bibliography teacher), Yale University Library; and J. M. Edelstein, UCLA Library.

My work has benefited from the help of bookdealers, and I thank the Argosy Bookshop, Robert

Black, Covent Garden Bookshop, I. D. Edrich, Walter Goldwater, Harold Graves, Guildhall Bookshop, Douglas Jacobs, Peter Keisogloff, Jack Neiburg, Michael Pappantonio, Paul Richards, Anthony Rota, John S. Van E. Kohn, L. A. Wallrich, Henry W. Wenning, and Robert Wilson. I thank the following collectors and scholars: Jeanne Bennett, Fredson Bowers, Allan Covici, Ben Grauer, James Meriwether, Henry Dan Piper, Landon T. Raymond, and R. L. Samsell. I thank the following students and research assistants: Jan Abrahamsen (especially Mrs. Abrahamsen), Pam Barrett, Linda Berry, Amy Boyd, Timothy Carpenter, I. S. Skelton, and James West.

I thank the following publishers and literary agents: Max Reinhardt and Guido A. Waldman, The Bodley Head; Philip Coleman, Charles Scribner's Sons; Ian Parsons and Norah Smallwood, Chatto & Windus; Ivan Von Auw, Jr. and Patricia Powell, Harold Ober Associates; Miss Patricia Cork, Hughes Massie Ltd.; Roger Mayer, Metro-Goldwyn-Mayer; Robert Nance, University of South Carolina Press; and F. T. Smith, William Collins Sons. I thank the following institutions and foundations for support: American Council of Learned Societies, American Philosophical Society, the Department of English of the University of South Carolina, and the University of South Carolina Research and Productive Scholarship Fund. I am indebted to John C. Guilds, formerly Head, Department of English, University of South Carolina. I thank Paul Jureidini for accompanying me on a hundred trips. And I thank Frederick A. Hetzel, Director of the University of Pittsburgh Press, for his support and Louise Craft, Associate Editor, for her final editing of the manuscript.

Introduction

A L L bibliographies are provisional. This bibliography is the product of the process of diminution and the process of accretion operating at the same time. It began as a more ambitious work, and at one point I planned to include an inventory of Fitzgerald's manuscripts. But 1961 became 1971—and still the bibliography was not published. More and more work on Fitzgerald was being done, and some of it might have been better if the authors had been able to consult a descriptive bibliography. An unpublished bibliography—no matter how comprehensive—is not usable: publication is the essential act of scholarship. An augmented edition of this bibliography is planned.

This descriptive bibliography of F. Scott Fitzgerald's writings is limited to writings by Fitzgerald. It does not list writings about Fitzgerald, except in cases where they include something by Fitzgerald published for the first time—see Section F.[1] There is also a brief alphabetical list of principal works about Fitzgerald in Appendix 10.

FORMAT

Section A lists chronologically all books, pamphlets, and broadsides wholly or substantially by

---

1. For writings about Fitzgerald, the reader is directed to Jackson R. Bryer, *The Critical Reputation of F. Scott Fitzgerald* (Hamden, Conn.: Archon Books, 1967).

Fitzgerald—including all printings of all editions in English. At the end of this section there is an AA supplemental list of collections of Fitzgerald's work which do not include any material by Fitzgerald published for the first time.

The numbering system for Section A indicates the edition and printing for each entry. Thus for *This Side of Paradise*, A 5.1.a indicates that it is the fifth title published by Fitzgerald, and that the entry is for the first edition (1), first printing (a). States are indicated by inferior numbers—thus *A 8.1.b₂* is the second state of the second printing of the first edition of *The Beautiful and Damned*. Issues are indicated by asterisks—thus *A 8.1.a** is the Canadian issue of the first printing of the first edition of *B&D*. Special problems are indicated by daggers—thus *A 6.1.a†* is the Australasian binding of the first-printing sheets of the first edition of *Flappers and Philosophers*.

Section B lists chronologically all titles in which material by Fitzgerald appears for the first time in a book or pamphlet. Items that were previously unpublished are so identified. The first printings only of these books are described, but the English editions are also noted. It has been difficult to set policy for Section B. There are many memoirs that quote recollected conversations with Fitzgerald or that quote bits of letters—sometimes from memory. Therefore, the B entries have been limited to the first book appearances of material that was unquestionably written by Fitzgerald. But there is a supplemental BB section of borderline items which are, in my judgment, important. This BB group is admittedly selective.

Section C lists chronologically the first publication in magazines and newspapers of material by Fitzgerald. The first English publication of stories is also noted. A few reprintings are noted in this section in cases where the fact of republication seems especially important   for example, syndication of a story or an article. It is a flaw of this bibliography that it does not list every reprinting of each item in Section C. A bibliography should provide evidence for tracing the development of an author's reputation and career in terms of the circulation of his work.[2]

Section D includes manuscript and typescript material by Fitzgerald quoted in auction, bookdealer, and library-exhibition catalogues. It does not include books listed in these catalogues unless the book is inscribed by Fitzgerald. Because some of these catalogues are now hard to obtain, I have taken the unusual step of requoting Fitzgerald's words printed in them. These entries are arranged chronologically, with the undatable catalogues at the end.

Section E lists chronologically interviews with Fitzgerald.

Section F lists—alphabetically by author—articles that include material by Fitzgerald. The compilation of this section involved many decisions about borderline cases.

Section G lists chronologically blurbs by Fitzgerald on dust jackets of books by other authors.

Section H lists chronologically keepsakes with material by Fitzgerald. A keepsake is here defined as a separately printed small item with a limited number of copies not offered for sale. The keepsakes listed in this section do not include any previously

---

2. The details about Fitzgerald's most frequently anthologized stories can help the scholar to understand the author's public image. This information would be especially useful in reconstructing the Fitzgerald revival. Which stories were reprinted between 1945 and 1951? How many were "flapper" stories? Which stories were included in American literature textbooks? What about the reprinting of stories in England? I intend to remedy this defect in an augmented edition.

unpublished material by Fitzgerald that can be considered either substantial or important. Some items that might be considered keepsakes are included in Sections A and B: see A 21, A 23, A 25, A 29, A 30, B 5, B 30, B 68.

Section I is a bibliography of Zelda Fitzgerald's publications. It lists chronologically all printings of all editions of *Save Me the Waltz* (in full description) and the first appearance of her contributions to magazines and newspapers. Zelda Fitzgerald's works are in the body of the bibliography, rather than being relegated to an appendix, because they were often intertwined with those of her husband. The items in which F. Scott Fitzgerald had a hand or shared the by-line are cross-referenced to Section C.

Appendix 1 lists English-language editions of Fitzgerald story collections published in Japan.[3]

Appendix 2 lists unlocated clippings with material by Fitzgerald that he preserved in his scrapbooks. It is a hunting list.

Appendix 3 lists the two published plays based on Fitzgerald stories.

Appendix 4 lists the unpublished plays by Fitzgerald produced in St. Paul, Minn.

Appendix 5 lists those mimeographed film scripts by Fitzgerald that I have seen.

Appendix 6 lists Fitzgerald's movie-writing assignments.

Appendix 7 lists movies made from Fitzgerald's stories and novels.

Appendix 8 lists Braille editions of Fitzgerald's writings.

---

3. It will no doubt be wondered why I have omitted translations of F. Scott Fitzgerald's work, for one of the things that may interest scholars is the spread of Fitzgerald's reputation abroad. A separate checklist of translations appears in the *Fitzgerald/Hemingway Annual 1972*.

Appendix 9 discusses the significance of Fitzgerald's contracts, and facsimiles those for his novels.

Appendix 10 lists in alphabetical order by author the principal works about Fitzgerald.

TERMS AND METHODS

Edition. All the copies of a book printed from a single setting of type—including all printings from standing type, from plates, or by offset.

Printing. All the copies of a book printed at one time (without removing the type or plates from the press).

State. States are created by an alteration not affecting the conditions of issue to some copies of a given printing (by stop-press correction or cancellation of leaves). *States* occur within printings and normally—but not invariably—result from prepublication changes. See A 8.1.b$_1$ and A 8.1.b$_2$; A 15.1.a$_1$ and A 15.1.a$_2$; A 17.1.a$_1$ and A 17.1.a$_2$.

Issue. Issues are created by an alteration affecting the conditions of publication or sale (usually a title-page alteration) to some copies of a given printing. *Issues* occur within printings and normally—but not invariably—result from changes made after initial publication of part of the printing. See A 8.1.a*, A 9.1.a*, and A 19.1.b*. *Simultaneous issues* are possible—for example, the English and American issues of a single printing or the original publisher's and a book club's issues when these are created by stop-press alteration of the title page. But there is no known case of simultaneous issue for Fitzgerald.[4]

---

4. It is possible to define *issue* in terms of distribution rather than in terms of printing. One could consider that an *issue* is created whenever a printing is introduced into a publisher's series, or released by a different publisher, or

The terms *issue* and *state* have been restricted to the sheets of the book. Binding or dust-jacket variants have no bearing on *state* and *issue* as properly applied. See A 6.1.a†.

Dust jackets for Section A entries have been described in detail because they are part of the original publication effort. There is, of course, no certainty that a jacket now on a copy of a book was always on it. Collectors and dealers frequently improve copies by transferring dust jackets.

The form of entry for first English editions is somewhat condensed from the full form for first American editions—for example, type size and typeface are omitted. Gaps are specified in English signings—thus *A-I K-U X-Z*[8]. Bibliographers normally assume that the reader will adjust for the use of a twenty-three-letter alphabet in books printed in England; but I believe it is better to be specific in these cases. See A 15.2.a for a case in which the twenty-three-letter system broke down.

For binding cloth designations I have used the same system as in Jacob Blanck, ed., *Bibliography*

---

even sold at a new price. Under this usage the Modern Library printing of *The Great Gatsby* (A 11.1.e) would be the Modern Library issue. This usage would also be applicable to the English so-called "cheap editions" of Fitzgerald—which are not new editions at all (A 9.2.b). The Chatto & Windus "cheap edition" of *Tender is the Night* is a remainder of the first printing with the price altered by a label on the dust jacket (A 14.2.a†). It represents a fresh attempt by the publisher to market (or issue) the title; but no changes were made to the sheets of the book, and no reprinting occurred. Since it is one of the afflictions of bibliography that its four basic terms (*edition, printing, issue,* and *state*) have been applied inconsistently and whimsically—*issue* has probably been the most abused of these terms—I have elected to use *issue* conservatively. It may very well be that a new term is needed to cover the situations that arise in twentieth-century publishing when plates are leased to another publisher—i.e., when a complete printing is reissued by a different publisher from the one who first made the plates. Perhaps a term like *printing-issue* would serve.

of American Literature (New Haven: Yale University Press, 1955), which in one system of book cloth manufacturers. These cloth grains are illustrated in each volume of the *BAL;* and I have provided a brief description after the symbols—thus V *cloth (fine linen-like grain).*

The spines of bindings or dust jackets are printed horizontally unless otherwise stated. But the reader is to assume that vertically printed spines read top to bottom unless otherwise stated.

The term *perfect binding* refers to books in which the pages are held together with an adhesive along the back edge after the folds have been trimmed off.

I am color-blind. All the color identifications have been supplied by Jennifer E. Atkinson under my instruction to keep the color terms simple.

In the descriptions of title pages, bindings, and dust jackets, the color of the lettering is black unless otherwise stated. The style of type is roman unless otherwise specified. A color designation holds for subsequent lines until a color change is specified. Thus for the front cover of *The Evil Eye* (see A 3):

'[orange outlined in black] THE · EVIL · EYE | [black] A Musical Comedy in Two Acts | [double rule] | PRESENTED BY | [orange] The Princeton University | Triangle Club | [black] 1915–1916 | [device] | BOOK BY | E. Wilson, Jr., '16 | LYRICS BY | F. Scott Fitzgerald, '17 | [device] | MUSIC BY | Paul B. Dickey, '17 | AND | F. Warburton Guilbert, '19 | [device] | PRODUCED UNDER THE DIRECTION OF | Lewis Hooper | [device] | THE JOHN CHURCH COMPANY | CINCINNATI NEW YORK LONDON | Metzerott 16'.

The first line is printed in orange outlined in black; the next three lines are in black; the next two lines are in orange; the remaining eighteen lines are in black.

Dates supplied in brackets do not appear on the title pages. Usually—but not invariably—they are taken from the copyright pages.

The descriptions do not provide the thickness of leaves and the bulk of the sheets because there is no case for Fitzgerald in which these measurements are required to differentiate printings.

Locations are given in the National Union Catalogue symbols—with these exceptions:

BM: British Museum
Bodleian: Bodleian Library
LC: Library of Congress
Lilly: Lilly Library, Indiana University
MJB: Collection of Matthew J. Bruccoli
RLS: Collection of R. L. Samsell

For BM deposit copies the words *deposit-stamp* precede the date to distinguish the date stamped in the book from the date in the deposit ledger.

The Scribners code is given for printings in which it appears. The first letter in this code designates the printing (or what Scribners regards as a new printing); the digits indicate month and year; and the bracketed letters indicate the printer. Thus *A-1.63 [Col]* means that the book is the first printing dated January 1963, and that it was printed at the Colonial Press.

Scribners almost certainly prepared salesmen's dummies and advance review copies of Fitzgerald's books; but I have never seen a dummy, and have seen only one advance copy in wrappers (A 14.1.a†).

For paperbacks, the serial number provided is that of the first printing. Paperback publishers often change the serial numbers in later printings; but such changes have not been noted in this bibliography.

Freak copies—that is, books with the gatherings out of order or with repeated gatherings—are without bibliographical significance and have been ignored in this bibliography.

It is desirable in bibliographical description to avoid end-of-line hyphens in transcriptions. Words should not be divided in a transcription unless they are divided in the original. Because of word length and a measured line, however, it is impossible always to achieve this optimum. End-of-line hyphens have been avoided wherever possible and always when a hyphen would create ambiguity in spelling.

First publication of material by Fitzgerald in individual numbers of the *Fitzgerald Newsletter* is listed in Section C, and articles about Fitzgerald that include previously unpublished material by him are listed in Section F. The bound volume (from a new setting of type) of the *Fitzgerald Newsletter* has been listed in Section B. The volumes of the *Fitzgerald/Hemingway Annual* have been similarly treated.

A bibliography is outdated the day it is published. Addenda and corrigenda are earnestly solicited.

The University of South Carolina
21 August 1971

A. Separate Publications

All books, pamphlets, and broadsides wholly or substantially by Fitzgerald, including all printings of all
editions in English, arranged chronologically. At the
end of Section A there is an AA supplemental list of
collections of Fitzgerald's work which do not include
any material by Fitzgerald published for the first
time.

A 1 "FIE! FIE! FI–FI–"
Script

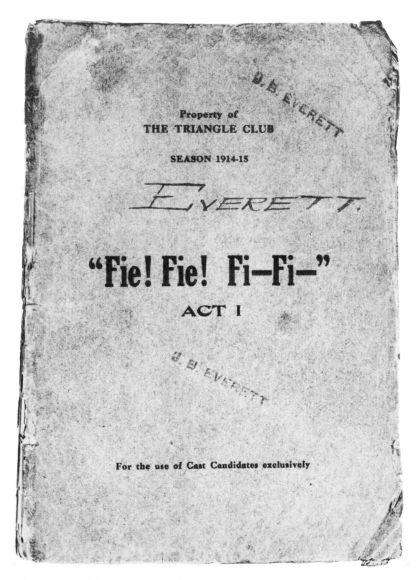

A 1: Cover title, Act 1, 9″ x 6″

Cover titles only for both acts.

A 1: Cover title, Act 2, 9" x 6"

Act 1

Fifty-two pages numbered 4–24, with fourteen blank leaves. Five unbound leaves of lyrics attached, printed on rectos only.

[1]²⁶

Act 2

Thirty-two pages numbered 2–14, with nine blank leaves.

[1]¹⁶

Typography and paper: Forty-four lines per page. Wove paper.

Binding: Act 1—tan gray wrappers; Act 2—gray wrappers. Both wrappers printed in black. Stapled.

Publication: Acting script; not for sale. Probably printed fall 1914. Number of copies unknown.

Locations: MJB (with attached leaves); NjP.

Notes: The book for the show was written by Fitzgerald and revised by Walker M. Ellis, who took full credit. All the lyrics were by Fitzgerald. See Bruccoli, "F. Scott Fitzgerald's First Book Appearance," *PBSA,* LIX (First Quarter 1965), 58.

A 2 FIE! FIE! FI-FI!

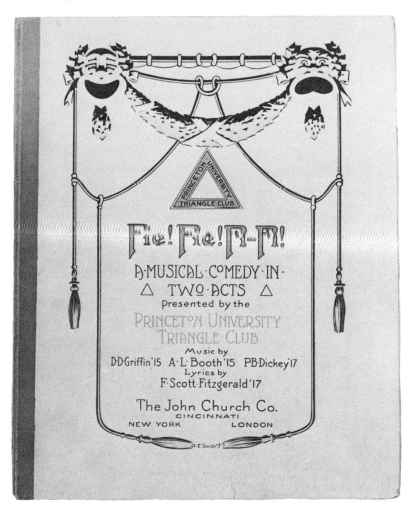

A 2: Cover title

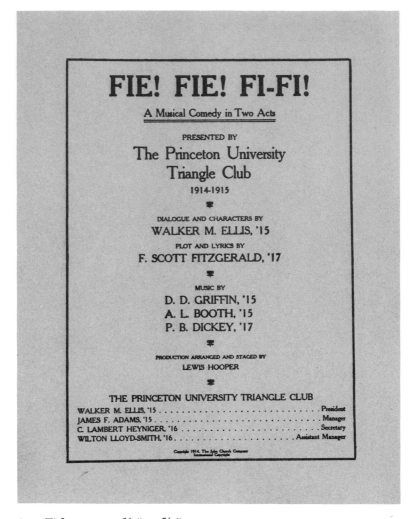

A 2: Title page, 12¹⁄₁₆″ x 9⁵⁄₁₆″

Copyright notice on p. 3 has year hand-corrected in ink: 'Copyright, MCMXIV, by The John Church Company | International Copyright'.

Plate number 17389 appears on every page of music.

[Cincinnati, New York, & London: The John Church Co., 1914.]

[i–ii] [1–2] 3–91 [92–94]

|1–6|⁸

Contents: pp. i–ii: blank; p. 1: title; p. 2: 'MUSICAL NUM-
BERS' [list of 19]; pp. 3–91: music and lyrics headed 'Opening Chorus Act I' [copyright notice at bottom of p. 3]; pp.
92–94: blank.

Lyrics by F. Scott Fitzgerald: Act I—"Opening Chorus,"
"Gentlemen Bandits We," "A Slave to Modern Improvements,"
"In Her Eyes," "What the Manicure Lady Knows," "Good-night
and Good-bye," "Round and Round," "Chatter Trio," "Finale";
Act II—"Rose of the Night," "Men," "In the Dark," "Love or
Eugenics," "Reminiscence," "Fie! Fie! Fi-Fi!," "The Monte Carlo
Moon," "Finale."

Paper: Wove paper.

Binding: White boards, printed on front cover in black and
orange: '[within frame consisting of tragic and comic masks
and curtain ropes] [Triangle Club device] | [orange outlined
in black] Fie! Fie! Fi-Fi! | [black] A·MUSICAL·CᵒMEDY·IN· |
△ TWᵒ·ACTS △ | Presented by the | [orange] PRINCETON·UNI-
VERSITY | TRIANGLE·CLUB | [black] Music by | D·D·Griffin '15
A·L·Booth '15 P·B·Dickey '17 | Lyrics by | F·Scott·Fitzgerald
'17 | The John Church Co. | CINCINNATI | NEW YORK LON-
DON | I·E·Swart'. Orange cloth spine. All edges trimmed.

Publication: Number of copies, publication date, and price
unknown. Sold at performances. Opening performance: 19
December 1914.

Locations: Lilly; MJB; NjP; OKentU.

Notes: Copyright notice hand-corrected in all copies seen. It
is impossible to tell in these copies what the original copyright date was.

Fitzgerald's lyrics are reprinted in A 32.

A 3 THE EVIL EYE

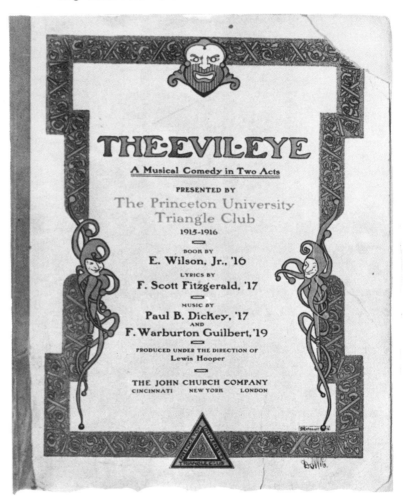

A 3: Cover title

Contents: pp. i–ii: blank; p. 1: title; p. 2: 'Musical Numbers' [list of eighteen]; pp. 3–92: music and lyrics headed ' "The Evil Eye" | Act I | Opening Chorus' [copyright notice at bottom of p. 3]; pp. 93–94: blank.

Lyrics by F. Scott Fitzgerald: Act I—"Opening," "I've Got My Eyes on You," "On Dreams Alone," "The Evil Eye," "What I'll Forget," "Over the Waves to Me," "On Her Eukalali," "Jump Off the Wall," "Finale"; Act II—"Opening," "Harris from Paris," "Twilight," "The Never, Never Land," "My Idea of Love," "Other Eyes," "The Girl of the Golden West," "With Me."

Paper: Wove paper.

Binding: White boards, printed on front cover in black and orange: '[within frame consisting of mask, jesters, arabesque decorations, and Triangle Club device] [orange outlined in black] THE·EVIL·EYE | [black] A Musical Comedy in Two Acts | [double rule] | PRESENTED BY | [orange] The Princeton University | Triangle Club | [black] 1915–1916 | [device] | BOOK BY | E. Wilson, Jr., '16 | LYRICS BY | F. Scott Fitzgerald, '17 | [device] | MUSIC BY | Paul B. Dickey, '17 | AND | F. Warburton Guilbert, '19 | [device] | PRODUCED UNDER THE DIRECTION OF | Lewis Hooper | [device] | THE JOHN CHURCH COMPANY | CINCINNATI NEW YORK LONDON | Metzerott 16'. Orange cloth spine. All edges trimmed.

Publication: Number of copies, publication date, and price unknown. Sold at performances. Opening performance: 18 December 1915.

Locations: MJB; NjP; OKentU.

Notes: A copy of the printed acting script is at the Princeton University Library. It includes none of Fitzgerald's lyrics.

Fitzgerald's lyrics are reprinted in A 32.

THE EVIL EYE

A Musical Comedy in Two Acts

PRESENTED BY

The Princeton University
Triangle Club
1915-1916

BOOK BY
E. WILSON, Jr., '16

LYRICS BY
F. SCOTT FITZGERALD, '17

MUSIC BY
PAUL B. DICKEY, '17
AND
F. WARBURTON GUILBERT, '19

PIANO SOLO ARRANGEMENTS AND ORCHESTRATIONS BY
RICHARD L. WEAVER

PRODUCED UNDER THE DIRECTION OF
LEWIS HOOPER

THE PRINCETON UNIVERSITY TRIANGLE CLUB
C. LAMBERT HEYNIGER, '16 . . . . President
WILTON LLOYD-SMITH, '16 . . . . Manager
P. MACKAY STURGES, '17 . . . . Assistant Manager

Copyright 1915, The John Church Company
International Copyright

A 3: Title page, 12″ x 9⅚₆″

Copyright notice on p. 3 reads: 'Copyright MCMXV by The John Church Company | International Copyright'.

Plate number 17623 appears on every page of music.

[Cincinnati, New York, & London: The John Church Co., 1915.]

[i–ii] [1–2] 3–92 [93–94]

[1–6]⁸

A 4 SAFETY FIRST

A 4: Cover title

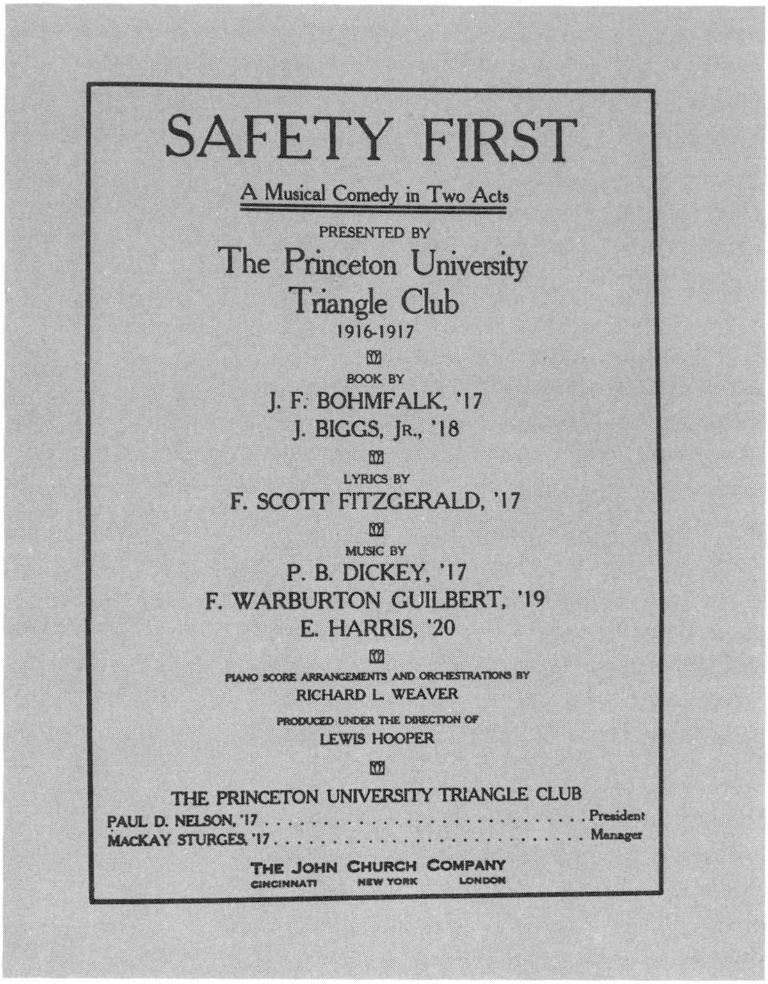
SAFETY FIRST

A Musical Comedy in Two Acts

PRESENTED BY

The Princeton University
Triangle Club
1916-1917

BOOK BY
J. F. BOHMFALK, '17
J. BIGGS, JR., '18

LYRICS BY
F. SCOTT FITZGERALD, '17

MUSIC BY
P. B. DICKEY, '17
F. WARBURTON GUILBERT, '19
E. HARRIS, '20

PIANO SCORE ARRANGEMENTS AND ORCHESTRATIONS BY
RICHARD L. WEAVER

PRODUCED UNDER THE DIRECTION OF
LEWIS HOOPER

THE PRINCETON UNIVERSITY TRIANGLE CLUB
PAUL D. NELSON, '17 . . . . President
MACKAY STURGES, '17 . . . . Manager

THE JOHN CHURCH COMPANY
CINCINNATI NEW YORK LONDON

A 4: Title page, 12″ x 9$\frac{5}{16}$″

Copyright notice on p. 5 reads: 'Copyright, MCMXVI, by The John Church Company | International Copyright'.

Plate number 17867 appears on every page of music.

[Cincinnati, New York, & London: The John Church Co., 1916.]

[1–4] 5–99 [100]

[1–5]⁸ [6]¹⁰

Contents: p. 1: title; p. 2: 'MUSICAL NUMBERS' [list of twenty-two]; p. 3: cast; p. 4: blank; pp. 5–99: music and lyrics headed 'Opening | (A) Prologue | Spirit of the Future' [copyright notice at bottom of p. 5]; p. 100: blank. The lyrics are out of order on pp. 51–52.

     Lyrics by F. Scott Fitzgerald: "Prologue," "Garden of Arden"; Act I—"Opening Chorus," "Send Him to Tom," "One-Lump Percy," "Where Did Bridget Kelly Get Her Persian Temperament?," "It Is Art," "Safety First," "Charlotte Corday," "Underneath the April Rain," "Finale—Dance, Lady, Dance"; Act II, Scene 1—"Safety First," "Hello, Temptation," "When That Beautiful Chord Came True," "Rag-Time Melodrama"; Scene 2 —"Opening," "Take Those Hawaiian Songs Away," "The Vampires Won't Vampire for Me," "The Hummin' Blues," "Down in Front," "Finale."

Paper: Wove paper.

Binding: White boards, printed on front cover in black, orange, yellow, red, and blue: '[two gowned women against oriental mask] [pale blue outlined in red] SAFETY FIRST! | PRESENTED BY | [black] V. NEWLIN '19 | [pale blue outlined in red] THE PRINCETON TRIANGLE CLUB'. Orange cloth spine. All edges trimmed.

Publication: Number of copies, publication date, and price unknown. Sold at performances. Opening performance: 15 December 1916.

Locations: MJB; NjP; OKentU.

Notes: A copy of the printed acting script is at the Princeton University Library. It includes none of Fitzgerald's lyrics.
     Fitzgerald's lyrics are reprinted in A 32.

A 5 THIS SIDE OF PARADISE

A 5.1.a
First edition, first printing (1920)

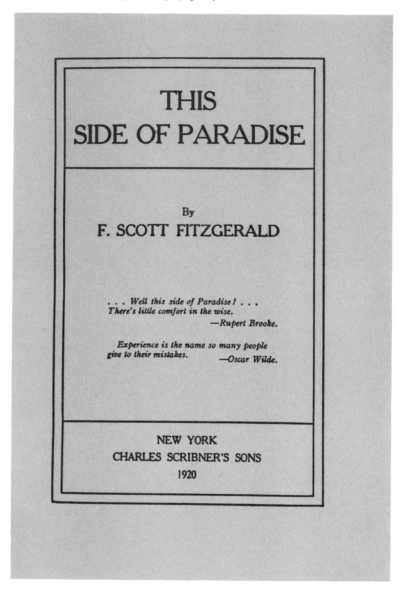

THIS
SIDE OF PARADISE

By
F. SCOTT FITZGERALD

. . . Well this side of Paradise! . . .
There's little comfort in the wise.
—*Rupert Brooke.*

Experience is the name so many people
give to their mistakes. —*Oscar Wilde.*

NEW YORK
CHARLES SCRIBNER'S SONS
1920

A 5.1.a: 7⁹⁄₁₆″ x 5⅛″

COPYRIGHT, 1920, BY
CHARLES SCRIBNER'S SONS

Published April, 1920

[i–viii] [1–2] 3–168 [169–170] 171–176 [177–178] 179–305 [306–312]

[1–20][8]

Contents: p. i: half title; p. ii: blank; p. iii: title; p. iv: copyright; p. v: 'TO | SIGORNEY FAY'; p. vi: blank; p. vii: contents; p. viii: blank; p. 1: 'BOOK ONE | THE ROMANTIC EGOTIST'; p. 2: blank; pp. 3–305: text, headed 'CHAPTER I | AMORY, SON OF BEATRICE', p. 169: 'INTERLUDE | MAY, 1917— FEBRUARY, 1919'; p. 177: 'BOOK TWO | THE EDUCATION OF A PERSONAGE'; pp. 306–312: blank.

Typography and paper: 11 point on 12, Old Style. 5¾″ (6¹⁄₁₆″) x 3½″; thirty-five (occasionally thirty-six) lines per page. Running heads: rectos, chapter titles; versos, 'THIS SIDE OF PARADISE'. Wove paper.

Binding: Green B cloth (linen-like grain). Front blindstamped: 'THIS SIDE OF | PARADISE | By F. Scott Fitzgerald'. Spine goldstamped: 'THIS | SIDE | OF | PARADISE | [rule] | Fitzgerald | SCRIBNERS'. White wove endpapers of sized stock. Top and bottom edges trimmed.

Dust jacket: Front has drawing of man and woman in evening dress against orange background, signed by W. E. Hill: '[white outlined in black] THIS SIDE OF | PARADISE | By F. Scott Fitzgerald'. Spine lettered in black: 'THIS | SIDE | OF | PARADISE | [rule] | Fitzgerald | SCRIBNERS'. Back has list of sixteen titles, starting with *Blacksheep! Blacksheep!* and ending with *Hiker Joy.* Front flap has blurb for *TSOP;* back flap has ad for *Scribner's Magazine.*

Publication: 3,000 copies of the first printing. Published 26 March 1920. $1.75.

Printing: Composed and printed by the Scribner Press; plates made by the New York Electrotyping Co. Bound by the Scribner Press.

Dust jacket for A 5.1.a

Locations: Lilly; MJD (dj); NjP. Fitzgerald's marked copy is owned by his daughter.

Note one: Revisions were made in the plates in the fourth (May 1920) and seventh (August 1920) printings. See Bruccoli, "A Collation of F. Scott Fitzgerald's *This Side of Paradise*," *Studies in Bibliography,* IX (1957), 263–265; also Bruccoli, "Fitzgerald's Marked Copy of *This Side of Paradise*," *Fitzgerald/Hemingway Annual 1971,* pp. 64–69.

Collation

[v]	SIGORNEY [SIGOURNEY	4		
3.1	trait [trait,	4		
3.2	few [few,	4		
4.1	Margaritta [Margherita	7		
6.7	raconteur [raconteuse	4		
7.33	Ashvill [Asheville	7		
17.3	'Casey-Jones ["Casey-Jones	4		
18.22	Ghunga Dhin [Gunga Dhin	7		
18.26	Rhinehart [Rinehart	4	[Rineheart	7
28.10	ex-ambassador [ex-minister	4		
51.9	Litt. [Lit.	4		
51.29	*Cumizza* [*Cunizza*	4		
56.2	*Litt.* [*Lit.*	4		
80.29	Cambell [Campbell	4		
116.6	flare [metier	4		
117.30	*Litt.* [*Lit.*	4		
119.4	*Booth. . .). [Booth. . .)*	4		
120.13	Dachari [Daiquiri	4		
154.20	CECELIA [CECILIA	7		
176.36	Johnston [Johnson	7		
180.24	*tickle-toe on the soft carpet* [*shimmy enthusiastically*	4		
182.27	*just* [*utterly*	4		
184.1	impeachable [unimpeachable	4		
224.24	Jenny Gerhardt [Jennie Gerhardt	4		
224.25	McKenzie [Mackenzie	4		
226.35	Benêt [Benét	4		
228.23	I restless [I am restless	4		
229.13	Kerenski [Kerensky	4		
229.17	Gunmeyer [Guynemer	4		
232.22	Gouveneer [Gouverneur	4		
233.14	Bennet [Bennett	7		
235.15	*sight,* [*sight*	4		
235.24	*life* [*Life*	4		

235.25   *One*   [—*one*   4
240.28   *langeur*   [*langueur*   7
242.26   Celleni   [Cellini   7
251.9   Stretch   [Scratch   4
252.34   tens   [teens   7
294.23   Mackeys   [Mackays   4
296.28   deep   [much   4
300.27   born   [borne   7
304.19   God's   [Gods   4

Note two: Cut versions of *This Side of Paradise* were serialized in several newspapers after book publication. The following serializations have been located:

Chicago Herald-Examiner, 23 January–11 March 1921
Atlanta Georgian, 24 February–18 April 1921
New York Daily News, 30 April–10 June 1923

Note three: TSOP was sold in Australia by Whitcombe & Tombs and in Canada by Copp, Clark Company (Whitney Darrow to Maxwell Perkins, 1 August 1922). No copies of these books have been located; and it is impossible to determine whether they were separate printings, the Scribners sheets issued with new title pages, or the Scribners sheets in special bindings. See A 6.1.a†, A 8.1.a*, and A 9.1.a*.

August 1, 1922

Memo for Mr. Perkins:

All Fitzgerald books have been published in Canada by Copp, Clark Company.

"This Side of Paradise" and "Flappers and Philosophers" were sold in Australia by Whitcomb and Tombs. "The Beautiful and Damned" in Australia was handled by the English publishers.

Whitney Darrow

Note four: An adaptation of TSOP by Sydney Sloane was performed at the Sheridan Square Playhouse in New York in 1962.

LATER PRINTINGS WITHIN THE FIRST
EDITION

A 5.1.b
Second printing: New York: Scribners, 1920. On copyright
page: 'Reprinted April, 1920'. 3,025 copies.

A 5.1.c
Third printing: New York: Scribners, 1920. On copyright
page: 'Reprinted twice in April, 1920'. 5,000 copies. Locations:
MJB; NjP.

An unknown number of copies of this printing have a tipped-in
glossy leaf bearing "The Author's Apology"—each signed by
Fitzgerald. These copies were prepared for a meeting of the
American Booksellers Association. One specially bound copy
in yellow cloth has been seen at ViU. See H 4, H 6.

A 5.1.d
Fourth printing: New York: Scribners, 1920. On copyright
page: 'Reprinted May, 1920'. Plate corrections. 5,000 copies.
Locations: MJB; ViU.

A 5.1.e
Fifth printing: New York: Scribners, 1920. On copyright
page: 'Reprinted May, June, 1920'. 5,050 copies.

A 5.1.f
Sixth printing: New York: Scribners, 1920. On copyright
page: 'Reprinted May [. . .] July, 1920'. 5,000 copies.

A 5.1.g
Seventh printing: New York: Scribners, 1920. On copyright
page: 'Reprinted May [. . .] August, 1920'. Plate corrections
5,000 copies. Locations: MJB; ViU.

A 5.1.h
Eighth printing: New York: Scribners, 1920. On copyright
page: 'Reprinted May [. . .] September, 1920'. 5,000 copies.

A 5.1.i
Ninth printing: New York: Scribners, 1920. On copyright
page: 'Reprinted May [. . .] October, 1920'. 5,000 copies.

A 5.1.j
Tenth printing: New York: Scribners, 1921. On copyright page: 'Reprinted May [. . .] February, 1921'. 3,000 copies.

A 5.1.k
Eleventh printing: New York: Scribners, 1921. On copyright page: 'Reprinted [. . .] March, 1921'. 3,000 copies.

A 5.1.l
Twelfth printing: New York: Scribners, 1921. On copyright page: 'Reprinted [. . .] October, 1921'. 2,000 copies.

OBSERVED FURTHER PRINTINGS WITHIN
THE FIRST EDITION

A 5.1.m
New York: Scribners, 1922. Possibly two printings in 1922 of 1,000 copies and 970 copies.

A 5.1.n
New York: A. L. Burt, [1923].

A 5.1.o
New York: Scribners, 1925. 270 copies.

A 5.1.p
New York: Scribners, 1931. 290 copies.

A 5.1.q
New York: Grosset & Dunlap, n.d. [1947].

A 5.1.r
New York: Scribners, 1951.

A 5.1.s
New York: Scribners, 1953.

A 5.1.t
New York: Scribners, 1953.

A 5.1.u
New York: Scribners, [1957]. I-6.57 [V].

A 5.1.v
New York: Scribners, [1959]. J-2.59 [V].

A 5.2.a
First English edition, first printing [1921]

THIS
SIDE OF PARADISE

by

F. SCOTT FITZGERALD

Well this side of Paradise! . . .
There's little comfort in the wise.
Rupert Brooke.

Experience is the name so many people
give to their mistakes.
Oscar Wilde.

LONDON: 48 PALL MALL
W. COLLINS SONS & CO. LTD.
GLASGOW MELBOURNE AUCKLAND

A 5.2.a: 7" x 5½"

Copyright page: 'Copyright 1921'.

P. 292: 'GLASGOW: W. COLLINS SONS AND CO. LTD.'

[i–vi] vii [viii] [1–2] 3–292 [293–296]

[A]⁸ B–I⁸ K–T⁸

Contents: p. i: half title; p. ii: list of four titles in Collins' First Novel Library; p. iii: title; p. iv: copyright; p. v: dedication; p. vi: blank; p. vii: contents; p. viii: blank; p. 1: 'Book I | THE ROMANTIC EGOTIST'; p. 2: blank; pp. 3–292: text, headed 'CHAPTER I | AMORY, SON OF BEATRICE'; pp. 293–296: ads.

Typography and paper: Thirty-eight lines per page. Wove paper.

Binding: Blue V cloth (fine linen-like grain). Redstamped. Front: '[within double-rule frame] THIS SIDE OF PARADISE | F. SCOTT FITZGERALD'. Spine: '[double rule] | THIS SIDE | OF | PARADISE | F. SCOTT | FITZGERALD | COLLINS | [double rule]'. White wove endpapers of heavier stock than text papers. All edges trimmed.

Dust jacket: Not seen.

Publication: Unknown number of copies of the first printing. Published 26 May 1921. 7s. 6d. Review copy so embossed on title page.

Locations: BM 12730.S.3. (deposit-stamp 21 July 1921); Bodleian (deposited July 1921); MJB (review copy).

Notes: The first English printing of *This Side of Paradise* varies unauthoritatively from the first Scribners printing of the novel in some 850 readings. This figure does not include variants caused by Collins's omission of periods after abbreviations or alteration of quotation marks. Of the 850 variants, 32 are substantive.

A 5.2.b
Second printing: London: W. Collins Sons, [1923]. On copyright page: 'First Impression, May, 1921 | Second ″ February, 1923'. Collins' 2/6 net Novels. Location: MJB.

The dust jacket for this printing uses the Hill drawing from the Scribners dust jacket. The only observed specimen of this dust jacket, seen in Fitzgerald's scrapbook, lacks the back cover and flaps.

A 5.2.c
Cheap reprint: London: W. Collins Sons, [1927]. Collins' 2/- Novels, #86.

This reprint was not seen; information is based on an ad in Collins's reprint of *TJA* and *The English Catalogue of Books*.

LATER EDITIONS

A 5.3
Second English edition

F. SCOTT FITZGERALD | THIS SIDE | OF | PARADISE | [two lines of italic type] | RUPERT BROOKE | [two lines of italic type] | OSCAR WILDE | THE GREY WALLS PRESS

London, 1948.

A 5.4
Second American edition

This Side | of Paradise | [decoration] | F. Scott Fitzgerald | *Author of:* | THE LAST TYCOON | THE GREAT GATSBY | TENDER IS THE NIGHT

New York: Dell, 1948. #D140.

A 5.5
Third American edition

[decoration] F. SCOTT FITZGERALD [decoration] | *This Side of Paradise* | [two lines of italic type] | —RUPERT BROOKE | [two lines of italic type] | —OSCAR WILDE | [decoration] | *New York* | CHARLES SCRIBNER'S SONS

1960. Scribner Library #SL60. Copyright page states 'RESET OCTOBER, 1960', but the 1960 first printing has not been seen. Reprints noted: A-8.62 [C]; D-10.63 [Col]; E-2.65 [Col]; F-2.66 [Col]; H-10.68 [Col]; I-1.70 [C].

A 5.6
Third English edition

THE | BODLEY HEAD | SCOTT | FITZGERALD | VOL. III | THIS SIDE OF PARADISE | [four lines of type] | THE BODLEY HEAD | LONDON

1960

A 5.7
Fourth English edition

This Side of Paradise | [tapered rule] | F. SCOTT FITZGERALD | PENGUIN BOOKS | *in association with the Bodley Head*

Harmondsworth, Middlesex, 1963. #1867. Reprinted 1965, 1967, 1970.

A 5.8
Fourth American edition

THIS SIDE | OF PARADISE | BY | F. SCOTT FITZGERALD | [six lines of italic type] | CHARLES SCRIBNER'S SONS *New York*

1970. Part of a four-volume set (with *GG, TITN, LT*) distributed by the Literary Guild of America and its associated books clubs.

[1–11] 12–144 [145–147] 148–152 [153–155] 156–255 [256]

A 5.9
First Japanese edition

F. Scott Fitzgerald | This Side of Paradise | Edited | with Introduction and Notes | by | Makoto Nagai | *Aoyama*

1970.

EXCERPT FROM TSOP

A 5.10
Readings in American Literature, ed. Sabina Jędraszko. Warsaw: Państwowe Wydawnictwo Naukowe, 1961. Excerpt, pp. 30–49.

A 6 FLAPPERS AND PHILOSOPHERS

A 6.*1*.a
First edition, first printing (*1920*)

FLAPPERS
AND PHILOSOPHERS

BY
F. SCOTT FITZGERALD
AUTHOR OF "THIS SIDE OF PARADISE"

NEW YORK
CHARLES SCRIBNER'S SONS
1920

A 6.1.a: 7⁷⁄₁₆″ x 5⅛″

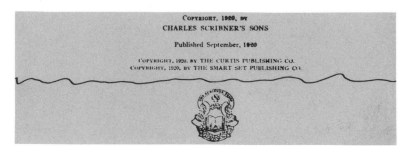

[i–viii] [1–2] 3–269 [270–272]

[1–17]⁸ [18]⁴

Contents: p. i: half title; p. ii: blank; p. iii: title; p. iv: copyright; p. v: 'TO ZELDA'; p. vi: blank; p. vii: contents; p. viii: blank; p. 1: half title; p. 2: blank; pp. 3–269: text, headed 'THE OFFSHORE PIRATE'; pp. 270–272: blank.

Stories.   "The Offshore Pirate," "The Ice Palace," "Head and Shoulders," "The Cut-Glass Bowl," "Bernice Bobs Her Hair," "Benediction," "Dalyrimple Goes Wrong," "The Four Fists."

Typography and paper: 12 point on 13, Old Style. 5⁹⁄₁₆″ (5⅞″) x 3½″; thirty-one lines per page. Running heads: rectos, story titles; versos, 'FLAPPERS AND PHILOSOPHERS'. Wove paper.

Binding: Green B cloth (linen-like grain) or T cloth (vertical lines); priority not established. Front blindstamped: 'FLAPPERS AND | PHILOSOPHERS | By F. Scott Fitzgerald'. Spine goldstamped: 'FLAPPERS | AND | PHILOSOPHERS | [rule] | Fitzgerald | SCRIBNERS'. White wove endpapers of sized stock. Top and bottom edges trimmed.

Dust jacket: Front has drawing of girl having hair bobbed against orange background, signed by W. E. Hill: '[white outlined in black] FLAPPERS AND | PHILOSOPHERS | By F. Scott Fitzgerald'. Spine lettered in black: 'FLAPPERS | AND | PHILOSOPHERS | [rule] | Fitzgerald | Scribners'. Back: 'NEW SCRIBNER FICTION [fourteen titles beginning with *Erskine Dale—Pioneer* and ending with *On a Passing Frontier*]'. Front flap has *F&P* blurb; back flap has *TSOP* blurb.

Publication: 5,000 copies of the first printing. Published 10 September 1920. $1.75.

Dust jacket for A 6.1.a

Printing: Composed and printed by the Scribner Press; plates made by the New York Electrotyping Co. Bound by the Scribner Press.

Location: LC (deposited 14 September 1920); Lilly (T cloth with dj); MJB (B cloth with dj and T cloth); NjP; PSt.

Note one: There is one textual variant in the plates, which first appeared in the fourth printing of December 1920.

152.23 panoply [panorama

Note two: F&P was sold in Canada by Copp, Clark Company (Whitney Darrow to Maxwell Perkins, 1 August 1922). No copy has been located; and it is impossible to determine whether it was a separate printing, the Scribners sheets issued with a Copp, Clark title page, or the Scribners sheets in a Copp, Clark binding. See A 5.1.a, A 8.1.a*, and A 9.1.a*.

A 6.1.a†
Australasian binding of first American printing

Sheets of the first Scribners printing were bound for distribution by Whitcombe & Tombs in Australia and New Zealand.

Same title page and copyright page as Scribners first printing. Same pagination and collation as Scribners first printing. Pages 271–272 are the rear pastedown endpaper.

Binding: Red V cloth (fine linen-like grain). Blackstamped. Front: 'FLAPPERS AND | PHILOSOPHERS | By F. Scott Fitzgerald'. Spine: 'FLAPPERS | AND | PHILOSOPHERS | [rule] | Fitzgerald | Whitcombe & Tombs | Limited.' White endpapers. All edges trimmed.

Dust jacket: If any, not seen.

Location: MJB.

LATER PRINTINGS WITHIN THE FIRST EDITION

A 6.1.b
Second printing: New York: Scribners, 1920. On copyright page: 'Reprinted September, 1920'. 3,000 copies.

A 0.1.c
Third printing: New York: Scrlbners, 1920. On copyright
page: 'Reprinted September, October, 1920'. 3,025 copies.

A 6.1.d
Fourth printing: New York; Scribners, 1920. On copyright
page: 'Reprinted September, October, December, 1920'. 2,000
copies.

A 6.1.e
Fifth printing: New York: Scribners, 1921. On copyright
page: 'Reprinted September, October, December, 1920; December, 1921.' 1,300 copies.

A 6.1.f
Sixth printing: New York: Scribners, 1922. On copyright
page: 'Reprinted [. . .] November, 1922.' 1,000 copies.

A 6.2.a
First English edition, first printing [1922]

FLAPPERS AND PHILOSOPHERS

by

F. SCOTT FITZGERALD

Author of 'This Side of Paradise'

LONDON: 48 PALL MALL
W. COLLINS SONS & CO. LTD.
GLASGOW MELBOURNE AUCKLAND

A 6.2.a: 7¼″ x 4⅞″

Copyright page: 'Copyright, 1922 | *Manufactured in Great Britain*'.

P. 272: 'GLASGOW: W. COLLINS SONS AND CO. LTD.'

[i–vi] vii [viii] [1–2] 3–45 [46–48] 49–71 [72–74] 75–99 [100–102] 103–137 [138–140] 141–175 [176–178] 179–207 [208–210] 211–246 [247–248] 249–271 [272–280]

[A]⁸ B–I⁸ K–S⁸

Contents: p. i: half title; p. ii: list of six new novels; p. iii: title; p. iv: copyright; p. v: dedication; p. vi: blank; p. vii: contents; p. viii: blank; p. 1: 'THE OFFSHORE PIRATE'; p. 2: blank; pp. 3–271: text, headed 'I'; pp. 272: colophon; pp. 273–280: ads.

Stories. Same stories as Scribners edition, but in this order: "The Offshore Pirate," "The Four Fists," "Dalyrimple Goes Wrong," "Head and Shoulders," "The Ice Palace," "The Cut-Glass Bowl," "Bernice Bobs Her Hair," "Benediction."

Typography and paper: Thirty-four lines per page. Wove paper.

Binding: Blue V cloth (fine linen-like grain). Redstamped. Front: '[within double-rule frame] FLAPPERS | AND PHILOSOPHERS | F. SCOTT FITZGERALD | [Collins device]'. Spine: '[double rule] | FLAPPERS | AND | PHILOSOPHERS | [fleuron] | F. SCOTT | FITZGERALD | COLLINS | [double rule]'. White wove endpapers of different stock from text paper. All edges trimmed.

Dust jacket: Not seen.

Publication: Unknown number of copies. Published 23 March 1922. 7s. 6d.

Location: BM 12730.S.2. (deposit-stamp 25 March 1922); Bodleian (deposited April 1922); MJB.

Note: The first Collins printing of *F&P* varies from the first Scribners printing in some 435 readings, of which 7 are substantives:

80.6 muddled [169.20 muffled
80.25–6 white, of brown [170.7–8 white, brown
89.12–13 clear- | cut [105.9–10 clean cut
97.15 leaning [112.26 looking
152.23 panoply [205.19 panorama

244.5   older   [98.29   elder
259.19   squared off   [62.19   squared up

A 6.2.b
Cheap reprint: London: W. Collins Sons, [1925]. Collins'
2/- novels, #40. Location: MJB.

A 6.3
Second American edition

Flappers and Philosophers | by F. SCOTT FITZGERALD |
CHARLES SCRIBNER'S SONS, *New York*

1959. A-6.59 [H]. Introduction by Arthur Mizener. Reprint
noted: F-5.66 [H].

A 7 THE SAINT PAUL DAILY DIRGE

A 7.1.a
(1922)

Weather   THE ST. PAUL DAILY DIRGE   Mortuary | [rule] |
Rotten   Edition
PRICE—A SWEET KISS. ST. PAUL, MINNESOTA, FRIDAY,
JANUARY 13, 1922. VOL. I. NO. 1. | [rule] | COTILLION IS
SAD FAILURE

Broadside, printed on recto only. Wove paper.

Publication: Written and privately printed by Fitzgerald as a
joke. Zelda Fitzgerald almost certainly had a part in this
project. Unknown number of copies. Distributed 13 January
1922 in St. Paul, Minn.

Locations: MJB; MnHi; OKentU; RLS.

A 7.1.b
Facsimile: 200 copies printed by the *Fitzgerald Newsletter*
(Columbus, Ohio, 1968).

A 7.1.a: 22¾" x 16½"

A 8 THE BEAUTIFUL AND DAMNED

A 8.1.a
First edition, first printing (1922)

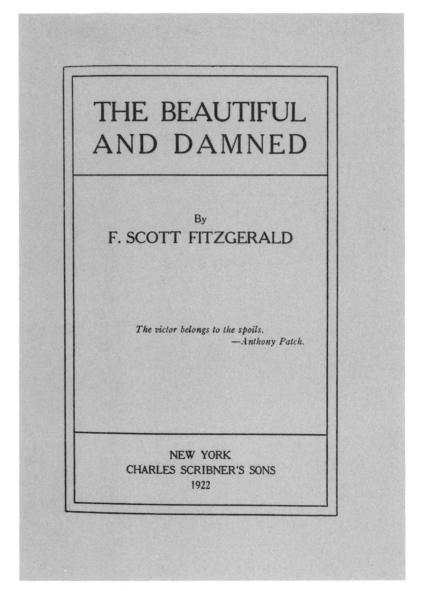

THE BEAUTIFUL
AND DAMNED

By
F. SCOTT FITZGERALD

The victor belongs to the spoils.
—Anthony Patch.

NEW YORK
CHARLES SCRIBNER'S SONS
1922

A 8.1.a: 7⅜" x 5⅛"

[i–x] [1–2] 3–128 [129–130] 131–309 [310–312] 313–449 [450]

[1]⁶ [2–29]⁸

Contents: p. i: blank; p. ii: 'BY F. SCOTT FITZGERALD | [three titles]'; p. iii: half title; p. iv: blank; p. v: title; p. vi: copyright; p. vii: 'TO | SHANE LESLIE, GEORGE JEAN NATHAN | AND MAXWELL PERKINS | IN APPRECIATION OF MUCH LITERARY HELP | AND ENCOURAGEMENT'; p. viii: blank; p. ix: contents; p. x: blank; p. 1: 'BOOK ONE'; p. 2: blank; pp. 3–449: text, headed 'CHAPTER I | ANTHONY PATCH'; p. 129: 'BOOK TWO'; p. 311: 'BOOK III'; p. 450: blank.

Typography and paper: 11 point on 12, Old Style. 5¹⁵⁄₁₆″ (6¼″) x 3½″; thirty-five lines per page. Running heads: rectos, chapter titles; versos, 'THE BEAUTIFUL AND DAMNED'. Wove paper.

Binding: Green B cloth (linen-like grain). Front cover blind-stamped: 'THE BEAUTIFUL | AND DAMNED | By F. Scott Fitzgerald'. Spine goldstamped: 'THE | BEAUTIFUL | AND | DAMNED | [rule] | Fitzgerald | SCRIBNERS'. White wove endpapers of sized stock. Top and bottom edges trimmed.

Dust jacket: Front has drawing of man and woman in evening dress against an orange circle, signed by W. E. Hill: '[white outlined in black] THE BEAUTIFUL | AND DAMNED | [solid black] BY THE AUTHOR OF | "THIS SIDE OF PARADISE" | F. Scott Fitzgerald'.[1] Spine lettered in black: 'THE | BEAUTI-

---

1. There is the front cover of what seems to be a trial dust jacket for *B&D* in Fitzgerald's scrapbook. This specimen has a blue green circle and omits the two lines 'BY THE AUTHOR OF | "THIS SIDE OF PARADISE"'. See Fitzgerald's letters to Perkins (*Dear Scott / Dear Max*, pp. 43, 49, 52–53): 14 October 1921, 16 December 1921, and 31 January 1922.

One copy of the orange-circle dust jacket has been seen with the title lettering on the front cover in solid black (Holtzman Collection).

Dust jacket for A 8.1.a

FUL | AND | DAMNED | [rule] | Fitzgerald | SCRIBNERS'. Back has signed photo of Fitzgerald with blurb. Front flap has blurbs for fifth printing of *F&P* and twelfth printing of *TSOP;* back flap lists ten Scribners titles.

Publication: 20,600 copies of the first printing were printed in January. Published 4 March 1922. $2.00.

Printing: Composed and printed by the Scribner Press; plates made by the New York Electrotyping Co. Bound by the Scribner Press.

Locations: LC (deposited 6 March 1922); Lilly (dj); MJB (dj); NjP (dj); OKentU.

Note one: For an analysis of the priority of the early printings and states, see Bruccoli, "Bibliographical Notes on F. Scott Fitzgerald's *The Beautiful and Damned," Studies in Bibliography,* XIII (1960), 258–261.

B&D was serialized in *Metropolitan Magazine,* LIV–LV (September 1921–March 1922). The serial was edited by the *Metropolitan* from Fitzgerald's original version; he then revised his original version for book publication.

The conclusion of the *Metropolitan* serial was omitted from the book.

THAT exquisite heavenly irony which has tabulated the demise of many generations of sparrows seems to us to be content with the moral judgments of man upon fellow man. If there is a subtler and yet more nebulous ethic somewhere in the mind, one might believe that beneath the sordid dress and near the bruised heart of this transaction there was a motive which was not weak but only futile and sad. In the search for happiness, which search is the greatest and possibly the only crime of which we in our petty misery are capable, these two people were marked as guilty chiefly by the freshness and fullness of their desire. Their disillusion was always a comparative thing—they had sought glamor and color through their respective worlds with steadfast loyalty—sought it and it alone in kisses and in wine, sought it with the same ingenuousness in the wanton moonlight as under the cold sun of inviolate chastity. Their fault was not that they had doubted but that they had believed.

The exquisite perfection of their boredom, the delicacy of their inattention, the inexhaustibility of their discontent—were disastrous extremes—that was all. And if, before Gloria yielded up her gift of beauty, she shed one bright feather of light so that someone, gazing up from the grey earth, might say, " Look! There is an angel's wing!" perhaps she had given more than enough in exchange for her tinsel joys.

. . . The story ends here.

Cut versions of *The Beautiful and Damned* were serialized in several newspapers after book publication. Two appearances have been found: *New York Daily News*, 29 January–26 March 1923; *Washington Herald*, 2 July 1922–26 October 1922.

Note two: *B&D* was sold in Australia by Collins (Whitney Darrow to Maxwell Perkins, 1 August 1922; Perkins to Fitzgerald, 6 July 1922). No copy has been located, and it is impossible to determine whether it was a separate printing or the Collins sheets issued with a new title page. See A 5.1.a (Note three) and 6.1.a†.

A 8.1.a*
Canadian Issue of American sheets (1922)

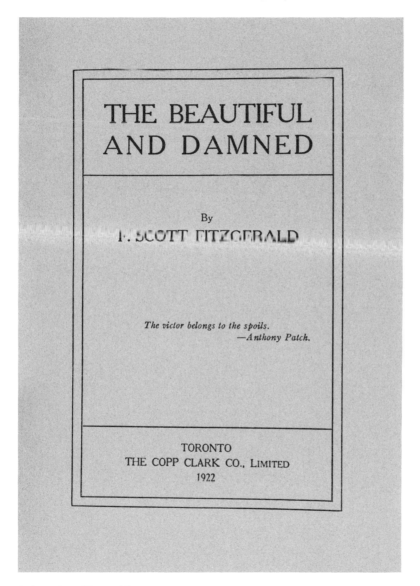

THE BEAUTIFUL
AND DAMNED

By
F. SCOTT FITZGERALD

The victor belongs to the spoils.
—Anthony Patch.

TORONTO
THE COPP CLARK CO., LIMITED
1922

A 8.1.a*: 7⅜″ x 5¼″

Same collation and pagination as Scribners first printing.

Contents: pp. i–ii: blank; p. iii: half title; p. iv: blank; p. v: title; p. vi: copyright; p. vii: dedication; p. viii: blank; p. ix: contents; p. x: blank; p. 1: 'BOOK ONE'; p. 2: blank; p. 3–449: text; p. 450: blank.

Binding: Green B cloth (linen-like grain). Front blind-stamped: 'THE BEAUTIFUL | AND DAMNED | By F. Scott Fitzgerald'. Spine goldstamped: 'THE | BEAUTIFUL | AND | DAMNED | [rule] | Fitzgerald | THE | COPP, CLARK CO. | LIMITED'. White wove endpapers of sized stock. Top and bottom edges trimmed.

Dust jacket: Not seen.

Locations: MJB; RLS.

Note: Probably first-printing sheets with a reset gathering [1]⁶ of preliminaries.

LATER PRINTINGS WITHIN THE FIRST
EDITION

A 8.1.b₁
Second printing, first state: New York: Scribners, 1922. 19,750 copies of states 1 and 2 printed in March 1922.

State 1 has same title page as first printing. Copyright page: 'COPYRIGHT, 1922, BY | CHARLES SCRIBNER'S SONS | [rule] | Printed in the United States of America | [rule] | Published March, 1922 | [rule] | COPYRIGHT, 1929, 1922, BY THE METROPOLITAN PUBLICATIONS, INC. | [Scribners seal]'.

[i–x] [1–2] 3–128 [129–130] 131–309 [310–312] 313–449
[450–454],

[1]⁸ [2–15]¹⁶

P. *451:* ad for twelfth printing of *TSOP;* p. 452: ad for fifth
printing of *F&P;* pp. 453–454: blank.

Binding: Green B cloth or FL cloth (checkered grain).

Locations: Lilly (B cloth); MJB (B and FL cloths).

Note: No textual variants noted between first and second
printings.

A 8.1.b₂
Second printing, second state

State 2 has same title page and copyright as state 1.

[i–x] [1–2] 3–128 [129–130] 131–309 [310–312] 313–449
[450]

[1]⁸ [2]¹⁶ [3]¹⁶ (–3₁₅,₁₆) [4–27]⁸; 2 leaves cancelled after p. 66,
not affecting pagination.

Binding: Green B or FL cloth.

Locations: MJB (B cloth); ViU (FL cloth).

Note: State 2 is made up of three gatherings from the
second printing and twenty-four gatherings from the first printing. In order to avoid duplicate pages, leaves 3₁₅,₁₆ were
cancelled. It is possible that the production of the Copp, Clark
Canadian issue of the first printing by the Scribner Press re-
sulted in extra sheets in 8's which were salvaged in this way.

A 8.1.c
Third printing: New York: Scribners, 1922. On copyright
page: 'Reprinted March, April, 1922' 10,000 copies.

A 8.1.d
Fourth printing(?): New York: Scribners, 1922. On copyright page: 'Reprinted March, April, 1922'. In A. L. Burt binding but with Scribners title page. Possibly remainder sheets of
the third printing.

A 8.1.e
Fifth printing: New York: A. L. Burt, 1924. On copyright
page: 'Reprinted March, April, 1922'.

A 8.1.f
Sixth printing (English)

[within triple-rule frame] THE BEAUTIFUL | AND DAMNED | F. SCOTT FITZGERALD | *The victor belongs to the spoils* | *Anthony Patch* | *London* | THE GREY WALLS PRESS

1950. Reprinted 1954.

A 8.1.g
Seventh printing: New York: Scribners, [1958]. AA-2.58 [MH].

With textual alterations; for collation see Bruccoli, "Bibliographical Notes on F. Scott Fitzgerald's *The Beautiful and Damned.*"

A 8.1.h
Eighth printing: New York: Scribners, [1963]. D-3.63 [MH].

A 8.1.i
Ninth printing: New York: Scribners [   ]. Scribner Library #SL90. First Scribner Library printing not seen. Reprints noted: C-10.65 [MCOL]; D-8.66 [MCOL].

A 8.2.a
First English edition, first printing [1922]

THE BEAUTIFUL AND DAMNED

by

F. SCOTT FITZGERALD

Author of " Flappers and Philosophers,"
" This Side of Paradise "

The victor belongs to the spoils.
—Anthony Patch.

LONDON: 48 PALL MALL
W. COLLINS SONS & CO. LTD.
GLASGOW MELBOURNE AUCKLAND

A 8.2.a: 7¼" x 4⅞"

Copyright page: 'Copyright 1922. | LONDON AND GLAS-GOW: W. COLLINS SONS AND CO. LTD.'

[i–vi] vii [viii] [1–2] 3–107 [108–110] 111–265 [266–268] 269–386 [387–392]

[A]⁸ B–I⁸ K–U⁸ X–Z⁸, 2A–2B⁸

Contents: p. i: half title; p. ii: list of six new novels; p. iii: title; p. iv: copyright; p. v: dedication; p. vi: blank; p. vii: contents; p. viii: blank; p. 1: 'BOOK ONE'; p. 2: blank; pp. 3–386: text, headed 'CHAPTER I | ANTHONY PATCH'; pp. 387–392: ads.

Typography and paper: Forty-two lines per page. Wove paper.

Binding: Blue V cloth (fine linen-like grain). Redstamped. Front: '[within double-rule frame] THE BEAUTIFUL | AND DAMNED | F. SCOTT FITZGERALD | [Collins device]'. Spine: '[double rule] | THE | BEAUTIFUL | AND | DAMNED | [fleuron] | F. SCOTT | FITZGERALD | [Collins device] | COLLINS | [double rule]'. White wove endpapers of different stock than text paper. All edges trimmed.

Dust jacket: Front has drawing of woman against blue background: '[lettered in black] THE [diamond] BEAUTIFUL [diamond] AND [diamond] DAMNED | F. SCOTT FITZGERALD'. Spine: '[red] THE | BEAUTIFUL | AND | DAMNED | [black] F. SCOTT | FITZGERALD | [price in white against red circle] | [black seal] | [black] COLLINS'. Front flap has blurb for *B&D;* back and back flap missing in only observed specimen, seen in Fitzgerald's scrapbook.

Publication: Unknown number of copies of the first printing. Published 28 September 1922. 7s.6d.[2]

Locations: BM 12730.S.1. (deposit-stamp 3 November 1922); Bodleian (deposited November 1922); MJB.

Note: The first Collins printing of *B&D* varies from the first Scribners printing in some 700 readings, of which 82 are substantives; 134 lines are omitted from the Collins text:

   20.14–30   (Collins p. 18)
   23.30–24.15 (Collins p. 20)

---

2. F. T. Smith, former editorial director of Collins, noted on 10 March 1966: "We sold 899 Home and 335 Export."

27.20–30.5   "A Flash-Back in Paradise"   (Collins p. 23)
?55 16–21   (Collins p. 219)

The authority for these cuts is unknown.

A 8.2.b
Second printing: London: W. Collins Sons, [1922]. On copy-right page: 'First Impression, September, 1922 | Second " Oc-tober, 1922'. Location: MJB.

A 8.2.c
Cheap reprint: London: W. Collins Sons, [1925]. Collins' 2/- novels, #44.

This reprint was not seen; information is based on ads in Col-lins's reprints of *F&P* and *TJA* and on *The English Catalogue of Books.*

LATER EDITIONS

A 8.3
Second American edition

F. SCOTT FITZGERALD | THE | BEAUTIFUL | AND | DAMNED | *The victor belongs to the spoils* | —ANTHONY PATCH | PERMABOOKS | *Garden City, New York*

1951. #P123.

A 8.4
Second English edition

THE | BODLEY HEAD | SCOTT | FITZGERALD | VOL. IV | THE BEAUTIFUL AND DAMNED | AND TWO SHORT STORIES | THE BODLEY HEAD | LONDON

1961.

A 8.5
Third English edition

The Beautiful and | Damned | F. Scott Fitzgerald | [penguin] | Penguin Books

Harmondsworth, Middlesex, 1966. #2414. Reprinted 1968.

A 9 TALES OF THE JAZZ AGE

A 9.1.a
First edition, first printing (1922)

TALES OF THE
JAZZ AGE

BY

F. SCOTT FITZGERALD

NEW YORK
CHARLES SCRIBNER'S SONS
1922

A 9.1.a: 7⁷⁄₁₆″ x 5¹⁄₁₆″

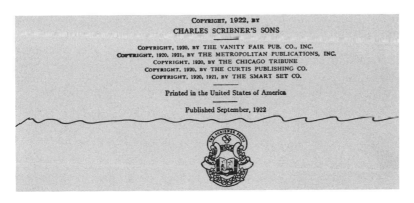

[A–B] [i–vi] vii–xi [xii] [1–2] 3–138 [139–140] 141–272 [273–274] 275–317 [318–322]

[1]⁸ [2–11]¹⁶

Contents: p. A: blank; p. B: 'BY F. SCOTT FITZGERALD | [four titles]'; p. i: half title; p. ii: blank; p. iii: title; p. iv: copyright; p. v: 'QUITE INAPPROPRIATELY | TO MY MOTHER'; p. vi: blank; pp. vii–xi: Fitzgerald's annotated contents; p. xii: blank; p. 1: 'MY LAST FLAPPERS'; p. 2: blank; pp. 3–317: text, headed 'THE JELLY-BEAN'; p. 139: 'FANTASIES'; p. 273: 'UN-CLASSIFIED MASTERPIECES'; pp. 318–322: blank.

Stories. *My Last Flappers*—"The Jelly-Bean," "The Camel's Back," "May Day," "Porcelain and Pink"; *Fantasies*—"The Diamond as Big as The Ritz," "The Curious Case of Benjamin Button," "Tarquin of Cheapside," "O Russet Witch!"; *Unclassified Masterpieces*—"The Lees of Happiness," "Mr. Icky," "Jemina."

Typography and paper: 11 point on 12, Old Style. 5¹³⁄₁₆″ (6¹⁄₁₆″) x 3½″; thirty-five lines per page. Running heads: rectos, story titles; versos, 'TALES OF THE JAZZ AGE'. Wove paper.

Binding: Green B cloth (linen-like grain). Front blindstamped: 'TALES OF THE | JAZZ AGE | By F. Scott Fitzgerald'. Spine goldstamped: 'TALES | OF THE | JAZZ AGE | [rule] | Fitzgerald | SCRIBNERS'. White wove endpapers of coated stock. Top and bottom edges trimmed.

Dust jacket: Front has drawing of figures on white background, signed by John Held, Jr.: '[black and white] TALES OF THE | JAZZ AGE | [orange] By the Author of | THE BEAUTIFUL | AND DAMNED | [black and white] F. SCOTT FITZGERALD'. Spine lettered in black: 'TALES | OF THE | JAZZ

AGE | [rule] | Fitzgerald | SCRIBNERS'. Back has excerpts from Fitzgerald's annotated contents. Front flap has blurb for *B&D;* back flap has blurbs for fifth printing of *F&P* and thirteenth printing of *TSOP*.

Publication: 8,000 copies of the first printing. Published 22 September 1922. $1.75.

Printing: Composed and printed by the Scribner Press; plates made by the New York Electrotyping Co. Bound by the Scribner Press.

Locations: Lilly (Scribner Press Bindery Office Copy); MJB (dj); NjP; OKentU; PSt.

Note: The Scribners records show three printings of *TJA* in 1922. These were not identified by the publisher and have not been differentiated by bibliographical tests. One textual revision has been discovered by machine collation:

   232.6   and   [an

But it has not been determined whether this plate change occurred between the first and second printings or between the second and third printings.

Dust jacket for A 9.1.a

A 9.1.a*
Canadian issue of American sheets (1922)

TALES OF THE
JAZZ AGE

BY

F. SCOTT FITZGERALD

TORONTO
THE COPP CLARK CO., Limited
1922

A 9.1.a*: 7⅜" x 5¼"

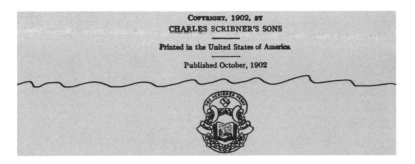

Same pagination and collation as Scribners first printing.

Contents: Preliminaries differ from Scribners issue only in that p. B is blank.

Binding: Green B cloth (linen-like grain). Front blindstamped: 'TALES OF THE | JAZZ AGE | By F. Scott Fitzgerald'. Spine goldstamped: 'TALES | OF THE | JAZZ AGE | [rule] | Fitzgerald | THE | COPP, CLARK CO. | LIMITED'. White wove endpapers of different stock from text paper. Top and bottom edges trimmed.

Dust jacket: Not seen.

Location: MJB.

Note: This issue consisted of Scribners sheets with a partly reset gathering [1]⁸ of preliminaries for Copp, Clark. The title and copyright pages are reset; the copyright page reads '1902' in error for 1922.

LATER PRINTINGS WITHIN THE FIRST
EDITION

A 9.1.b
Second printing: New York: Scribners, 1922. Not differentiated on copyright page. October 1922. 3,000 copies.

A 9.1.c
Third printing: New York: Scribners, 1922. Not differentiated on copyright page. October 1922. 3,000 copies.

A 9.1.d
Pirated reprint: In 1971 an unauthorized facsimile printing of *TJA* was offered for sale by Folcroft Library Editions, Folcroft, Pa. Not seen.

A 9.2.a
First English edition, first printing [1923]

TALES OF THE JAZZ AGE

by

F. SCOTT FITZGERALD

Author of "This Side of Paradise," "The Beautiful and Damned,"
"Flappers and Philosophers."

LONDON: 48 PALL MALL
W. COLLINS SONS & CO. LTD.
GLASGOW MELBOURNE AUCKLAND

A 9.2.a: 7¾6″ x 4⅞″

Copyright page: 'Copyright, 1923 | *Manufactured in Great Britain*'.

P. 318: 'GLASGOW: W. COLLINS SONS AND CO. LTD.'

[i–vi] vii–xii [1–2] 3–138 [139–140] 141–272 [273–274] 275–317 [318–324]

[A]⁸ B–I⁸ K–U⁸ X⁸

Contents: p. i: half title; p. ii: list of six new novels; p. iii: title; p. iv: copyright; p. v: dedication; p. vi: blank; pp. vii–xii: contents; p. 1: 'MY LAST FLAPPERS'; p. 2: blank; pp. 3–317: text, headed 'THE JELLY-BEAN | I'; p. 318: colophon; pp. 319–324: ads.
Same stories as the Scribners edition.

Typography and paper: Thirty-six lines per page. Wove paper.

Binding: Blue V cloth (fine linen-like grain). Redstamped. Front: '[within double-rule frame] TALES OF | THE JAZZ AGE | F. SCOTT FITZGERALD'. Spine: '[double rule] | TALES | OF THE | JAZZ AGE | [fleuron] | F. SCOTT | FITZGERALD [Collins device] | COLLINS | [double rule]'. White wove endpapers of different stock from text paper. All edges trimmed.

Dust jacket: Front has drawing of dancers and jazz musicians against yellow square, signed by C. Morse [?]: '[black and white lettering] TALES OF THE | JAZZ AGE | [red] *by* | [black and white] F. SCOTT | FITZGERALD | [red] Author of THE BEAUTIFUL AND DAMNED'. Spine: '[red] TALES | OF THE | JAZZ | AGE | [black] F. SCOTT | FITZGERALD | AUTHOR OF | "THE BEAUTIFUL AND DAMNED" etc. | [white price against red circle] | [black seal] | [black] COLLINS'. Back and flaps are missing in only observed specimen, seen in Fitzgerald's scrapbook.

Publication: Unknown number of copies. Published 28 March 1923. 7s. 6d. Review copy so embossed on title page.

Location: BM 12731.c.37. (deposit-stamp 28 March 1923); Bodleian (deposited April 1923); MJB (review copy).

A 9.2.b
Cheap reprint: London: W. Collins Sons, [1927]. Collins' 2/- novels, #72. Location: MJB.

LATER EDITION

A 9.3.a
Second American edition (revised contents)

SIX| TALES | OF | THE | JAZZ | AGE | [decoration] | *AND OTHER STORIES* | By F. SCOTT FITZGERALD | CHARLES SCRIBNER'S SONS, *New York.*

1960. A-1.60 [H]. Reprint noted: B-4.60 [H].

Contents: "The Jelly Bean" (*TJA*), "The Camel's Back" (*TJA*), "The Curious Case of Benjamin Button" (*TJA*), "Tarquin of Cheapside" (*TJA*), " 'O Russet Witch!' " (*TJA*), "The Lees of Happiness" (*TJA*), "The Adjuster" (*ASYM*), "Hot and Cold Blood" (*ASYM*), "Gretchen's Forty Winks" (*ASYM*).

Introduction by Frances Fitzgerald Lanahan includes facsimile of Fitzgerald's 1923 "Monthly Expenditure," p. 8.

A 9.3.b
New York: Scribners, [   ]. Scribner Library #SL157. First Scribner Library printing not seen. Reprints noted: B-1.69 [Col]; C-11.70 (c).

A 10 THE VEGETABLE

A 10.1.a
First edition, first printing (1923)

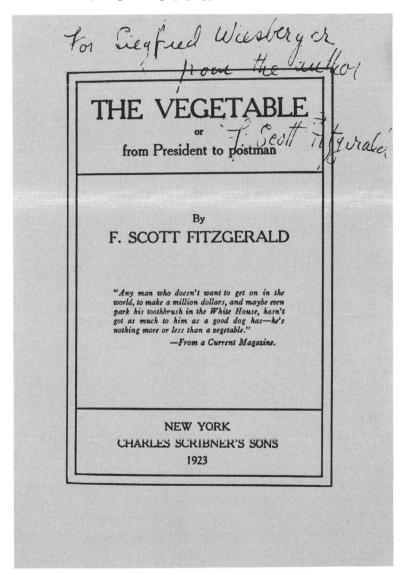

A 10.1.a: 7⁷⁄₁₆″ x 5¼″

[i–viii] [1–2] 3–145 [146–152]

[1–10]^8

Contents: p. i: blank; p. ii: 'BY F. SCOTT FITZGERALD | [five titles]'; p. iii: half title; p. iv: blank; p. v: title; p. vi: copyright; p. vii: 'TO | KATHERINE TIGHE AND EDMUND WILSON, JR. | WHO DELETED MANY ABSURDITIES | FROM MY FIRST TWO NOVELS I RECOMMEND | THE ABSURDITIES SET DOWN HERE'; p. viii: blank; p. 1: half title; p. 2: blank; pp. 3–145: text, headed 'THE VEGETABLE | ACT I'; p. 146: blank; pp. 147–148: ads for *B&D, TSOP, TJA,* and *F&P;* pp. 149–152 blank.

Typography and paper: 11 point on 13, Old Style. 5³⁄₁₆″ (5⁷⁄₁₆″) x 3½″; twenty-five lines per page. Running heads: rectos and versos, 'THE VEGETABLE'. Wove paper.

Binding: Green B cloth (linen-like grain). Front blindstamped: 'THE | VEGETABLE | By F. Scott Fitzgerald'. Spine gold-stamped: 'THE | VEGETABLE | [rule] | Fitzgerald | SCRIB-NERS'. White wove endpapers of sized stock. Top and bottom edges trimmed.

Dust jacket: Front has drawing of figures against red background, signed by John Held, Jr.: '[white] 'THE | VEGETABLE | BY | F. SCOTT FITZGERALD'. Spine lettered in black: 'THE | VEGETABLE | [rule] | Fitzgerald | SCRIBNERS'. Back has blurb for *Veg.* Front flap has blurbs for *B&D* and *TJA;* back flap has blurbs for fifth printing of *F&P* and thirteenth printing of *TSOP.*

Publication: 7,650 copies. Published 27 April 1923. $1.50.

Printing: Composed and printed by the Scribner Press; plates made by the New York Electrotyping Co. Bound by the Scribner Press.

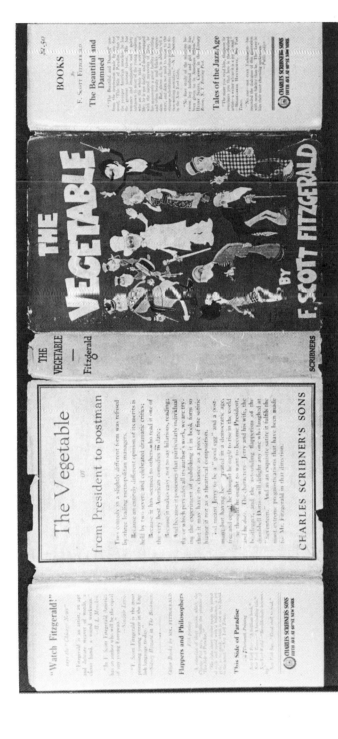

Dust jacket for A 10.1.a

Locations: LC (deposited 30 April 1923); Lilly (dj); MJB (dj);
NjP (Fitzgerald's marked copy); OKentU; PSt.

Note: *The Vegetable* premiered at the Apollo Theatre, Atlantic
City, N.J., 19 November 1923.

A 10.1.b
Pirated reprint: In 1971 an unauthorized facsimile reprint of
The Vegetable was offered for sale by Folcroft Library Editions,
Folcroft, Pa. This piracy is on laid paper and bound in gold-
stamped maroon buckram. It facsimiles the original title page
and copyright page. Location: MJB.

A 11   THE GREAT GATSBY

A 11.1.a
First edition, first printing (1925)

THE GREAT GATSBY

BY

F. SCOTT FITZGERALD

Then wear the gold hat, if that will move her;
If you can bounce high, bounce for her too,
Till she cry "Lover, gold-hatted, high-bouncing lover,
I must have you!"
—Thomas Parke D'Invilliers.

NEW YORK
CHARLES SCRIBNER'S SONS
1925

A 11.1.a: 7 7/16″ x 5 1/8″

[i–vi] 1–218

[1–14]⁸

Contents: p. i: half title; p. ii: 'BY F. SCOTT FITZGERALD |
[six titles]'; p. iii: title; p. iv: copyright; p. v: 'ONCE AGAIN |
TO | ZELDA'; p. vi: blank; pp. 1–218: text, headed 'THE GREAT
GATSBY | CHAPTER I'.

Typography and paper: 12 point on 14, Old Style. 5⁹⁄₁₆″
(5¹³⁄₁₆″) x 3½″; twenty-nine lines per page. Running heads: rectos and versos, 'THE GREAT GATSBY'. Wove paper.

Binding: Green B cloth (linen-like grain). Front blindstamped:
'THE GREAT | GATSBY | By F. Scott Fitzgerald'. Spine gold-
stamped: 'THE | GREAT | GATSBY | [rule] | Fitzgerald | SCRIB-
NERS'. White wove endpapers of sized stock. Top and bottom
edges trimmed.

Dust jacket: Front has drawing of woman's face above amuse-
ment park night scene, signed by F. Cugat: '[white lettering]
[swash] The [roman] GREAT | GATSBY | F ᐃ SCOTT ᐃ FITZGER-
ALD'. Spine lettered in white: '[swash] The | [roman] GREAT |
GATSBY | FITZGERALD | SCRIBNERS'. Back has blurb for *GG*. In
first printing of jacket there is a lowercase 'j' in 'jay Gatsby' on
the back at line 14; it is hand-corrected in ink in most copies
seen. (The second printing of the jacket corrects this error.)
Front flap lists books by Fitzgerald; back flap lists books by Ring
W. Lardner. A later printing of the jacket quotes from reviews
on the flaps and back.

Publication: 20,870 copies of the first printing. Published 10
April 1925. $2.00.

Printing: Composed and printed by the Scribner Press; plates
made by the New York Electrotyping Co. Bound by the Scribner
Press.

Dust jacket for A 11.1.a

Locations: LC (deposited 2 June 1925); Lilly; MJB (dj with hand-corrected lowercase 'j', dj with capital 'J', dj with reviews); NjP (Fitzgerald's marked copy); OKentU (dj with capital 'J'); PSt.·

Note one: For studies of the text see Bruce Harkness, "Bibliography and the Novelistic Fallacy," in *Bibliography and Textual Criticism,* ed. O M Brack, Jr., and Warner Barnes (Chicago: University of Chicago Press, [1969]), pp. 23–40; Bruccoli, "A Further Note on the First Printing of *The Great Gatsby*," *Studies in Bibliography,* XVI (1961), 244; Bruccoli, " 'A Might Collation': Animadversions on the Text of F. Scott Fitzgerald," in *Editing Twentieth-Century Texts,* ed. Francess G. Halpenny (Toronto: University of Toronto Press, [1972]), pp. 28–50; Jennifer E. Atkinson, "Fitzgerald's Marked Copy of *The Great Gatsby*," *Fitzgerald/Hemingway Annual 1970,* pp. 28–33; "Editorial," *Fitzgerald/Hemingway Annual 1970,* pp. 265.

There are six textual variants between the first and second printings:

> 60.16   chatter   [echolalia
> 119.22   northern   [southern
> 165.16   it's   [its
> 165.29   away   [away.
> 205.9–10   sick in tired   [sickantired
> 211.7–8   Union Street station   [Union Station

Note two: The novel was serialized after book publication in *Famous Story Magazine,* III (April, May, June, July, August 1926). It was reprinted in England in *Argosy,* XXII (August 1937), 54–93. *GG* may have been serialized by the Bell Syndicate in 1925 (see *Dear Scott/Dear Max,* p. 119).

Note three: *GG* was dramatized by Owen Davis. It opened at the Ambassador Theatre in New York on 2 February 1926 and ran for 112 performances. The play version was not published; but a typescript is at LC (PS3507/.A745G7/Rare Bk. Coll.). See Burns Mantle, *The Best Plays of 1925–26* (New York: Dodd, Mead, 1926).

A 11.1.b
Second printing: New York: Scribners, 1925. Not differentiated on copyright page. August 1925. 3,000 copies. Locations: Lilly; MJB.

Identical with first printing, except for the six textual variants listed above. The second printing retains the Scribners seal on the copyright page.

A 11.1.c
First English printing, from American plates [1926]

THE GREAT GATSBY

BY

F. SCOTT FITZGERALD

Then wear the gold hat, if that will move her,
If you can bounce high, bounce for her too,
Till she cry "Lover, gold-hatted, high-bouncing lover,
I must have you!"
—Thomas Parke D'Invilliers.

LONDON
CHATTO & WINDUS

A 11.1.c: 7⅜" x 4⅞"

Copyright page: 'PUBLISHED 1926 | PRINTED IN GREAT BRITAIN | ALL | RIGHTS RESERVED'.

Same pagination and collation as first Scribners printing.

Contents: p. i: half title; p. ii: blank; p. iii: title; p. iv: copyright; p. v: dedication; p. vi: blank; pp. 1–218: text, headed 'THE GREAT GATSBY | CHAPTER I'.

Paper: Laid unwatermarked paper. Vertical chain lines 1″ apart.

Binding: Dark blue V cloth (fine linen-like grain). Spine goldstamped: 'THE GREAT | GATSBY | F. | SCOTT FITZGERALD | CHATTO & WINDUS'. Also tan V cloth, spine blackstamped. Also light blue cloth-like boards, spine blackstamped—possibly a remainder binding or a cheap reprint (see A 11.1.d). The dark blue cloth binding seems to be the primary binding. White wove endpapers. All edges trimmed.

Dust jacket: Not seen.

Publication: Unknown number of copies. Published February 1926. 7s.

Locations: BM 12730.s.4. (deposit-stamp 10 February 1926; dark blue V cloth); Bodleian (deposited 15 February 1926); Lilly; MJB (three bindings); NjP (dark blue V cloth).

Note: The first English publication of *GG* is not a new edition, but is a separate printing in England from the plates of the American edition—the third printing of the first edition. It includes the six emendations from the second Scribners printing.

A 11.1.d
Cheap reprint (?):   London: Chatto & Windus, [1927]. 2s.

350 sets of gatherings were bound in a cheaper binding. It cannot be determined whether these were remainder gatherings or a new printing. Not seen—information is based on *The English Catalogue of Books*.

LATER PRINTINGS WITHIN THE FIRST EDITION

A 11.1.e
Fourth printing (Modern Library)

[within double-rule frame] THE | GREAT GATSBY | [rule] | BY | F. SCOTT FITZGERALD | [rule] | WITH A NEW INTRODUCTION | BY | F. SCOTT FITZGERALD | [rule] | [four-line verse epigraph] | —THOMAS PARKE D'INVILLIERS. | [device] | [rule] | BENNETT A. CERF·DONALD S. KLOPFER | THE MODERN LIBRARY | NEW YORK

On copyright page: 'First Modern Library Edition | 1934'.

Binding: Noted in blue, green, brown, or red cloth gold-stamped.

Dust jacket. Some jackets are stamped in ink 'DISCONTIN-UED TITLE'.

Publication: One Modern Library printing only. Probably 5,000 copies. Published 13 September 1934. 95¢. See B 19. First publication of Fitzgerald's introduction, pp. vii–xi.

A 11.1.f
Fifth printing: New York: Scribners, 1942. Published August 1942. Location: MJB.

A 11.1.g
Sixth printing: New York: New Directions, [1946]. New Classics, #9. Introduction by Lionel Trilling. Published December 1945.

A 11.1.h
Seventh printing: New York: Grosset & Dunlap, [1949], Dust jacket has wraparound band promoting the 1949 Paramount film.

SECOND EDITION

A 11.2.a
Second American edition

The Last Tycoon . . . Together With The Great Gatsby And Selected Stories. New York: Scribners, 1941. Reprinted 1945.

See A 18.1.a for main entry.

REPRINTS

A 11.2.b
The Last Tycoon . . . Together With The Great Gatsby. New York: Scribners, 1951. Omits stories. See A 18.1.c.

A 11.2.c
Modern Standard Authors Three Novels of F. Scott Fitzgerald. New York: Scribners, [1953]. Reprints *GG*, second edition setting. See AA 4.

LATER EDITIONS

A 11.3
Third American edition (Armed Services)

[within double-rule frame] [to the left of a vertical rule] PUBLISHED BY ARRANGEMENT WITH | CHARLES SCRIBNER'S SONS, NEW YORK | COPYRIGHT, 1925, | BY CHARLES SCRIBNER'S SONS | [to the right of a vertical rule; the first three lines in script] The | Great Gatsby | by | F. SCOTT FITZGERALD | *Editions for the Armed Services, Inc.* | A NON-PROFIT ORGANIZATION ESTABLISHED BY | THE COUNCIL ON BOOKS IN WARTIME, NEW YORK | [outside frame] 862

Probably distributed in 1945. 155,000 copies. Not for sale. Locations: LC (received 16 April 1946); MJB. See *Editions for the Armed Services, Inc. A History* (New York: Editions for the Armed Services, n.d.).

A 11.4
Fourth American edition (Portable)

The Portable F. Scott Fitzgerald, selected by Dorothy Parker and with an introduction by John O'Hara. New York: Viking, 1945. Reprinted 1945, 1949. Also published as *The Indispensable F. Scott Fitzgerald* (New York: The Book Society, 1949 and 1951). See AA 1.

A 11.5
Fifth American edition

[within double-rule frame] THE GREAT | GATSBY | F. SCOTT FITZGERALD | [four-line verse epigraph] | —Thomas Parke D'Invilliers | [rooster] | New York | BANTAM BOOKS

1945. #8. Reprinted 1946 (twice), 1951, 1952, 1954. In 1949 a dust jacket was put on this edition, showing Alan Ladd in a scene from the Paramount film.

A 11.6
Sixth American edition

[first two lines in swash] Great American | Short Novels | EDITED BY | WILLIAM PHILLIPS | [swash] A Permanent Library Book | [line of decorations with seal in center] | 1946 | DIAL PRESS: *NEW YORK*

1950 fifth printing and undated sixth printing noted. Includes *GG*, pp. 453–575.

A 11.7
First English edition

F. SCOTT FITZGERALD | [star] | The Great | GATSBY | [star] | THE GREY WALLS PRESS

London, 1948. Reprinted 1949.

A 11.8
Second English edition

THE GREAT GATSBY | [tapered rule with decoration in middle] | *F Scott Fitzgerald* | PENGUIN BOOKS | HARMONDSWORTH·MIDDLESEX

1950. #746. Reprinted 1954, 1958, 1961, 1962, 1963, 1964, 1966, 1967, 1968 (twice), 1969 (twice).

A 11.9
First Swedish edition

[within single-rule frame] F. SCOTT FITZGERALD | *The Great*

| *Gatsby* | [tapered rule] | THE POLYGLOT CLUB | STOCKHOLM | 1950

English text with Swedish gloss. Location: MJB.

A 11.10.a
Seventh American edition

The Great Gatsby | BY | F. SCOTT FITZGERALD | [four line verse epigraph] | —THOMAS PARKE D'INVILLIERS | *CHARLES SCRIBNER'S SONS* | *New York*

1957. Student's Edition: A-8.57 [C]. Reprint noted: B-1.58 [C].

A 11.10.b
In 1960 the Student's Edition was incorporated into the Scribner Library (#SL1); A-1.60 [C]. Reprints noted: D-3.61 [C]; G-4.63 [Col]; H-10.63 [Col]; J-9.64 [Col]; J-2.65 [Col] (duplicate plates); N-8.68 [Col]; O-5.69 [C]; P-9.69 [C]; R-10.70 [C]. Also clothbound: C-7.59 [H].

A 11.11
Third English edition

THE BODLEY HEAD | SCOTT | FITZGERALD | WITH AN INTRODUCTION BY | J. B. PRIESTLEY | VOL. I | THE GREAT GATSBY | THE LAST TYCOON, AND SOME | SHORTER PIECES | THE BODLEY HEAD | LONDON

1958.

A 11.12
First Japanese edition

[rule] | *Kairyudo's Mentor Library No. 11* | [rule] | F. SCOTT FITZGERALD | THE GREAT GATSBY | Edited and Annotated | by | NAOTARO TATSUNOKUCHI | and | NOBUYUKI KIUCHI | KAIRYUDO | TOKYO

1960. Location: MJB.

A 11.13
Eighth American edition

THE | *Great Gatsby* | [decoration] | BY F. SCOTT FITZGERALD | [four-line verse epigraph] | —THOMAS PARKE D'INVILLIERS |

CHARLES SCRIBNER'S SONS | 597 *Fifth Avenue, New York 17, New York*

1961. School Edition: A-9.61 [V]. Foreword and study guide by Albert K. Ridout. Paperbound reprint: A-1.68 [M].

A 11.14
Ninth American edition

The | FITZGERALD | *Reader* | Edited by *ARTHUR MIZENER* | Charles Scribner's Sons | *New York*

1963. 3.63 [H]. Includes *GG*, pp. 105–238. See AA 9.

A 11.15
Tenth American edition

A QUARTO | OF MODERN | LITERATURE | *Edited by* | LEONARD BROWN | *FIFTH EDITION* | CHARLES SCRIBNER'S SONS *New York*

1964. A-3.64 [V]. Includes *GG*, pp. 212–267.

A 11.16
Eleventh American edition

[two-page title; the following on the left page] Three | Great | American | Novels | [the following on the right page] The Great Gatsby | F. SCOTT FITZGERALD | WITH AN INTRODUCTION BY MALCOLM COWLEY | [six lines of type] | MODERN STANDARD AUTHORS | CHARLES SCRIBNER'S SONS | NEW YORK

1967. A-9.67 [c].

A 11.17
Fourth English edition

THE BODLEY HEAD SERIES | The | Great Gatsby | F. SCOTT FITZGERALD | *with commentary* | *and notes by* | J. F. WYATT | M.A. | THE BODLEY HEAD | LONDON SYDNEY | TORONTO

1967.

A 11.18
Fifth English edition

THE GREAT GATSBY | F. SCOTT FITZGERALD |

ILLUSTRATIONS BY CHARLES RAYMOND | [rule] | THE
FOLIO SOCIETY·LONDON·1968

Introduction by Tim Andrews.

A 11.19
Twelfth American edition

The Great Gatsby | BY | F. SCOTT FITZGERALD | [four-line
verse epigraph] | —THOMAS PARKE D'INVILLIERS | *CHARLES
SCRIBNER'S SONS* | *New York*

1968. Scribners Large Type Edition: A-5.68 [C].

A 11.20
Thirteenth American edition

HENRY DAN PIPER | Southern Illinois University, Carbondale
| FITZGERALD'S *The Great Gatsby:* | The Novel, The
Critics, The Background | [lamp] SCRIBNER | RESEARCH |
ANTHOLOGIES | CHARLES SCRIBNER'S SONS | New York

1970. A-3.70 [H].

A 11.21
Fourteenth American edition

THE | GREAT GATSBY | BY | F. SCOTT FITZGERALD | [four-
line verse epigraph] | —THOMAS PARKE D'INVILLIERS |
CHARLES SCRIBNER'S SONS | *New York*

1970. Part of a four-volume set (with *TSOP, TITN,* LT) distributed by The Literary Guild of America and its associated book
clubs.

[1–7] 8–159 [160]

EXCERPTS FROM GG

A 11.22
The Great American Parade. Garden City, N.Y.: Doubleday,
Doran, 1935. Includes excerpt from *GG,* "The Guy Who Fixed
the World Series," pp. 496–499.

A 11.23
North, East, South, West, ed. Charles Lee. New York: Howell
Soskin, [1945]. Includes opening of *GG,* pp. 224–225.

A 11.24
I Wish I'd Written That, ed. Eugene J. Woods. New York and London: Whittlesey House, [1946]. John Dos Passos selected the description of Myrtle's party, pp. 368–380.

See *write and rewrite*, B 66, B 67.

A *12.1.a*
First edition, first printing (*1926*)

ALL THE SAD
YOUNG MEN

By
F. SCOTT FITZGERALD

NEW YORK
CHARLES SCRIBNER'S SONS
1926

A 12.1.a: 7½" x 5⅛"

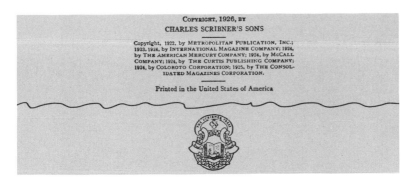

[i–viii] 1–267 [268]

[1–16]⁸ [17]¹⁰

Contents: p. i: half title; p. ii: 'BY F. SCOTT FITZGERALD | [seven titles]'; p. iii: title; p. iv: copyright; p. v: 'TO | RING AND ELLIS LARDNER'; p. vi: blank; p vii: contents; p. viii: blank; pp. 1–267: text, headed 'THE RICH BOY'; p. 268: blank.

Stories. "The Rich Boy," "Winter Dreams," "The Baby Party," "Absolution," "Rags Martin-Jones and the Pr-nce of W-les," "The Adjuster," "Hot and Cold Blood," " 'The Sensible Thing'," "Gretchen's Forty Winks."

Typography and paper: 12 point on 13, Old Style. 5½″ (5¹³⁄₁₆″) x 3½″; thirty-one lines per page. Running heads: rectos, story titles; versos, 'ALL THE SAD YOUNG MEN'. Wove paper.

Binding: Green B cloth (linen-like grain). Front blindstamped: 'ALL THE | SAD YOUNG MEN | By F. Scott Fitzgerald'. Spine goldstamped: 'ALL | THE SAD | YOUNG | MEN | [rule] | Fitzgerald | SCRIBNERS'. White wove endpapers of sized stock. Top and bottom edges trimmed.

Dust jacket: Front has drawing in green and black of woman holding a globe, signed by CLEON: '[lettered in black against tan background] ALL THE SAD | YOUNG MEN | F·SCOTT FITZGERALD'. Spine lettered in black: 'ALL | THE SAD | YOUNG | MEN | [rule] | Fitzgerald | SCRIBNERS'. Back has blurb about Fitzgerald. Front flap has blurbs by Broun, Jones, Woollcott, and Hergesheimer; back flap has ad for Ring Lardner's *The Love Nest*. The lips of the woman on the front show progressive batter.

Publication: 10,100 copies of the first printing. Published 26 February 1926. $2.00.

Dust jacket for A 12.1.a

Printing: Printed by the Scribner Press from plates made from type set by the Scribner Press. Bound by the Scribner Press.

Locations: LC (not deposit copy); Lilly (dj); MJB (dj); NjP; PSt.

Note one: The Scribners records show three printings of *ASYM* in 1926. These were not identified by the publisher and have not been differentiated by bibliographical tests. No textual variants have been discovered by machine collation of copies with sharp type against copies with worn type. Batter has been noted at 38.6–9 (left margin), 248.21–24 (left margin), and 90 (folio).

Note two: Three of the stories in *ASYM* were included in *Six Tales of the Jazz Age and Other Stories* (1960). A 9.3.a.

A 12.1.b
Second printing: New York: Scribners, 1926. Not differentiated on copyright page. March 1926. 3,020 copies.

A 12.1.c
Third printing: New York: Scribners, 1926. Not differentiated on copyright page. May 1926. 3,050 copies.

A 12.1.d
Pirated reprint: In 1969 copies of an unauthorized offset reprint of *ASYM* were sold by Quality Books of Philadelphia. This piracy had the original title page but can be identified by its blank copyright page. The copy seen is bound in light blue buckram, with goldstamped spine. Location: ScU (PZ/3/.F5754/A1/c.2). A later printing of this piracy was offered for sale in 1971 by Folcroft Library Editions, Folcroft, Pa. This printing is bound in goldstamped maroon buckram and has a special title page, which is the 1926 Scribners title page with a new imprint substituted: '[double rule] | ALL THE SAD | YOUNG MEN | *By* | F. SCOTT FITZGERALD | [rule] | [decoration] | [rule] | THE FOLCROFT PRESS [device]'. On verso: 'Reprinted 1970'. Location: MJB.

A 13 JOHN JACKSON'S ARCADY
Only printing [1928]

John Jackson's Arcady

By

F. SCOTT FITZGERALD

A Contest Selection

Arranged by
LILIAN HOLMES STRACK

BOSTON
Walter H. Baker Company
PUBLISHERS

A 13: 7⅜″ x 4⅞″

[1–3] 4–8

[1]⁴

Contents: p. 1: title; p. 2: copyright; pp. 3–8: text, headed: '[ornamental bar] | John Jackson's Arcady'.

Typography and paper: Double columns, forty-two lines per column. Running heads. rectos and versos, '*JOHN JACKSON'S ARCADY*'. Laid unwatermarked paper.

Binding: Orange wrappers printed on front in black and gray: '[within double-rule frame, first four lines within decorative compartment] [black] John Jackson's Arcady | BY | F. SCOTT FITZGERALD | [gray script] Baker's Manuscript Readings | [within a gray scrollwork compartment] [black Baker seal] | [gray] WALTER H·BAKER COMPANY··BOSTON'. Number on back wraper: '18992'.

Publication: Unknown number of copies. Published 2 August 1928. 50¢.

Location: LC (received 9 August 1928); Lilly; MJB; NjP.

Note: Presumably one printing only. Fitzgerald's story was revised and cut for public reading by Lilian Holmes Strack.

A 14 TENDER IS THE NIGHT

A 14.1.a
First edition, first printing (1934)

TENDER IS THE
NIGHT
A ROMANCE

By

F. Scott Fitzgerald

DECORATIONS BY
EDWARD SHENTON

NEW YORK
CHARLES SCRIBNER'S SONS
1934

A 14.1.a: 7⅜″ x 5⅛″

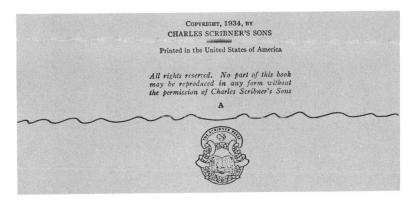

[ì–x] [1–2] 3–148 [149–150] 151–306 [307–308] 309–408 [409–410]

[1–25]⁸ [26]¹⁰

Contents: p. i–iii: blank; p. iv: 'BY F. SCOTT FITZGERALD | [eight titles]'; p. v: half title; p. vi: epigraph from "Ode to a Nightingale"; p. vii: title; p. viii: copyright; p. ix: 'TO | GERALD AND SARA | MANY FÊTES'; p. x: blank; p. 1: 'TENDER IS THE NIGHT | BOOK ONE'; p. 2: blank; pp. 3–408: text; p. 149: 'BOOK II'; p. 307: 'BOOK III'; pp. 409–410: blank.

Typography and paper: 10½ point on 11½, Old Style. Pen and ink decorations by Edward Shenton. 5½" (6") x 3¹¹⁄₁₆"; thirty-three lines per page. Running heads: rectos and versos, 'TENDER IS THE NIGHT'. Wove paper.

Binding: Green B cloth (linen-like grain) or T cloth (vertical lines). Front has blindstamped single-rule frame. Spine gold-stamped: 'TENDER | IS THE | NIGHT | [rule] | Fitzgerald | SCRIBNERS'. White wove endpapers of coated stock. Top and bottom edges trimmed.

Dust jacket: Front has drawing of Riviera scene: '[yellow] F. SCOTT FITZGERALD | [white rule] | [red] TENDER IS | THE NIGHT'. Spine: '[red] TENDER | IS THE | NIGHT | [yellow] F. SCOTT | FITZGERALD | [red] SCRIBNERS'. Back has profile drawing of Fitzgerald and blurb for *TITN*. Front flap has blurbs by Eliot, Mencken, and Rosenfeld; back flap lists books by Fitzgerald.

Publication: 7,600 copies of the first printing. Published 12 April 1934. $2.50.

Dust jacket for A 14.1.a

Printing: Printed by the Scribner Press from plates made and type set by Brown Bros. Linotypers. Bound by the Scribner Press. (The cost of composition and electrotyping was $712.07; the cost of corrections was $318.56.)

Locations: LC (B cloth, deposited 14 April 1934); Lilly (B cloth, dj); MJB (B cloth and T cloth, both with dj); NjP; ViU.

Note: See M. J. Bruccoli, *The Composition of Tender is the Night* (Pittsburgh: University of Pittsburgh Press, 1963) and "Material for a Centenary Edition of *Tender is the Night*," *Studies in Bibliography*, XVII (1964), 177–193.

A 14.1.a†

One copy bound in wrappers made from the dust jacket has been located at ViU (PS3511/.19T4/1934 copy 5). It may have been used as an advance or review copy. The Scribners records indicate that 500 copies in wrappers were ordered; but since only one copy has been located, it seems doubtful that these copies were actually prepared.

A 14.1.b

Second printing: New York: Scribners, 1934. Not differentiated on copyright page, except that the 'A' is removed. April 1934. 5,075 copies.

A 14.1.c

Third printing: New York: Scribners, 1934. Not differentiated on copyright page. May 1934. 2,520 copies. There is one plate alteration between the second and third printings:

320.17   Charles   [Devereux

Location: NjP (Fitzgerald's marked copy).

A 14.1.d

Fourth printing: New York: Scribners, 1951.

The following plate alterations were made:

vii   FÊTES   [FÉTES (*possibly batter*)
344.7   Saland   [Salaud

A *14.2.a*
First English edition, first printing (1934)

TENDER
IS THE NIGHT
A ROMANCE

By

F. Scott Fitzgerald

1934
CHATTO & WINDUS
LONDON

A 14.2.a: 7⅜″ x 4⅞″

Copyright page: 'PRINTED IN GREAT BRITAIN | ALL RIGHTS RESERVED'.

P. 408: 'Printed in Great Britain by Butler & Tanner Ltd., Frome and London'.

[i–viii] [1–2] 3–148 [149–150] 151–306 [307–308] 309–408

[A]⁴ B–I⁸ K–U⁸ X–Z⁸, AA–CC⁸ DD⁴; four-page gathering of ads inserted at rear.

Contents: p. i: half title; p. ii: blank; p. iii: title; p. iv: copyright; p. v: dedication; p. vi: blank; p. vii: epigraph; p. viii: blank; p. 1: 'BOOK I'; p. 2: blank; pp. 3–408: text, headed 'I'.

Typography and paper: Thirty-five lines per page. Running heads: rectos, book and chapter; versos, 'TENDER IS THE NIGHT'. Laid paper, vertical chainmarks 15/16″ apart.

Binding: Blue V cloth (fine linen-like grain). Spine yellow-stamped: 'TENDER | IS THE | NIGHT | [star] | F. SCOTT | FITZGERALD | CHATTO & WINDUS'. White wove endpapers. Top and front edges trimmed.

Dust jacket: Front has drawing of man and woman in bathing suits against blue background with yellow stars, signed by THÉA: '[white] TENDER | IS THE NIGHT | [red] BY F. SCOTT FITZGERALD'. Spine: '[red] TENDER | IS THE | NIGHT | [woman's head in a star] | BY | F. SCOTT | FITZGERALD | [blue] CHATTO & | WINDUS'. Back: 'NEW FICTION' [nine titles]. Front flap has blurb for *TITN;* back flap blank.

Publication: Unknown number of copies. Published September 1934. 7s. 6d.

Locations: BM 12730.s.5. (deposit-stamp 12 September 1934); Bodleian (deposited September 1934); MJB (dj); NjP.

Note: The first Chatto & Windus printing of *TITN* varies from the first Scribners printing in some 860 readings, of which 6 are substantives:

    61.10   words   [61.10   worlds
    133.4–5 this name [133.3   his name
    169.17 may I add [168.9   may add
    347.3   lay own   [346.31 lay, down
    362.2   with insincerity [361.24 within sincerity
    396.9   her raging [395.16 her, raging

The authority for these alterations is unknown.

A 14.2.a†
Butler & Tanner Ltd. prepared a "cheap edition" from remainder copies in September 1936 by pasting a printed label
'2/6' on the spine of the dust jacket. Location: MJB (publisher's office copy, dj). 250 sets of gatherings were bound in a
cheaper binding—not seen.

A 14.2.a‡
Proof Copy

Printed on thin wove paper and bound in brown paper
wrappers. White label printed in black on front wrapper:
'TENDER IS THE | NIGHT | F. SCOTT FITZGERALD | [deco-
ration] | CHATTO & WINDUS | [rule] | Butler & Tanner Ltd.,
Frome and London'. Possibly used as a review copy. Location:
MJB.

LATER EDITIONS OF THE 1934 TEXT

A 14.3
Second American edition

The Portable F. Scott Fitzgerald, selected by Dorothy Parker
and with an introduction by John O'Hara. New York: Viking,
1945. See AA 1.

A 14.4
Second English edition

TENDER | IS THE NIGHT | [tapered rule] | by | F. SCOTT
FITZGERALD | THE GREY WALLS PRESS LTD. | Crown
Passage, Pall Mall | London

1948.

A 14.5
Third American edition

[two-page title] [script] Tender is the Night | [wavy rule] |
[roman] by | F. Scott Fitzgerald | [wavy rule] | [rooster]
BANTAM BOOKS·New York

1951. #A867. Reprinted February and April 1951.

A 14.6
Fourth American edition

F. SCOTT FITZGERALD | *Tender is the Night* | [four lines of italic type] | —ODE TO A NIGHTINGALE [decorations] | NEW YORK | *CHARLES SCRIBNER'S SONS*

1960. A–1.60 [C]. Scribner Library #SL2. Reprints noted: E–8.61 [C]; H–10.63 [Col]; I–9.64 [Col]; L–2.67 [Col]; N–5.69 [C].

A 14.7
Fifth American edition

TENDER | IS THE | NIGHT | F. SCOTT | FITZGERALD | [four lines of italic type] | —*ODE TO A NIGHTINGALE* | BANTAM BOOKS [rooster] NEW YORK

1962. #S2385 / 5. Reprinted four times.

A 14.8
Sixth American edition

TENDER | IS THE NIGHT | BY | F. SCOTT FITZGERALD | [four lines of italic type] | —ODE TO A NIGHTINGALE | CHARLES SCRIBNER'S SONS *New York*

1970. Part of a four-volume set (with *TSOP, GG, LT*) distributed by The Literary Guild of America and its associated book clubs.

[1–9] 10–128 [129–131] 132–263 [264–267] 268–349 [350–352]

A 15 TENDER IS THE NIGHT
Revised edition

A *15.1.a₁*
First printing, first state (1951)

Tender is the Night

A ROMANCE

By

F. Scott Fitzgerald

With the Author's Final Revisions
PREFACE BY
MALCOLM COWLEY

CHARLES SCRIBNER'S SONS
NEW YORK
1951

A 15.1.a₁: 8¼″ x 5½″

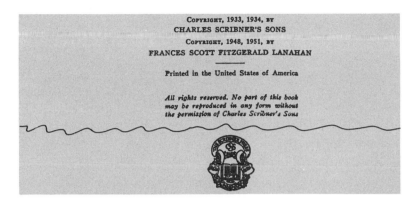

[i–viii] ix–xviii [xix–xx] [1–2] 3–50 [51–52] 53–114 [115–116] 117–183 [184–186] 187–253 [254–256] 257–356

[1–11]¹⁶ [12]¹²

Contents: p. i: half title; p. ii: 'BY F. SCOTT FITZGERALD | [five titles]'; p. iii: title; p. iv: copyright; p. v: dedication; p. vi: blank; p. vii: contents; p. viii: blank; pp. ix–xviii: 'INTRO-DUCTION'; p. xix: epigraph; p. xx: blank; p. 1: 'BOOK I | CASE HISTORY | 1917–1919 | [tapered rule]'; p. 2: blank; pp. 3–334: text, headed 'TENDER IS THE NIGHT | CHAPTER I'; p. 51: 'BOOK II | ROSEMARY'S ANGLE | 1919–1925 | | [tapered rule]'; p. 115: 'BOOK III | CASUALTIES | 1925 | [tapered rule]'; p. 185: 'BOOK IV | ESCAPE | 1925–1929 | [tapered rule]'; p. 255: 'BOOK V | THE WAY HOME | 1929–1930 | [tapered rule]'; pp. 335–348: 'APPENDIX | [swash] The Manuscripts of "Tender" '; pp. 349–356: '[swash] Notes'.

Typography and paper: Thirty-eight lines per page. Running heads: rectos and versos, 'TENDER IS THE NIGHT'. Wove paper.

Binding: Tan V cloth (fine linen-like grain). Spine black-stamped with four red compartments: '[three rules] | TENDER | IS THE | NIGHT | [three rules] | F. SCOTT | FITZGERALD | [three rules] | AUTHOR'S | FINAL | REVISION | [six rules] | SCRIBNERS | [three rules]'. White wove endpapers of different stock from text paper. All edges trimmed.

Dust jacket: Tan laid paper. Front has seventeen lines of type in red and black: 'THE AUTHOR'S FINAL VERSION, COMPLETELY | RESET, AND NOW PUBLISHED FOR THE FIRST TIME | F. SCOTT FITZGERALD | [red] *Tender is the*

Night | [twelve lines of type printed in black quoting Fitzgerald's 24 December 1938 letter to Perkins and Fitzgerald's note in his own copy of *TITN*] | WITH AN INTRODUCTION BY *Malcolm Cowley'*. Spine: '[black script] Tender | is the | Night | [red] F. SCOTT | FITZGERALD | [black] SCRIBNERS'. Back has list of five volumes by Fitzgerald. Front flap has blurb for *TITN;* back flap has blurb for *Stories*.

Publication: 5,075 copies of the first printing. Published 12 November 1951. $3.50.

Printing: Composed and printed from plates by the Scribner Press. Bound by the Scribner Press.

Locations: LC (deposited 21 November 1951); Lilly (second state, dj); MJB (first and second states, both with dj); NjP (second state).

Note: A mimeographed *Erratum Slip for Reviewers* on Scribner letterhead was inserted in review copies and lists the four errata noted under A 15.1.a₂.

A 15.1.a₂
First printing, second state

$[1]^{16}(\pm 1_{6,7,9})\ [2-11]^{16}\ [12]^{12}$

Three leaves were cancelled in Cowley's introduction to correct four errors:

```
xi.18      xett  [   text
xiv.19     tsandards  [   standards
xviii.23   b each  [   beach
xviii.24   accompanied  [   accomplished
```

LATER PRINTINGS WITHIN THE REVISED TEXT

A 15.1.b
New York: Scribners, 1953.

A 15.1.c
Modern Standard Authors Three Novels of F. Scott Fitzgerald.
New York: Scribners, [1953]. See AA 4.

A 15.1.d
New York: Scribners, 1956.

A 15.1.e
New York: Scribners, [1959]. J-9.59 [MH].

A 15.1.f
New York: Scribners, [1970]. O-5.70 [MC]. Scribner Library #SL2. The Scribner Library series normally used the original text, but in the "O" printing of 1970, the plates of the revised text were used inadvertently.

A 15.2.a
Revised edition, first English edition, first printing [1953]

TENDER
IS THE NIGHT

by

F. SCOTT FITZGERALD

With the author's final revisions
and a preface. by

MALCOLM COWLEY

LONDON
THE GREY WALLS PRESS

A 15.2.a: scant 7¼″ x 4¹³⁄₁₆″

*This new edition published in 1953
by The Grey Walls Press Limited
6 & 7 Crown Passage, Pall Mall,
London, S.W.1*

*Printed in Great Britain
by The Alcuin Press,
Welwyn Garden City.
All rights reserved*

[i–x] xi–xxii [1–2] 3–55 [56–58] 59–131 [132–134] 135–213 [214–216] 217–297 [298–300] 301–407 [408] 409–418

[A]⁸ B:I⁸ K:Y⁸, AA:CC⁸ DD⁴

Contents: p. i: half title; p. ii: '*by the same author* | [three titles]'; p. iii: title; p. iv: copyright; p. v: dedication; p. vi: blank; p. vii: epigraph; p. viii: blank; p. ix: contents; p. x: blank; pp. xi–xxii: '*INTRODUCTION*'; p. 1: section title; p. 2: blank; pp. 3–392: text, headed 'I'; pp. 57, 133, 215, 299: section titles; pp. 393–407: '*APPENDIX*'; pp. 409–418: 'Notes'.

Typography and paper: Thirty-five lines per page. Wove paper.

Binding: Pinkish tan V cloth (fine linen-like grain) or gold tan paper-covered boards. Priority of bindings undetermined. Spine goldstamped: '*TENDER* | *IS THE* | *NIGHT* | [asterisk] | *F. SCOTT* | *FITZGERALD* | *GREY* | *WALLS* | *PRESS*'. White wove endpapers of different stock from text paper. All edges trimmed.

Dust jacket: City night scene in shades of black, gray, and white on front, spine, and back, signed by PAGRAM. Front: '[white] TENDER IS THE | NIGHT | F. Scott Fitzgerald'. Spine: '[black] Tender | is the | Night | [white] *by* | F. Scott | Fitzgerald | [black] GREY | WALLS | PRESS'. Front flap has blurb for *TITN;* back flap lists four other Fitzgerald titles, '*Catalogue No. R.6714.*'

Publication: Unknown number of copies. Published 30 July 1953. 12s. 6d.

Locations: Bodleian (deposited 7 December 1953); MJB (both bindings with dj).

A 15.3
Second English edition

F. SCOTT FITZGERALD | TENDER IS THE NIGHT |
A ROMANCE | [double rule] | WITH THE AUTHOR'S
FINAL REVISION | PREFACE BY | MALCOLM COWLEY |
PENGUIN BOOKS

Harmondsworth, Middlesex, 1955. #906. Reprinted 1958, 1961,
1963, 1964, 1966, 1968, 1970. There are two errors on the
copyright page: *TITN* was not first published in 1939, and the
revised version was not published in 1948.

A 16 THE TRUE STORY OF APPOMATTOX
(*1934*)

THE TRUE STORY OF APPOMATTOX

Columnist Discovers That It Was Grant Who Surrendered To Lee Instead Of Lee Surrendering To Grant

Circumstances Divulged For The First Time By Captain X

We have learned that when Grant had decided to surrender his milk-fed millions to Lee's starving remnants and the rendezvous was arranged at Appomattox Court House, Lee demanded that Grant put his submission into writing. Unfortunately Grant's pencil broke, and, removing his cigar from his mouth, he turned to General Lee and said with true military courtesy: "General, I have broken my pencil; will you lend me your sword to sharpen it with?" General Lee, always ready and willing to oblige, whipped forth his sword and tendered it to General Grant.

It was unfortunately just at this moment that the flashlight photographers and radio announcers got to work and the picture was erroneously given to the world that General Lee was surrendering his sword to General Grant.

The credulous public immediately accepted this story. The bells that were prepared to ring triumphantly in Loudoun county were stilled while the much inferior Yankee bells in Old North Church in Boston burst forth in a false pæan of triumph. To this day the legend persists, but we of the Welbourne *Journal* are able to present to the world for the first time the real TRUTH about this eighty-year-old slander that Virginia lost its single-handed war against the allied Eskimos north of the Mason and Dixon line.

A 16: 8½″ x 1¹⁵⁄₁₆″

THE   TRUE | STORY   OF | APPOMATTOX | [rule] |
Columnist Discovers That It | Was Grant Who Surrendered |
To Lee Instead of Lee | Surrendering To Grant | [rule] |
Circumstances Divulged For | The First Time By | Captain X |
[rule]

Thirty-eight-line newspaper clipping. Newsprint. Cropped sections of news items on verso. July 1934.

Locations: NjP; ViU.

Fitzgerald to Perkins, 30 July 1934: "I managed to have my
joke about Grant and Lee taken down on paper. Then last night
I had it faked up by the *Sun* here in Baltimore and I am going
to send one to Elizabeth [Lemmon] framed. Please return the
one herewith enclosed for your inspection."

See A 32.

A 17 TAPS AT REVEILLE

A 17.1.a₁
First edition, only printing, first state (1935)

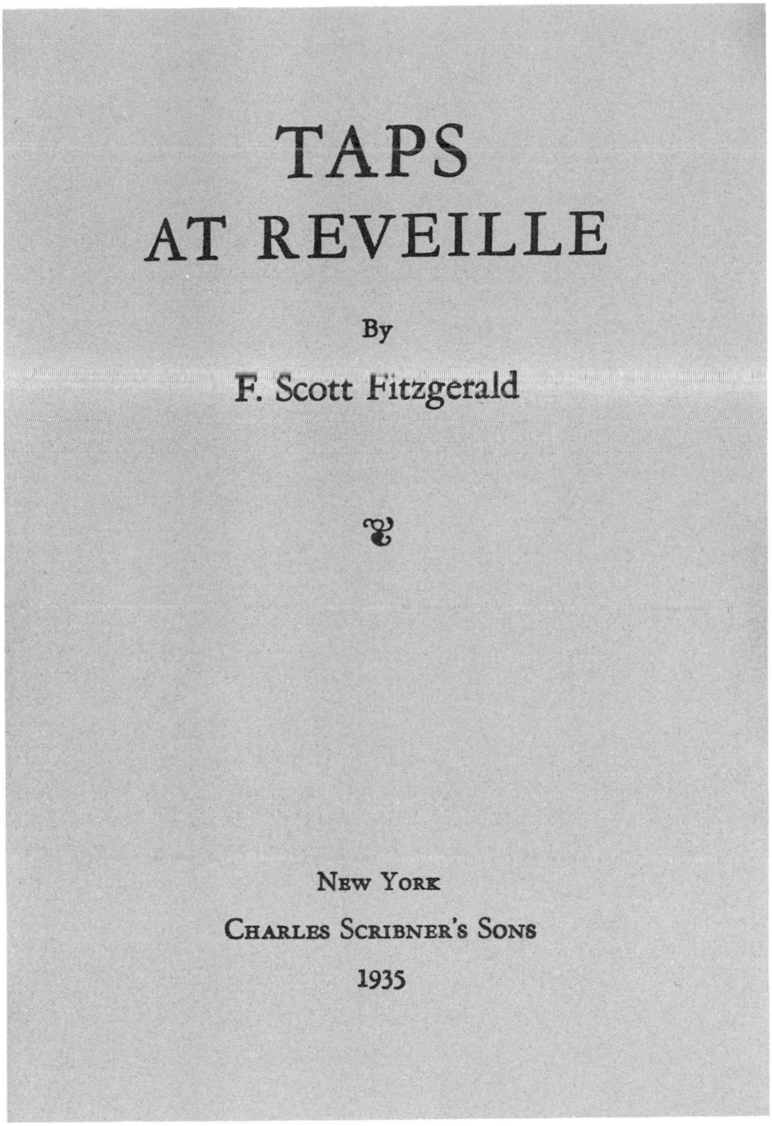

TAPS
AT REVEILLE

By

F. Scott Fitzgerald

ॐ

New York
Charles Scribner's Sons
1935

A 17.1.a₁: 7⁵⁄₁₆″ x 5⅛″

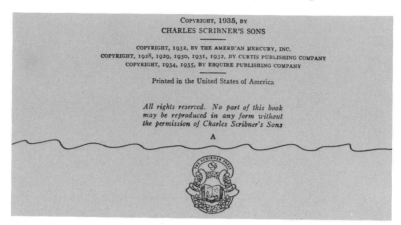

[i–xii] 1–407 [408]

[1–25]⁸ [26]¹⁰

Contents: p. i: blank; p. ii: 'BY F. SCOTT FITZGERALD |
[nine titles]'; p. iii: half title; p. iv: blank; p. v: title page; p. vi:
copyright; p. vii: 'TO | HAROLD OBER'; p. viii: blank; p. ix:
contents; p. x: blank; p. xi: half title; p. xii: blank; pp. 1–407:
text, headed 'BASIL | THE SCANDAL DETECTIVES | I'; p. 408:
blank.

  Stories. Basil—"The Scandal Detectives," "The Freshest
Boy," "He Thinks He's Wonderful," "The Captured Shadow,"
"The Perfect Life"; *Josephine*—"First Blood," "A Nice Quiet
Place," "A Woman With A Past"; "Crazy Sunday," "Two
Wrongs," "The Night of Chancellorsville," "The Last of the
Belles," "Majesty," "Family in the Wind," "A Short Trip Home,"
"One Interne," "The Fiend," "Babylon Revisited."

Typography and paper: 10½ point on 11½, Old Style. 5¹¹⁄₁₆″
(6⅛″) x 3¹¹⁄₁₆″; thirty-three lines per page. Running heads: rectos, story titles; versos, section title for Basil and Josephine
stories, story titles for the rest. Wove paper.

Binding: Green B cloth (linen-like grain). Front has blind-
stamped single-rule frame. Spine goldstamped: 'TAPS | AT |
REVEILLE | [rule] | Fitzgerald | SCRIBNERS'. White wove
endpapers of sized stock. Top and bottom edges trimmed.

Dust jacket: Front has drawings of figures from stories
against orange background, signed by Doris Spiegel: '[black
outlined in white] [first two lines in script] Taps at Reveille |
Stories | F. SCOTT FITZGERALD'. Spine lettered in black:

"You feel as you read it that you will never forget it," said Gilbert Seldes of

F. Scott Fitzgerald's most recent novel

Tender Is the Night

"The people are men and women of tremendous passions," he continued, "doing fine things and ignoble things," living."

"Shows its author's distinctive gift—a romantic imagination, a swiftness of movement, and a sense of enchantment in people and places, all of which combine to give the great merit of being always entertaining."
— Mary Colum in The Forum

"A continually pleasurable performance... An exciting and psychologically apt study in the disintegration of a marriage."
— John Chamberlain in The New York Times

Taps at Reveille
—
FITZGERALD

Taps at Reveille
Stories
F. SCOTT FITZGERALD

SCRIBNERS

TAPS AT REVEILLE

by
F. Scott Fitzgerald

Author of «Tender Is the Night», «The Great Gatsby», etc

In these eighteen stories, chosen by Mr. Fitzgerald as his best short-story writing in the past decade, the author not only brings together in one volume the exploits and adventures of two of his most vividly delineated characters, but adds ten tales which, with one exception, portray various phases of American life from the beginning of the aureate twenties to the bitter end of the age of gold. That one exception is a story, here printed for the first time, that tells what happened to a pair of light ladies who followed the Federal armies to the Civil War battle-field of Chancellorsville—and back. It is among the most remarkable stories that have come from the pen of an acknowledged master in the field.

The book begins with five stories about Basil Duke Lee, the freshest, most disturbingly real adolescent who was ever young in the days when "The Quaker Girl" played on Broadway and folks were singing "Everybody's Doing It." These tragically amusing and uncannily perceptive tales of the pre-war 'teen age are followed by three stories of Josephine, not much older than Basil in years, but as old as Lilith in feminine wiles. She is the complete picture of the eternal feminine, in years when the deadliness of the female was perhaps more celebrated than it is today.

The ten stories which make up the rest of the book include such brilliant pieces as "The Last of the Belles," "Family in the Wind," "A Short Trip Home," and—one of the best of all Fitzgerald stories—"Babylon Revisited."

Scott Fitzgerald's fame as a writer rests quite as securely on his short stories as on his novels. This collection contains much of his finest work, and something for every reader of American fiction.

Published by CHARLES SCRIBNER'S SONS, *New York*

TAPS AT REVEILLE

by F. Scott Fitzgerald

Other short-story collections by Mr. Fitzgerald

Tales of the Jazz Age

"The more you read him, the more he convinces you that here is the destined artist... He is a writer whom it is a joy to read." — New York Times

All the Sad Young Men

"Originality, freshness, intriguing plot, natural yet unexpected surprises, and an easy manner of writing that carries one along without consciousness of the mechanics of the story-writer's trade."
— Boston Transcript

A description of "Taps at Reveille" appears on the back of this jacket.

Dust jacket for A 17.1.a₁

'[first two lines in script] Taps at | Reveille | [rule] | FITZ-GERALD | SCRIBNERS'. Back has blurb for *TAR*. Front flap has blurbs for *TITN;* back flap has blurbs for *TJA* and *ASYM.* The price, which is rubberstamped on the front flap of the jacket of some copies, has been noted in two sizes: ³⁄₁₆″ and ⅛″ high.

Publication: 5,100 copies. Published 20 March 1935. $2.50.

Printing: Printed by the Scribner Press from plates made and type set by Brown Bros., Linotypers. Bound by the Scribner Press.

Locations: BM (deposit-stamp 25 March 1935); LC (first state; deposited 25 March 1935); Lilly (first state, dj); MJB (first and second states; dj without price, dj with small stamp, dj with large stamp); NjP (first state; second state with dj); OKentU (second state); PSt (second state).

A 17.1.a₂
Second state

$[1-22]^8 [23]^8 (\pm 23_{5,6}) [24-25]^8 [26]^{10}$

The cancellation of pp. 349–352 introduces three revisions in "One Interne":

  350.5–7   —he need not base himself on the adding ma-chine-calculating machine-probability machine-St. Francis of Assis machine any longer.   [—need not base himself upon that human mixture of adding machines and St. Francis of Assis any longer.
  351.15   —and was   [—was
  351.29–30   "Oh, catch it—oh, catch it and take it—oh, catch it," she sighed. "I   ["Oh, things like that happen whenever there are a lot of men together. I

A 17.2.a
Second edition

TAPS | AT REVEILLE | *by* F. SCOTT FITZGERALD | [deco-ration] | *CHARLES SCRIBNER'S SONS New York*

1960. A–6.60 [H]. The first state of the text.

A 17.2.b
New York: Scribners, [1971]. Scribner Library #SL274. A–9.71 [M].

A 18 THE LAST TYCOON

A 18.1.a
First edition, first printing (1941)

THE LAST TYCOON

AN UNFINISHED NOVEL

BY

F. SCOTT FITZGERALD

TOGETHER WITH

THE GREAT GATSBY

AND SELECTED STORIES

NEW YORK

CHARLES SCRIBNER'S SONS

1941

A 18.1.a: 8³⁄₁₆″ x 5⅝″

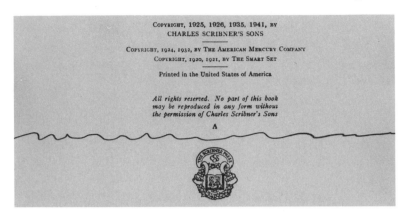

[i–viii] ix–xi [xii] [1–2] 3–163 [164–166] 167–301 [302–304] 305–355 [356–358] 359–398 [399–400] 401–437 [438–440] 441–456 [457–458] 459–476

[1–29]⁸ [30]⁴ [31]⁸

Contents: p. i: blank; p. ii: 'BY F. SCOTT FITZGERALD | [ten titles]'; p. iii: half title; p. iv: blank; p. v: title; p. vi: copyright; p. vii: contents; p. viii: blank; pp. ix–xi: '*FORE-WORD*'; p. xii: blank; p. 1: half title; p. 2: blank; pp. 3–476: text, headed 'THE LAST TYCOON | CHAPTER I'.

Includes *The Last Tycoon*, Notes for *The Last Tycoon*, *The Great Gatsby*, "May Day," "The Diamond as Big as the Ritz," "The Rich Boy," "Absolution," "Crazy Sunday."

Typography and paper: 11 point on 12, Granjon. 6½" (6¾") x 4"; thirty-eight lines per page. Running heads: rectos and versos, section titles. Wove paper.

Binding: Blue V cloth (fine linen-like grain). Front gold-stamped: '[first two lines in script] The | Last Tycoon | [arch consisting of two branches with leaves] | F. SCOTT FITZ-GERALD'. Spine goldstamped: '*THE | LAST | TYCOON* | [line of leaves] | [three rules] | [script] Fitzgerald | [roman] SCRIBNERS'. White wove endpapers of sized stock. Top and bottom edges trimmed. Top edge stained red.

Dust jacket: Front lettered against blue background: '[red border] | [white] F. SCOTT |FITZGERALD | [red arch consisting of two branches with leaves] | [red script] The | Last Tycoon | [white script] An Unfinished Novel, together with | The Great Gatsby, and | Selected Short Stories | [red border signed Neely]'. Spine: '[red border] | [white] F. SCOTT |

Dust jacket for A 18.1.a

FITZGERALD | [red decoration] | [red script] The | Last Tycoon |
[white] *An Unfinished Novel,* | *together with* | *The Great
Gatsby,* | *and Selected* | *Short Stories* | [red rule] | [red]
SCRIBNERS | [red border]'. Back has photo of Fitzgerald by
Eareckson. Front flap has blurb for *LT;* back flap has notes on
Fitzgerald.

Publication: Unknown number of copies of the first printing.
Published 27 October 1941. $2.75.

Printing: Printed by the Scribner Press from plates made
and type set by Brown Bros., Linotypers. Bound by the Scribner
Press.

Locations: LC (received 16 October 1941); Lilly (Scribner
Press Bindery Office Copy); MJB (dj); OKentU (dj).

Note: Abridged in *Omnibook,* IV (January 1942), 97–128;
also in *The Australian Omnibook,* no. 8 (September 1948),
72–123.

LATER   PRINTINGS   WITHIN   THE   FIRST
EDITION

A 18.1.b
Second printing: New York: Scribners, 1945. The copyright
page omits the 'A', but retains the seal.

A 18.1.c
New York: Scribners, 1951. *The Last Tycoon* and *The Great
Gatsby* only; stories omitted. See A 11.2.b.

A 18.1.d
Modern Standard Authors Three Novels of F. Scott Fitzgerald.
New York: Scribners, [1953]. See AA 4.

A 18.1.e
New York: Scribners, [1958]. A–4.58 [MH].

A 18.1.f
New York: Scribners, [1959]. B–4.59 [MH].

A 18.1.g
New York: Scribners, [1960]. C–6.60 [MH].

A 18.1.h
New York: Scribners, [1963]. D–3 63 [MH]

A 18.1.i
New York: Scribners, [1965]. E–3.65 [MH].

A 18.1.j
New York: Scribners, [1970]. Scribner Library #SL242. A–9.70 [M].

A 18.2.a
First English edition, first printing [1949]

THE LAST TYCOON

AN UNFINISHED NOVEL

BY

F. SCOTT FITZGERALD

LONDON
THE GREY WALLS PRESS LTD
Crown Passage, Pall Mall

A 18.2.a: 7¼″ x 4¾″

[1–4] 5–7 [8] 9–189 [190–192]

[A]⁴ B–I⁸ K–M⁸

Contents: p. 1: half title; p. 2: list of three titles by Fitzgerald; p. 3: title; p. 4: copyright; pp. 5–7: 'FOREWORD'; p. 8: blank; pp. 9–189: text, headed 'CHAPTER 1'; pp. 190–192: blank.

Typography and paper: Thirty-six lines per page. No running heads. Wove paper.

Binding: Yellow V cloth (fine linen-like grain). Spine gold-stamped: 'THE | LAST | TYCOON | [double rule] | F. Scott | Fitzgerald | [double rule] | Grey | Walls | Press'. White wove endpapers of different stock than text paper. All edges trimmed.

Dust jacket: Front has drawing of man on pedestal above throng, with female face looking down from above, signed by McConnell: '[to right of figure, in red] THE LAST | TYCOON | [dark green] F. Scott Fitzgerald'.

Spine: '[white] F. | SCOTT | FITZ- | GERALD | [red] THE | LAST | TY- | COON | [dark green] GREY | WALLS | PRESS'. Back has notes on Fitzgerald. Front flap has blurb for *LT*; back flap: 'Catalogue No. R.6716.'

Publication: Unknown number of copies. Published July 1949. 8s. 6d.

Locations: BM (deposit-stamp 16 July 1949); MJB (dj); PSt (dj).

A 18.2.b
Second printing: London: Grey Walls, [1949]. On copyright page: '*Second Impression 1949.*'

LATER EDITIONS

A 18.3
Second English edition

The Last Tycoon | [tapered rule] | F. SCOTT FITZGERALD | PENGUIN BOOKS

Harmondsworth, Middlesex, 1960. #1495. Reprinted 1962, 1963; with Foreword by Edmund Wilson and Notes, 1965, 1968.

A 18.4
Second American edition

THE | LAST TYCOON | *An Unfinished Novel* | BY | F. SCOTT FITZGERALD | CHARLES SCRIBNER'S SONS *New York*

[1–5] 6–7 [8–9] 10–165 [166–167] 168–190 [191–192]

1970. Part of a four-volume set (with *TSOP, GG, TITN*) distributed by The Literary Guild of America and its associated book clubs.

A 19 THE CRACK UP

A 19.1.a
First edition, first printing [1945]

THE CRACK-UP

F. SCOTT FITZGERALD

With other Uncollected Pieces,
Note-Books and Unpublished Letters

Together with Letters to Fitzgerald from Gertrude Stein, Edith
Wharton, T. S. Eliot, Thomas Wolfe
and John Dos Passos

And Essays and Poems by Paul
Rosenfeld, Glenway Wescott, John
Dos Passos, John Peale Bishop and
Edmund Wilson

Edited by 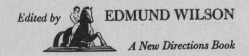 EDMUND WILSON

A New Directions Book

A 19.1.a: lines 3–12 and device in red brown; the rest in
black; 9¾₆″ x 5⁹⁄₁₆″

Acknowledgments

Of the pieces by F. Scott Fitzgerald reprinted here, Echoes of the Jazz Age *first appeared in* Scribner's Magazine; Ring *in* The New Republic; Early Success *in* American Cavalcade; *and all the rest in* Esquire. *The poem called* Lamp in the Window *and the introductory verses by the editor were published first in* The New Yorker. *The essay by Mr. Rosenfeld is reprinted from his book* Men Seen. *The poem by Mr. Bishop, the essay by Mr. Wescott, and part of the essay by Mr. Dos Passos originally appeared in* The New Republic. *Acknowledgment is due* Cosmopolitan Magazine *for permission to include* My Lost City, *which was bought but never published by it.*

The editor is indebted to Mrs. Samuel Lanahan, Miss Peggy Wood Weaver, Mr. Gerald Murphy and the late John Peale Bishop for supplying him with letters from Fitzgerald; to Miss Gertrude Stein, Mr. T. S. Eliot, Mr. John Dos Passos and the literary executors of Thomas Wolfe and Edith Wharton for permission to print letters written to Fitzgerald; and to Mr. Harold Ober and Mr. Maxwell Perkins for help in collecting Fitzgerald's articles.

Copyright 1931 by Charles Scribner's Sons
Copyright 1933 by Editorial Publications, Inc.
Copyright 1934 and 1936 by Esquire, Inc.
Copyright 1935 by F-R Publishing Corporation
Copyright 1945 by New Directions

Manufactured in the United States.
New Directions Books are published by James Laughlin.
New York Office: 67 West 44, New York City 18.

[i–ii] [1–6] 7–9 [10–12] 13–242 [243–244] 245–347 [348–350]

[1–22]⁸

Contents: pp. i–ii: blank; p. 1: half title; p. 2: blank; p. 3: title; p. 4: acknowledgments and copyrights; pp. 5–6: contents; pp. 7–9: 'DEDICATION'; p. 10: blank; p. 11: 'Autobiographical Pieces'; p. 12: blank; pp. 13–347: text, headed 'ECHOES OF THE JAZZ AGE'; p. 348: colophon, ' "THE CRACK-UP" WAS PRINTED FOR NEW DIRECTIONS | BY PETER BEILENSON, MOUNT VERNON, N.Y. | IN WAVERLY AND BULMER TYPES'; pp. 349–350: blank.

Includes "Echoes of the Jazz Age," "My Lost City," "Ring," " 'Show Mr. and Mrs. F. to Number ——'," "Auction—Model 1934," "Sleeping and Waking," "The Crack-Up," "Handle With Care," "Pasting It Together," "Early Success," "The Note-Books" [twenty-one sections], "Letters to Friends," "Letters to

Frances Scott Fitzgerald," "Three Letters about 'The Great Gatsby'," "A Letter from John Dos Passos," "A Letter From Thomas Wolfe," "F. Scott Fitzgerald" by Paul Rosenfeld, "The Moral of Scott Fitzgerald" by Glenway Wescott, "A Note on Fitzgerald" by John Dos Passos, "The Hours" by John Peale Bishop.

First book publication for all except "Ring." First appearance of "My Lost City." The titles of "Handle With Care" and "Pasting It Together" are transposed: the essay here titled "Handle With Care" is actually "Pasting It Together" and vice versa.

Typography and paper: 6⅞₆″ (6¹²⁄₁₆″) x 3¹¹⁄₁₆″; thirty-nine lines per page. No running heads. Wove paper.

Binding: Paper-covered boards of light red brown with wall-paper-like pattern in dark red brown. Dark red brown V cloth spine with printed light red brown label: '[dark red brown border] | [the following seven lines in black] The | Crack-up | by F. Scott | Fitzgerald | EDITED BY | EDMUND | WILSON | [dark red brown] New Directions | [dark red brown border]'. Off-white wove endpapers of different stock from text paper. All edges trimmed. Top edge stained dark red brown.

Dust jacket: Light red brown laid paper. Front: '[border of dark red brown squares] | [black] The Crack-up | F. SCOTT FITZGERALD | [ten lines of type describing contents] | *Edited by* [dark red brown device] EDMUND WILSON | *A New Directions Book.*' Spine: '[border of dark red brown squares] | [black] The | Crack-up | by F. Scott | Fitzgerald | EDITED BY | EDMUND | WILSON | New Directions | [border of dark red brown squares]'. Back: 'SOME UNUSUAL BOOKS' [titles by Brecht, Miller, Nabokov, Williams]. Front flap has blurb for *CU;* back flap has 'The Makers of Modern Literature Series' [titles by Levin, Daiches, Trilling, Honig, Nabokov].

Publication: 2,520 copies of the first printing. Published 12 August 1945. $3.50.

Printing: Printed by the Walpole Printing Offices from type set (or plates made) by Walpole. Bound by Russell Rutler Co.

Locations: LC (deposited 12 July 1945); Lilly (dj); MJB (dj); NjP (dj).

Note: The Crack-Up was originally announced for spring 1942 publication by the Colt Press (*Publishers' Weekly* [31 January 1942], Spring Book Index).

The Crack-up
F. SCOTT FITZGERALD

With other Uncollected Pieces,
Note-Books and Unpublished Letters

Together with Letters to Fitzgerald from Gertrude Stein, Edith
Wharton, T. S. Eliot, Thomas Wolfe
and John Dos Passos

And Essays and Poems by Paul
Rosenfeld, Glenway Wescott, John
Dos Passos, John Peale Bishop and
Edmund Wilson

Edited by EDMUND WILSON · A New Directions Book

New Directions

Spine: The Crack-up by F. Scott Fitzgerald · EDITED BY EDMUND WILSON · New Directions

---

The Crack-up
F. SCOTT FITZGERALD

SOME UNUSUAL BOOKS

THE PRIVATE LIFE OF THE MASTER RACE
by Bertolt Brecht

THE BOOKS OF HENRY MILLER

THE REAL LIFE OF SEBASTIAN KNIGHT
by Vladimir Nabokov

FIRST ACT by William Carlos Williams

PUBLISHED BY

NEW DIRECTIONS
67 WEST 44 STREET, NEW YORK 18

The Makers of Modern
Literature Series

JAMES JOYCE by Harry Levin

VIRGINIA WOOLF
by David Daiches

E. M. FORSTER by Lionel Trilling

FEDERICO GARCÍA LORCA
by Edwin Honig

NIKOLAI GOGOL
by Vladimir Nabokov

NEW DIRECTIONS

Dust jacket for A 19.1.a

LATER PRINTINGS WITHIN THE FIRST
EDITION

A 19.1.b
Clothbound

New York and Norfolk, Conn.: New Directions, [1945–1960].
Four offset reprintings of the first edition were manufactured
between 1945 and 1960. These printings are undifferentiated
by the publisher, but may be distinguished from the first
printing by the following points: title page all in black; colophon removed; bound in tan V cloth (fine linen-like pattern)
with spine vertically blackstamped or beige V cloth with spine
vertically brownstamped. At least one of these reprints has the
publisher's address on the copyright page changed to '333
Sixth Avenue'.

A 19.1.b*
First English issue of American copies

Undated reprint of the New Directions edition with printed
paper label pasted on p. 2: 'THIS IS | A NEW DIRECTIONS
BOOK | distributed | throughout the British Empire | from | 7
Crown Passage, Pall Mall | London S.W.1'. Issued August 1947
by the Falcon Press. The copyright page gives the address of
New Directions as '67 *West* 44, *New York City* 18.'

Publication: Unknown number of copies distributed in
England in 1947. 17s. 6d.

Locations: BM (deposit-stamp 12 August 1947); MJB;
OKentU.

A 19.1.c
Paperbound

New York and Norfolk, Conn.: New Directions, [1956]. New
Directions Paperbook No. 54. Offset reprinting of the first
edition. Reprints noted on copyright page: 'Fifth Printing,
1962'; 'SIXTH PRINTING'; 'SEVENTH PRINTING'.

A *19.2.a*
First English edition, first printing [*1965*]

The Crack-Up
with other Pieces and Stories

F. Scott Fitzgerald

 Penguin Books

A 19.2.a: 7⅛″ x 4⅜″

Penguin Books Ltd, Harmondsworth, Middlesex, England
Penguin Books Pty Ltd, Ringwood, Victoria, Australia

'Echoes of the Jazz Age' first published 1931
'My Lost City' first published 1945
'Ring' first published 1933
'The Crack-Up' first published 1936
'Early Success' first published 1937
'Gretchen's Forty Winks' first published 1924
'The Last of the Belles' first published 1929
'Babylon Revisited' first published 1931
'Pat Hobby Himself' first published 1940
'Financing Finnegan' first published 1938
Published together as Volume 2 of *The Bodley Head Scott Fitzgerald*
  (1958–63)
Published in Penguin Books 1965

'Echoes of the Jazz Age' copyright © Estate of F. Scott Fitzgerald, 1931
'My Lost City' copyright © Estate of F. Scott Fitzgerald, 1945
'Ring' copyright © Estate of F. Scott Fitzgerald, 1933
'The Crack-Up' copyright © Estate of F. Scott Fitzgerald, 1936
'Early Success' copyright © Estate of F. Scott Fitzgerald, 1937
'Gretchen's Forty Winks' copyright © Estate of F. Scott Fitzgerald, 1924
'The Last of the Belles' copyright © Estate of F. Scott Fitzgerald, 1929
'Babylon Revisited' copyright © Estate of F. Scott Fitzgerald, 1931
'Pat Hobby Himself' copyright © Estate of F. Scott Fitzgerald, 1940
'Financing Finnegan' copyright © Estate of F. Scott Fitzgerald, 1938

Made and printed in Great Britain by
Hazell Watson & Viney Ltd, Aylesbury, Bucks
Set in Linotype Granjon

[1–8] 9–62 [63–66] 67–154 [155–160]

Perfect binding

Contents: p. 1: biographical note on Fitzgerald, headed 'Penguin Book 2326'; p. 2: blank; p. 3: title; p. 4: copyright; p. 5: contents; p. 6: blank; p. 7: 'Autobiographical Pieces'; p. 8: blank; pp. 9–155: text, headed 'Echoes of the Jazz Age'; p. 65: 'Stories'; p. 156: blank; p. 157: Penguin ad; p. 158: blank; p. 159: ad for *The Diamond as Big as the Ritz;* p. 160: ad for *GG.*

Essays and stories. "Echoes of the Jazz Age," "My Lost City," "Ring," "The Crack-Up" (with "Handle With Care" and "Pasting It Together"), "Early Success," "Gretchen's Forty Winks," "The Last of the Belles," "Babylon Revisited," "Pat Hobby Himself," "Financing Finnegan."

Typography and paper: Thirty-five lines per page. Wove paper.

Binding: Wrappers. Front has photo of Fitzgerald and Scottie against orange and green gold panels divided by vertical white line: '[black] [penguin] a Penguin Book 3'6 | [white] The Crack-Up | [black] with other pieces and stories | [white] F. Scott Fitzgerald'. Spine: '[vertically] [white] F. Scott Fitzgerald [black] The Crack-up with Other Pieces and Stories | [horizontally] [penguin] | 2326'. Back has blurb for *CU*. All edges trimmed.

Publication: 35,000 copies. Published 29 July 1965. 3s. 6d.

Locations: BM (deposit-stamp 5 July 1965); MJB.

Notes: The copyright-page statement that the contents of this volume was 'Published together as Volume 2 of *The Bodley Head Scott Fitzgerald* | (1958–63)' is incorrect. The biographical note on p. 1 is also incorrect.

A copy purchased from Australia in 1967 is identical with the copy described, except that the price on the front cover is 5s. 6d.

The Penguin edition follows the New Directions edition in transposing the titles of "Handle With Care" and "Pasting It Together."

LATER PRINTINGS

A 19.2.b
Second printing: Harmondsworth, Middlesex: Penguin, [1968]. 15,000 copies.

A 19.2.c
Third printing: Harmondsworth, Middlesex: Penguin, [1971]. 12,500 copies.

A 20 THE STORIES OF F. SCOTT FITZGERALD

A 20.1.a
First edition, first printing (1951)

THE STORIES OF

F. Scott Fitzgerald

A Selection of 28 Stories
With an Introduction by
MALCOLM COWLEY

CHARLES SCRIBNER'S SONS
NEW YORK
1951

A 20.1.a: 8³⁄₁₆″ x 5⅝″

[i–iv] v–xxv [xxvi] [1–2] 3–172 [173–174] 175–304 [305–306] 307–380 [381–382] 383–473 [474]

[1–15]¹⁶ [16]¹⁰

Contents: p. i: half title; p. ii: blank; p. iii: title; p. iv: copyright; pp. v–vi: contents; pp. vii–xxv: 'INTRODUCTION'; p. xxvi: blank; p. 1: section title, 'I | Early Success'; p. 2: blank; pp. 3–4: 'EDITOR'S NOTE'; pp. 5–473: text, headed 'THE DIAMOND AS BIG | AS THE RITZ'; p. 173: section title, 'II | Glamor and Disillusionment'; p. 305: section title, 'III | Retrospective: Basil and Josephine'; p. 381: section title, 'IV | Last Act and Epilogue'; p. 474: blank.

Stories. "The Diamond as Big as the Ritz," "Bernice Bobs Her Hair," "The Ice Palace," "May Day," "Winter Dreams," "'The Sensible Thing'," "Absolution," "The Rich Boy," "The Baby Party," "Magnetism,"* "The Last of the Belles," "The Rough Crossing,"* "The Bridal Party,"* "Two Wrongs,"* "The Scandal Detectives," "The Freshest Boy," "The Captured Shadow," "A Woman with a Past," "Babylon Revisited," "Crazy Sunday," "Family in the Wind," "An Alcoholic Case,"* "The Long Way Out,"* "Financing Finnegan,"* "A Patriotic Short,"*

* Previously uncollected, having first book publication here.

"Two Old-Timers,"* "Three Hours Between Planes,"* "The Lost Decade."*

Typography and paper: 6¹¹⁄₁₆″ (7″) x 4⅛″; forty-four lines per page. Running heads: rectos and versos, story titles. Wove paper.

Binding: Black paper-covered boards (imitation V cloth). Front blindstamped with facsimile of Fitzgerald's signature. Spine goldstamped: 'THE STORIES | OF | F. SCOTT | FITZ-GERALD | [leaf] | WITH AN | INTRODUCTION | BY | MAL-COM | COWLEY | SCRIBNERS'. Also black C cloth with the spine stamped 'MALCOLM'. Priority undetermined. White wove endpapers of different stock from text paper. All edges trimmed.

Dust jacket: Front: '[black against red background] THE STORIES OF | [white against black background] F. SCOTT | FITZGERALD | [black against beige background] A SELEC-TION OF TWENTY-EIGHT | STORIES WITH AN INTRO-DUCTION | *by* MALCOLM COWLEY'. Spine lettered in black against beige background: 'THE | STORIES OF | F. SCOTT | FITZGERALD | [wide black band] SELECTED | BY | MAL-COLM | COWLEY | SCRIBNERS'. Back lists five Fitzgerald titles. Front and back flaps have blurb for *Stories.*

Publication: 7,510 copies of the first printing. Published 19 March 1951. $3.75.

Printing: Printed by the Scribner Press from type set by Brown Bros., Linotypers. Bound by the Scribner Press.

Locations: LC (deposited 28 March 1951); MJB ('MALCOM' and 'MALCOLM', both with dj); OKentU ('MALCOM', dj).

LATER PRINTINGS WITHIN THE FIRST EDITION

A 20.1.b
Second printing: New York: Scribners, 1951. March: 5,045 copies.

A 20.1.c
Third printing: New York: Scribners, 1951. April: 5,050 copies.

A 20.1.d
Fourth printing: New York: Scribners, 1953. Not seen. 2,500 copies.

A 20.1.e
Fifth printing: New York: Scribners, 1954. Not seen. 2,000 copies.

A 20.1.f
New York: Scribners, n.d. 'BOOK CLUB | 592 EDITION' is so identified on front flap of dust jacket. The Literary Guild of America held a lease on *Stories* from July 1964 to July 1966.

A 20.1.g
New York: Scribners, [1959]. H–7.59 [H].

A 20.1.h
New York: Scribners, [1963]. J–4.63 [H].

A 20.1.i
New York: Scribners, [1965]. K–9.65 [H].

A 20.1.j
New York: Scribners, [1966]. Scribner Library #SL135. A–6.66 [Col]. Reprint noted: C–12.68 [Col].

A 20.1.k
New York: Scribners, [1968]. L–2.68 [Col].

Λ 21 TURKEY REMΛINS
First edition, only printing [1956]

A 21: type decorations printed in red; lettering in black; 8¼″ x 5⁵⁄₁₆″

Reprinted through the kind permission of 'New Directions', Copyright 1945

Colophon: 'This keepsake | has been composed and printed | by the type of craftsmen of | COOPER & BEATTY, LIMITED, TORONTO | as a Christmas memento | for their friends | MCMLVI'

[A–B] [i–iv] v [vi] 1–5 [6–8]

[1]^8

Contents: pp. A–B: blank; p. i: half title; p. ii: 'Reprinted through the kind permission of "New Directions", Copyright 1945'; p. iii: title; p. iv: blank; p. v: text; p. vi: blank; pp. 1–6: text; pp. 7–8: blank.

Typography and paper: No running heads. Wove paper.

Binding: Red wrappers. Front has drawing of black turkey circled by gray decorations. Enclosed in protective white cover printed with publisher's Christmas greetings in black and two shades of green.

Publication: 2,000 copies printed in the fall of 1956. Not for sale.

Location: MJB (in cover).

Note: From *The Crack-Up*, pp. 193–195.

A 22 AFTERNOON OF AN AUTHOR

A 22.1.a
First edition, first printing (1957)

Afternoon of an Author

A Selection of
Uncollected Stories and Essays

By F. Scott
Fitzgerald

WITH AN INTRODUCTION AND NOTES
BY ARTHUR MIZENER

PRINCETON, NEW JERSEY
PRINCETON UNIVERSITY LIBRARY
1957

A 22.1.a: decorative frame around the author's name in brown;
the rest in black; 9¾₁₆″ x 6⅟₁₆″

The publication of this volume
has been made possible by the kind permission of
Mrs. Samuel J. Lanahan and Mr. Harold Ober,
to whom the Princeton University Library
expresses its gratitude

❖

Copyright, 1957, by Princeton University Library
Copyright, 1920 (renewed), 1924 (renewed), 1928 (renewed), 1929 (renewed),
1930, 1933, by Curtis Publishing Company
Copyright, 1926, by George H. Doran Company;
Copyright, 1953, by Frances Scott Fitzgerald Lanahan
Copyright, 1928, by Century Company;
Copyright, 1956, by Frances Scott Fitzgerald Lanahan
Copyright, 1936, 1939, 1940, by Esquire, Inc.
Copyright, 1948, by Reed Whittemore
Copyright, 1929, by Princeton Alumni Weekly
Copyright, 1927, by Collegiate World Publishing Company;
Copyright, 1955, by Frances Scott Fitzgerald Lanahan

❖

Published under the sponsorship of
the Friends of the Princeton Library
Design by P. J. Conkwright
Printed in the United States of America
by Princeton University Press at Princeton, New Jersey
Collotypes by Meriden Gravure Company

[i–x] [1–2] 3–11 [12–14] 15–30 [31] 32–68 [69] 70–79 [80–82] 83–85 [86] 87–98 [99] 100–121 [122–124] 125–135 [136] 137–165 [166–168] 169–175 [176] 177–201 [202] 203–210 [211] 212–226 [227–230]

[1–5]¹⁶ [6]⁸ [7–8]¹⁶; four leaves of illustrations sewn in between pp. 166 and 167 (after the sixth gathering).

Contents: pp. i–ii: blank; p. iii: half title; p. iv: blank; p. v: title; p. vi: copyright; p. vii: contents; p. viii: blank; p. ix: list of illustrations; p. x: blank; p. 1: half title; p. 2: blank; pp. 3–12: 'INTRODUCTION'; p. 13: 'PART I'; p. 14: blank; pp. 15–226: text, headed 'A Night at the Fair'; p. 81: 'PART II'; p. 123: 'PART III'; p. 167: 'PART IV'; p. 227: list of Princeton Library publications; pp. 228–230: blank.

Stories and essays. "A Night at the Fair," "Forging Ahead," "Basil and Cleopatra," "Princeton," "Who's Who—and Why," "How to Live on $36,000 a Year," "How to Live on Practically Nothing a Year," "How to Waste Material," "Ten Years in the Advertising Business," "One Hundred False Starts," "Outside the Cabinet-Maker's," "One Trip Abroad," " 'I Didn't Get Over'," "Afternoon of an Author," "Author's House," "Design in Plaster," "Boil Some Water—Lots of It," "Teamed with Genius," "No Harm Trying," "News of Paris—Fifteen Years Ago." First book appearance for all except "Princeton" and "Design in Plaster."

Typography and paper: Thirty-nine lines per page. Running heads: rectos and versos, titles of stories or essays. Wove paper.

Binding: Red brown V cloth (fine linen-like grain). Spine stamped vertically: '[dark red brown decoration] [silver] F. Scott Fitzgerald [dark red brown decoration] [silver] Afternoon of an Author.' White wove sized endpapers of different stock from text paper. All edges trimmed.

Dust jacket: Gray paper printed in red brown. Front: '[within five rule frames] Afternoon | of an Author | A Selection of | Uncollected Stories and Essays | [following two lines within decorative frame] By F. Scott | Fitzgerald | WITH AN INTRO- DUCTION AND NOTES | by Arthur Mizener'. Spine printed vertically: '[decoration] F. Scott Fitzgerald [decoration] After- noon of an Author'. Back has list of publications of The Friends of the Princeton Library. Front and back flaps have blurb for *AOAA*.

Publication: 1,500 copies of the first printing. Published 4 December 1957. $5.00.

Printing: Printed by the Princeton University Press. Collo- types printed by Meriden Gravure. Bound by J. C. Valentine.

Locations: LC (deposited 16 December 1957); Lilly (dj); MJB (dj); NjP (dj); OKentU (dj).

A 22.1.b
Second printing (trade)

Afternoon of an Author | A Selection of | Uncollected Stories and Essays | [following two lines within gray decorative frame] By F. Scott | Fitzgerald | WITH AN INTRODUCTION AND NOTES | BY ARTHUR MIZENER | CHARLES SCRIBNER'S SONS | NEW YORK

1958. A.2–58 [MH]. Omits illustrations. Published 25 April 1958. $4.50.

Location: LC (Received 28 March 1958); MJB (dj).

A 22.1.c
Third printing: New York: Scribners, [1972]. Scribner Library #SL 332. A–1.72 [M].

A 22.2
First English edition, first printing [1958]

AFTERNOON OF AN AUTHOR

A SELECTION OF UNCOLLECTED STORIES AND ESSAYS WITH AN INTRODUCTION AND NOTES BY ARTHUR MIZENER

F. Scott Fitzgerald

THE BODLEY HEAD
LONDON

Printed in Great Britain for
THE BODLEY HEAD LTD
10 Earlham Street, London W.C.2
by The Stellar Press Ltd, Barnet
Set in Monotype Plantin
First published in Great Britain 1958

[1–8] 9–20 [21–22] 23–103 [104–106] 107–155 [156–158] 159–209 [210–212] 213–284 [285–288]

[A]¹⁶ B–I¹⁶; four leaves of illustrations sewn in between pp. 96 and 97 (after gathering C). I₁₆ is rear paste-down endpaper.

Contents: p. 1: half title; p. 2: blank; p. 3: list of six titles by Fitzgerald; p. 4: blank; p. 5: title; p. 6: copyright; p. 7: contents; p. 8: list of illustrations; pp. 9–20: '[within frame of dots] INTRODUCTION'; p. 21: section title; p. 22: blank; pp. 23–284: text, headed '[within frame of dots] A NIGHT | AT THE FAIR'; pp. 285–288: blank. The final leaf (pp. 287–288) is the rear pastedown endpaper.

Typography and paper: Thirty-five lines per page. Laid paper, vertical chainmarks 1¹⁄₁₆″ apart.

Binding: Red paper-covered boards (imitation V cloth). Spine goldstamped: 'F. | Scott | Fitz- | gerald | [rule] | AFTER- | NOON | OF AN | AUTHOR | [rule] | BODLEY | HEAD'. White wove front endpapers. All edges trimmed.

Dust jacket: Lettered in black against solid red background. Front: 'F. Scott Fitzgerald | [tapered rule] | AFTER-NOON | OF AN | AUTHOR | [photo of Fitzgerald by Van Vechten within white frame] | WITH AN INTRODUCTION BY ARTHUR MIZENER'. Spine: '[horizontally] AFTER- | NOON | OF AN | AUTHOR | [vertically within frame] F. Scott Fitzgerald | [horizontally] BODLEY | HEAD'. Back has blurb for The Bodley Head Fitzgerald. Front flap has blurb for *AOAA* and '3/2100'; back flap has publisher's name and address.

Publication: 5,000 copies of the first printing. Published 6 October 1958. 16s.

Locations: BM (deposit-stamp 18 September 1958); Lilly (dj); MJB (dj); NjP (dj).

A 23 THE MYSTERY OF THE RAYMOND
MORTGAGE
First edition, only printing (1960)

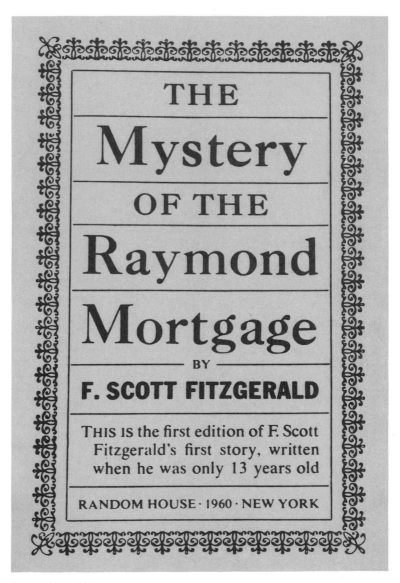

A 23: 8″ x 5⅝₁₆″

Statement of limitation: 'This first edition of | F. SCOTT FITZ-GERALD'S | *The Mystery of the Raymond Mortgage* | was privately printed | and limited to | 750 copies'

Cover title only.

[1–12]

[1]⁶

Contents: p. 1: statement of limitation; p. 2: blank; pp. 3–10: text, headed 'F. Scott Fitzgerald | The Mystery of the Raymond Mortgage'; pp. 11–12: blank.

Typography and paper: Forty lines per page. Running heads: rectos, *The Mystery of the Raymond Mortgage;* versos, *F. Scott Fitzgerald.* Wove paper.

Binding: Gray blue wrappers, printed in black on front.

Publication: Unknown number of copies. Distributed 2 September 1960 by Random House as promotional material for *Ellery Queen's 15th Mystery Annual.* Not for sale.

Locations: LC (received 13 September 1960); MJB; NjP; PSt.

Note: See "Editorial Note by Ellery Queen" in *Ellery Queen's 15th Mystery Annual* (1960) for alterations in text. See B 52.

A 24 THE PAT HOBBY STORIES

A 24.1.a
First edition, first printing [1962]

The
PAT
HOBBY
Stories

by F. SCOTT FITZGERALD

with an introduction by
Arnold Gingrich

CHARLES SCRIBNER'S SONS *New York*

A 24.1.a: 7$\frac{15}{16}$" x 5$\frac{3}{8}$"

[i–v] vi [vii–viii] ix–xxiii [xxiv] 1–159 [160–168]

[1–6]^{16}

Contents: p. i. half title; p. ii: 'BY F. SCOTT FITZGERALD | [eleven titles]'; p. iii: title; p. iv: copyright; pp. v–vi: contents; p. vii: half title; p. viii: blank; pp. ix–xxiii: 'INTRODUCTION'; p. xxiv: blank; pp. 1–158: text, headed 'PAT HOBBY'S | CHRISTMAS | WISH'; pp. 159–166: 'APPENDIX'; pp. 167–168: blank.

Stories. "Pat Hobby's Christmas Wish," "A Man in the Way," " 'Boil Some Water—Lots of It' " (*AOAA*), "Teamed with Genius" (*AOAA*), "Pat Hobby and Orson Welles," "Pat Hobby's Secret," "Pat Hobby, Putative Father," "The Homes of the Stars," "Pat Hobby Does His Bit," "Pat Hobby's Preview," "No Harm Trying" (*AOAA*), "A Patriotic Short" (*Stories*), "On the Trail of Pat Hobby," "Fun in an Artist's Studio," "Two Old-Timers" (*Stories*), "Mightier than the Sword," "Pat Hobby's College Days." Appendix has revised version of "A Patriotic Short." Introduction quotes Fitzgerald's letters to Arnold Gingrich. Five of the stories were previously collected in *The Stories of F. Scott Fitzgerald* (1951) and *Afternoon of an Author* (1957).

Typography and paper: Thirty-two lines per page. Running heads: rectos, story titles; versos, 'THE PAT HOBBY STORIES'. Wove paper.

Binding: Blue V cloth (fine linen-like grain). Spine gold-stamped: '[vertically] F. SCOTT | FITZGERALD | [horizontal rules and decorations] | [vertically] *The Pat Hobby* | *Stories* | [horizontal rules and decorations] [horizontally] Scribners | [horizontal rules and decorations]'. White wove endpapers of different stock than text paper. All edges trimmed.

Dust jacket: Front lettered in white on panels of green and blue filmstrip: 'F. Scott | Fitzgerald | The | PAT HOBBY | Stories | with an introduction by | ARNOLD GINGRICH'. Spine lettered in black and blue: '[vertically] [black] F. Scott Fitzgerald [blue] The PAT HOBBY Stories | [horizontally] [black] Scribners'. Back lists twelve Fitzgerald titles. Front and back flaps have blurb for *Hobby*.

Publication: 8,000 copies of the first printing. Published 27 June 1962. $3.50.

Printing: Book produced by Vail-Ballou Press.

Locations: LC (deposited 25 July 1962); Lilly (dj); MJB (dj); NjP (dj).

LATER PRINTINGS WITHIN THE FIRST EDITION

A 24.1.b
New York: Scribners, [1966]. C-12.66 [V]. Second printing not seen.

A 24.1.c
New York: Scribners, [1969]. D-11.69 [V].

A 24.1.d
New York: Scribners, [1970]. Scribner Library #SL216. A-6.70 [c].

A 24.2
First English edition, first printing [1967]

F. Scott Fitzgerald

The Pat Hobby Stories

With an introduction
by Arnold Gingrich

Penguin Books

A 24.2: 7$\frac{1}{16}$" x 4$\frac{3}{8}$"

Penguin Books Ltd, Harmondsworth,
Middlesex, England
Penguin Books Australia Ltd, Ringwood,
Victoria, Australia

First published in the U.S.A. 1962
Published in Penguin Books 1967
Copyright © Charles Scribner's Sons, 1962
Except for the original version of 'A Patriotic
Short' in the Appendix, all the stories in this
volume appeared first in *Esquire*. Copyright
1939, 1940, 1941 Frances S. F. Lanahan.
The following four stories are published
with permission of The Bodley Head: 'Boil Some
Water – Lots of It'; 'Teamed with Genius';
'A Patriotic Short'; 'Two Old-Timers'.

Made and printed in Great Britain by
Cox & Wyman Ltd, London, Reading and Fakenham
Set in Linotype Pilgrim

[1–7] 8–23 [24–25] 26–35 [36] 37–42 [43] 44–50 [51]
52–61 [62] 63–71 [72] 73–79 [80] 81–88 [89] 90–97 [98]
99–107 [108] 109–116 [117] 118–127 [128] 129–133 [134]
135–138 [139] 140–146 [147] 148–152 [153] 154–159
[160] 161–167 [168–176]

Perfect binding.

Typography and paper: Thirty-four lines per page. Wove
paper.

Binding: Printed paper wrappers. Front has photo of man
gesturing at woman on movie screen against purple background: '[penguin in orange oval] [white] F. Scott
4'6 | Fitzgerald | [yellow lettering with orange dots re-
sembling theater marquee] THE PAT HOBBY | STORIES'.
Spine: '[on orange background] [vertically] [white] F. Scott
Fitzgerald [black] The Pat Hobby Stories | [horizontally]
[penguin] | 2589'. Back cover has blurb printed in white and
yellow against purple background, with photo of Fitzgerald.
All edges trimmed.

Publication: 30,000 copies. Published March 1967. 4s. 6d.

Locations: BM (deposit-stamp 0 April 1967); MJB.

Note: A copy purchased from Australia in 1967 is identical with the copy described above, except that the price printed on the front wrapper is '80c'.

A 25 LETTER TO PERKINS
Scribners [1963]

599 Summit Ave.
St. Paul, Minn
Sept 18th, 1919

Dear Mr Perkins:

    Of course I was delighted to get your letter and I've been in a sort of trance all day; not that I doubted you'd take it but at last I have something to show people. It has enough advertisement in St. Paul

A 25: 6⅜″ x 5⅛″

Four leaves: pp. 2–4 numbered by Fitzgerald.

[1 2]?

Typography and paper: Printed in blue ink on white wove paper.

Location: MJB.

Note: Facsimile of letter from Fitzgerald to Maxwell E. Perkins, 18 September 1919. Not for sale. Unknown number of copies. Printed by Scribners as promotional piece for Turnbull's *The Letters of F. Scott Fitzgerald* (1963), in which this letter appears on pp. 139–140. The original letter was written in black ink.

A 26 THE LETTERS OF F. SCOTT FITZGERALD

A 26.1.a
First edition, first printing [1963]

*The Letters
of F. Scott Fitzgerald*

* * *

Edited by
ANDREW TURNBULL

CHARLES SCRIBNER'S SONS

New York

A 26.1.a: 8¹⁵⁄₁₆″ x 6″

[A–B] [i–xi] xii–xiii [xiv] xv–xviii [xix–xx] [1–2] 3–102 [103–104] 105–133 [134–136] 137–291 [292–294] 295–313 [314–316] 317–349 [350–352] 353–368 [369–370] 371–379 [380–382] 383–388 [389–390] 391–408 [409–410] 411–420 [421–422] 423–430 [431–432] 433–445 [446–448] 449–605 [606–608] 609–615 [616 618]. Frontispiece and eight pages of illustrations inserted.

[1–20]^{16}

Contents: pp. A-B: blank; p. i: 'BOOKS BY F. SCOTT FITZ-GERALD | [twelve titles]'; p. ii: blank; p. iii: half title; p. iv: blank; frontispiece tipped in before p. v: title page; p. vi: copyright; p. vii: 'ACKNOWLEDGMENTS'; p. viii: blank; p. ix: 'CHRONOLOGY'; p. x: blank; pp. xi–xiii: chronology; p. xiv: blank; pp. xv–xviii: 'INTRODUCTION'; p. xix: 'CONTENTS'; p. xx: blank; p. 1: '*I* | Letters | to Frances Scott Fitzgerald'; p. 2: blank; pp. 3–605: text; p. 606: blank; p. 607: section title, 'INDEX'; p. 608: blank; pp. 609–615: index; pp. 616–618: blank. Section titles: pp. 1, 103, 135, 293, 315, 351, 369, 381, 389, 409, 421, 431, 447.

Typography and paper: Thirty-nine lines per page. Running heads: rectos, section titles; versos, 'THE LETTERS OF F. SCOTT FITZGERALD'. Wove paper.

Binding: Green V cloth (fine linen-like grain). Front gold-stamped: 'SCOTT FITZGERALD'. Spine: '[black] TURNBULL | [two lines of black type decoration] | [goldstamped] *The Letters | of | F. Scott | Fitzgerald* | [three lines of black type decoration] | [black] Scribners'. White wove endpapers of different stock from text paper. All edges trimmed.

Dust jacket: Front cover printed against solid black background: '[line of green type decoration] | [green rule] | [gold]

The Letters of | [green rule] | [white] F. Scott | Fitzgerald | [green rule] | [gold] EDITED AND WITH AN INTRODUC-TION BY | ANDREW TURNBULL | [green rule] | [line of green type decoration]'. Spine: '[horizontal line of green type decoration] | [vertically] [green rule] | [gold] The Letters of [white] F. Scott Fitzgerald | [gold] EDITED AND WITH AN INTRODUCTION BY ANDREW TURNBULL [green] SCRIB-NERS | [green rule] | [horizontal line of green type decoration]'. Back has blurbs for *Scott Fitzgerald* and photo of Turnbull with biographical information. Front flap has blurb for *Letters;* back flap has list of titles by Fitzgerald.

Publication: 10,000 copies of the first printing. Published 26 September 1963. $10.

Printing: Book produced by Vail-Ballou Press.

Locations: LC (deposited 4 October 1963); Lilly (dj); MJB (dj); NjP (dj).

Note: Andrew Turnbull, *Thomas Wolfe* (New York: Scribners, [1967]), p. 274, adds four sentences to Fitzgerald's July 1937 letter to Wolfe, which appears on p. 552 of *Letters.*

LATER PRINTINGS WITHIN THE FIRST EDITION

A 26.1.b
New York: Scribners, [1963]. B-10.63 [V].

A 26.1.c
New York: Scribners, [1963]. C-11.63 [V].

A 26.1.d
THE LETTERS | OF | F. SCOTT | FITZGERALD | Edited by Andrew Turnbull | [Delta device] | A Delta Book 1965

New York: Dell, 1965. #4745. With chronological index by Jeremy Larner.

A 26.2
First edition, first English printing [1964]

THE LETTERS OF

F. Scott Fitzgerald

EDITED BY

ANDREW TURNBULL

THE BODLEY HEAD
LONDON

A 26.2: 9⁹⁄₁₆" x 6"

The text of this first English printing is offset from the first American edition.

[A-B] [i–xi] xii–xiii [xiv] xv–xviii [1–2] 3–102 [103–104] 105–133 [134–136] 137–291 [292–294] 295–313 [314–316] 317–349 [350–352] 353–368 [369–370] 371–379 [380–382] 383–388 [389–390] 391–408 [409–410] 411–420 [421–422] 423–430 [431–432] 433–445 [446–448] 449–605 [606–608] 609–615 [616–620]. Frontispiece and six pages of illustrations inserted.

$[1]^{16}$ 2–20^{16}

Contents: pp. A-B: blank; p. i: half title; p. ii: headed 'BY ANDREW TURNBULL'; p. iii: title page; p. iv: copyright; p. v: 'CONTENTS'; p. vi: blank; p. vii: 'ACKNOWLEDGMENTS'; p. viii: blank; p. ix: 'CHRONOLOGY', p. x: blank; pp xi–xiii: chronology; p. xiv: blank; pp. xv–xviii: 'INTRODUC-TION'; p. 1: 'I | Letters to | Frances Scott Fitzgerald'; p. 2: blank; pp. 3–605: text; p. 606: blank; p. 607: section title, 'INDEX'; p. 608: blank; pp. 609–615: index; pp. 616–620: blank.

Typography and paper: Same type and running heads as Scribners edition. Wove paper.

Binding: Brown paper-covered boards (imitation V cloth). Spine goldstamped: '[decoration] | *The* | *Letters of* | F. Scott | *Fitzgerald* | [decoration] | BODLEY HEAD'. White wove endpapers of different stock than text paper. Top edge stained yellow. All edges trimmed.

Dust jacket: Front lettered in yellow, red, and white against brown background: '[yellow] The | [red] LETTERS | [yellow] of F. Scott | Fitzgerald | [white] Edited with an introduction | by Andrew | [red] TURNBULL | [white] BODLEY HEAD'. Spine lettered in white, yellow, and red against brown: '[vertically, bottom to top] [white] LETTERS [yellow] of Scott | Fitzgerald [red] TURNBULL'. Back has blurbs for *Scott Fitzgerald*. Front flap has blurb for *Letters* and '521'; back flap has blurb for *The Bodley Head Fitzgerald*.

Publication: 4,000 copies of the first printing. Published 7 May 1964. 50s.

Locations: BM (deposit-stamp 27 April 1964); Lilly (dj); MJB (dj).

LATER EDITIONS

A 26.3
Second American edition

[two-page title, within frame] [on left] *Edited and with an* | *Introduction by* | *Andrew Turnbull* | [on right] *The Letters of* | *F. Scott Fitzgerald* | [below frame] [fleuron] A LAUREL EDITION

New York: Dell, 1966. #4745.

A 26.4
Second English edition

THE LETTERS OF | F. SCOTT FITZGERALD | EDITED BY | ANDREW TURNBULL | [penguin] | PENGUIN BOOKS

Harmondsworth, Middlesex, 1968. #2612.

Note: See AA 10 for separate edition of *Letters to His Daughter.*

A 26.5
Third American edition

The Letters of | F. Scott Fitzgerald | Edited by | ANDREW TURNBULL | [seal] | A NATIONAL GENERAL COMPANY

New York: Bantam, 1971. #Y6775.

A 27 THE APPRENTICE FICTION OF F. SCOTT
FITZGERALD
First edition, only printing [1965]

The Apprentice Fiction of

F. SCOTT FITZGERALD

1909–1917

Edited with an introduction by John Kuehl

Rutgers University Press

New Brunswick   *New Jersey*

A 27: 8¾₁₆″ x 5⅞₁₆″

[i–vi] vii–viii [1–2] 3–174 [175–182] 183–184. Four pages of illustrations inserted after third gathering.

[1 8]¹⁰

Contents: p. i: half title; p. ii: blank; p. iii: title; p. iv: copyright; p. v: contents; p. vi: blank; pp vii–viii: '*Preface*'; p. 1: half title; p. 2: blank; pp. 3–16: "*Introduction*"; pp. 17–174: text, headed '*The Mystery of the | Raymond Mortgage*'; pp. 175–182: appendix; pp. 183–184: index.

Stories. "The Mystery of the Raymond Mortgage"; "Reade, Substitute Right Half"; "A Debt of Honor"; "The Room With the Green Blinds"; "A Luckless Santa Claus"; "The Trail of the Duke"; "Pain and the Scientist"; "Shadow Laurels"; "The Ordeal"; "The Debutante"; "The Spire and the Gargoyle"; "Tarquin of Cheepside"; "Babes in the Woods"; "Sentiment—and the Use of Rouge"; "The Pierian Springs and the Last Straw"; "Appendix—The Death of My Father" (facsimile of manuscript).

Typography and paper: Thirty-six lines per page. Running heads across facing rectos and versos: '*The Apprentice Fiction of F. Scott Fitzgerald*'. Wove paper.

Binding: Red paper-covered boards; black V cloth shelfback, vertically goldstamped: 'KUEHL *The Apprentice Fiction | of* F. Scott Fitzgerald, 1909–1917 | [horizontally] *Rutgers*'. Black endpapers. All edges trimmed.

Dust jacket: Front has photo of young Fitzgerald against solid black background, lettered in white and red: '[white] THE APPRENTICE | FICTION OF | [red] F. SCOTT | *Fitz-*

gerald | [white] 1909–1917 | [white] EDITED WITH AN INTRODUCTION BY [red] JOHN KUEHL'. Spine lettered in white and red: '[horizontal in white] KUEHL | [vertical in red] THE APPRENTICE FICTION OF F. SCOTT FITZ-GERALD, 1909–1917 | [horizontal in white] RUTGERS'. Back has photo of Kuehl and biographical notes. Front and back flaps have blurb for *Apprentice Fiction.*

Publication: 5,000 copies published 15 March 1965. $5.00.

Printing: Book produced by Quinn & Boden.

Locations: LC (deposited 3 September 1965); Lilly (dj); MJB (dj); NjP (dj).

Dust jackets for (left-hand column, top to bottom) A 20.1.a, A 28, A 21, A 13, (right-hand column) A 22.1.a, A 24.1.a, and A 27

A 28   THOUGHTBOOK OF FRANCIS SCOTT KEY
FITZGERALD
First edition, only printing (1965)

Thoughtbook
of
Francis Scott Key Fitzgerald

with an Introduction by
John R. Kuehl

PRINCETON UNIVERSITY LIBRARY

PRINCETON, N. J., 1965

A 28: 9¼″ x 6¹⁄₁₆″

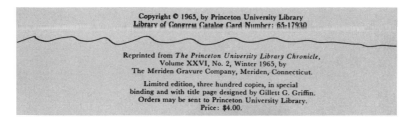

Unpaged: [1–44]

[1]⁶ [2–3]⁸

Contents: p. 1: half title; p. 2: blank; p. 3: title; p. 4: copyright; pp. 5–11: introduction; p. 12: blank; p. 13: half title; p. 14: seven-line note on facsimile; pp. 15–42: facsimiles; pp. 43–44: blank.

Paper: No running heads. Wove paper.

Binding: White paper-covered boards with blue lines. Front cover printed in facsimile of Fitzgerald's handwriting in black 'Thoughtbook | of | Francis Scott Key Fitzgerald | of | St Paul Minn. U S.A.' White endpapers on same stock as prelims. Issued in unprinted glassine jacket. All edges trimmed.

Publication: 300 copies. Published April 1965. $4.00.

Locations: Lilly (dj); MJB; NjP (dj); OKentU.

A 29 EXHIBITION CATALOGUE
(1965)

A 29: scant 9" x 4"

Colophon: 'Two Hundred And Fifty Copies—Of Which Twenty-Five Are Numbered And Signed—Printed By The F. J. Heer Printing Company For The Tauser Head Press. . . .'

Unpaged: Single sheet folded twice to make six pages.

Paper: Tan wove paper.

Publication: 250 copies distributed at exhibition marking the twenty-fifth anniversary of Fitzgerald's death. 21 December 1965. Not for sale.

Location: MJB; NjP.

Note: This catalogue describes twenty-five items from the Bruccoli Collection; the following are published for the first time: #20 (Inscription to Dorothy Parker), #22 (Inscription to Carroll Davis), #24 (Inscription to Annah Williamson), #25 (Inscription to J. Ellingham Brookes). It also quotes statement on Huck Finn, two letters to Shane Leslie, and letter to Alice Wooton

A 30 LETTER TO PERKINS
Princeton (1967)

Cottage Club-

Dear Mr. Perkins:
     Can't work here so have just about decided to quit work and become an ash-man. Still working on that SmartSet novellette.

     Everyone in college -- I mean *literally* everyone in college seems to have read Head + Shoulders so I wish you'd have the following ad inserted in "The Daily Princetonian" the first two days after my book appears

THE FIRST NOVEL of

F Scott Fitzgerald '17

THIS SIDE OF PARADISE

a story about a Princeton man

Chas. Scribners Sons $1.75 Princeton Univ Store

See you about the 17th

Scott Fitz—

A 30: 11" x 8½"

Broadside, printed on one side only in black ink on gray wove paper. Watermarked 'ATLANTIC BOND | 20'.

Facsimile of Fitzgerald letter to Maxwell E. Perkins, March 1920. Not included in *Letters*. Not for sale. Unknown number of copies. At lower left—'FACSIMILE OF ORIGINAL LETTER IN PRINCETON | UNIVERSITY LIBRARY. DISTRIBUTED JUNE 1967 | ON THE OCCASION OF THE FIFTIETH REUNION OF | SCOTT FITZGERALD'S CLASS. WITH THE PER- | MISSION OF HAROLD OBER ASSOCIATES AND | CHARLES SCRIBNER'S SONS. PROTECTED BY | COPYRIGHT.'

Locations: MJB; NjP.

A 31 DEARLY BELOVED
First edition, only printing (1969)

DEARLY BELOVED

A SHORT STORY BY F. SCOTT FITZGERALD

WITH GRAPHICS BY BYRON BURFORD

And a Note by Matthew J. Bruccoli

The Windhover Press of The University of Iowa

Iowa City 1969

A 31: 13⅞″ x 10″

Colophon: 'This edition of Dearly Beloved was printed | by hand at The Windhover Press in Octo- | ber and November of 1969. The handset | type is Bembo, a face adapted by the Mono- | type Corporation from one cut by Francesco | Griffo in the late fifteenth century. The | paper is Ruysdael Rag. | Of an edition lim- | ited to three hundred numbered copies, | 1 through 30 have been signed by the artist. | This is number

[1–16]

[1]⁸

Contents: pp. 1–2: blank; p. 3: title; p. 4: 'Copyright 1969 by Frances Fitzgerald Smith'; p. 5: illustration; p. 6: blank; p. 7: half title; pp. 8–9: text; p. 10: blank; p. 11: illustration; p. 12: blank; p. 13: 'Note' and 'Colophon'; pp. 14–16: blank

Typography and paper: Thirty-seven lines per page. No running heads. Wove paper.

Binding: Green paper-covered boards; black leather spine, goldstamped vertically: 'DEARLY BELOVED'. Top edge trimmed.

Publication: Signed copies $35; unsigned copies $6.50.

Locations: MJB (signed and unsigned); NjP (signed and unsigned).

Note: This story first appeared in the *Fitzgerald/Hemingway Annual 1969* and was reprinted in the *New York Times* (20 August 1969), 42. The *Times* article was reprinted in other papers: *Paris International Herald-Tribune* (21 August 1969), *Courier-Journal* (Louisville) (21 August 1969), *Akron Beacon-Journal* (14 September 1969), *San Francisco Examiner* (21 September 1969), *London Daily Telegraph Magazine* (28 November 1969).

A 32 F. SCOTT FITZGERALD IN HIS OWN TIME
[*1971*]

In His Own Time: A Miscellany

EDITED BY

Matthew J. Bruccoli
University of South Carolina

Jackson R. Bryer
University of Maryland

The Kent State University Press

A 32: 9″ x 6″

[i–vi] vii–xxii [1–3] 4–74 [75] 76–100 [101] 102–111 [112–113] 114–151 [152–153] 154–160 [161] 162–178 [179] 180–211 [212–213] 214–225 [226–227] 228–239 [240–243] 244–299 [300–301] 302–399 [400–401] 402–446 [447] 448–465 [466–467] 468–481 [482]

[1–14]^{16} [15]^{12} [16]^{16}

Contents: p. i: half title; p. ii: blank; p. iii: title; p. iv: copyright; p. v: dedication; p. vi: 'ABOUT THE EDITORS'; pp. vii–x: 'Foreword'; pp. xi–xxii: 'Contents'; p. 1: 'PART 1 | Miscellany by Fitzgerald'; p. 2: blank, pp. 3–401. text, headed 'Poems and Lyrics'; p. 241: 'Part Two | Miscellany about | Fitzgerald'; p. 482: blank.

Part 1 includes the following material by Fitzgerald: " 'Football' ";* *Fie! Fie! Fi-Fi!*—"Opening Chorus," "Gentlemen Bandits We," "A Slave to Modern Improvements," "In Her Eyes," "What the Manicure Lady Knows," "Good Night and Good Bye," " 'Round and 'Round," "Chatter Trio," "Finale Act I," "Rose of the Night," "Men," "In the Dark," "Love or Eugenics," "Reminiscence," "Fie! Fie! Fi-Fi!," "The Monte Carlo Moon," "Finale Act II"; "A Cheer for Princeton"; *The Evil Eye*—"Act I Opening Chorus," "I've Got My Eyes on You," "On Dreams Alone," "The Evil Eye," "What I'll Forget," "Over the Waves to Me," "On Her Eukalali," "Jump Off the Wall," "Finale Act I," "Act II Opening Chorus," "Harris from Paris," "Twilight," " 'The Never, Never Land,' " "My Idea of Love," "Other Eyes," "The Girl of the Golden West," "With Me", *Safety First!*—"(A) Prologue," "(B) Garden of Arden," "Act I Opening Chorus," "Send Him to Tom," "One-Lump Percy," "Where Did Bridget Kelly Get Her Persian Temperament?," "It Is Art," "Safety First," "Charlotte Corday," "Underneath the April Rain," "Dance, Lady, Dance," "(A) Safety First," "(B) Hello Temptation," "When That Beautiful Chord Came True," "Rag-Time Melodrama," "Scene II," "Take Those Hawaiian Songs Away," "The Vampires Won't Vampire for Me," "The Hummin'

---

* Asterisk indicates first book publication.

Blues," "Down in Front," "Finale"; "To My Unused Greek Book";* "Rain Before Dawn";* "Princeton—The Last Day";* "On a Play Twice Seen";* "The Cameo Frame";* "City Dusk";* "My First Love"; "Marching Streets"; "The Pope at Confession"; "A Dirge";* "Sleep of a University"; "To Anne";* untitled poem;* "Lamp in a Window"; "Obit on Parnassus"; "There was once a second group student . . .";* "May Small Talk";* "How They Head the Chapters";* "The Conquest of America";* "Yais"; "Little Minnie McCloskey";* "One from Penn's Neck";* "A Litany of Slang";* " 'Triangle Scenery by Bakst' ";* "Futuristic Impressions of the Editorial Boards";* " 'A glass of beer kills him' ";* "Oui, le backfield est from Paris"; * " 'When you find a man doing a little more' ";* "Things That Never Change Number 3333";* "The Old Frontiersman";* "Boy Kills Self Rather Than Pet";* "Precaution Primarily";* "Things That Never Change. No. 3982";* "McCaulay Mission—Water Street";* "Popular Parodies—No. 1";* "The Diary Of A Sophomore";* "Undulations Of An Undergraduate";* "Yale's swimming team will take its maiden plunge to-night";* "Kenilworth Socialism";* "True Democracy";* "A Few Well-Known Club Types And Their Futures";* "The Prince of Pests";* " 'These rifles *** will probably not be used . . .' ";* " 'It is assumed that the absence of submarines . . .' ";* "Ethel had her shot of brandy . . .";* "The Staying Up All Night";* "Intercollegiate Petting Cues";* "Our American Poets";* "Cedric the Stoker";* "Our Next Issue";* "The Usual Thing";* "Jemina"; review of *Penrod and Sam;** review of *David Blaize;** review of *The Celt and the World;** review of *Verses in Peace and War;** review of *God, The Invisible King;** review of *Prejudices. Second Series;** review of *Three Soldiers;** "Three Cities";* review of *Brass;** review of *Crome Yellow;** review of *Gentle Julia;** review of *Margey Wins the Game;** review of *The Oppidan;** review of *The Love Legend;** review of *Many Marriages;** review of *Being Respectable;** review of *Through the Wheat;** "How to Waste Material"; "F. Scott Fitzgerald Is Bored by Efforts at Realism in 'Lit' ";* blurb for *Babel;* blurb for *Lily-Iron;* introduction to *GG;* blurb for *Cast Down the Laurel;* foreword to *Colonial and Historic Homes of Maryland;* blurb for *What Makes Sammy Run?;* blurb for *The Day of the Locust;* self-interview;* "The Author's Apology"; "The Credo of F. Scott Fitzgerald";* "What I Was Advised To Do—And Didn't";* "How I Would Sell My Book If I Were a Bookseller";* "Confessions"; "In Literary New York";* "Censorship or Not";* "Fitzgerald

Sets Things Right About His College";* "Unfortunate 'Tradition' ";* "False and Extremely Unwise Tradition";* "Confused Romanticism";* "An Open Letter to Fritz Crisler";* comments on stories; statement on Huck Finn; "Anonymous '17";* letter to Harvey H. Smith;* " 'Why Blame It on the Poor Kiss if the Girl Veteran of Many Petting Parties Is Prone to Affairs After Marriage?' ";* "Does a Moment of Revolt Come Sometime to Every Married Man?";* "What Kind of Husbands Do 'Jimmies' Make?";* " 'Wait Till You Have Children of Your Own!' ";* "What Became of Our Flappers and Sheiks?";* "Girls Believe in Girls";* "What I Think and Feel at 25";* "A Short Autobiography"; "This is a Magazine";* "Reminiscences of Donald Stewart";* *The St. Paul Daily Dirge;* "The Most Disgraceful Thing I Ever Did"; "Salesmanship in the Champs-Elysées";* "The True Story of Appomattox";* "A Book of One's Own";* testimonial for Constant Tras.

Typography and paper: Thirty-nine lines per page. Running heads: rectos, section titles; versos, 'Miscellany by Fitzgerald' or 'Miscellany about Fitzgerald'. Wove paper, watermarked 'WARREN'S OLDE STYLE'.

Binding: White and black V cloth (fine linen-like grain). Front: '[facsimile signature in black against white cloth] F Scott Fitzgerald | [magenta against black cloth] In His Own Time: A Miscellany'. Spine: '[vertically] [facsimile signature in black against white cloth] F Scott Fitzgerald [magenta against black] In His Own Time: A Miscellany | [horizontal seal]'. Magenta endpapers. All edges trimmed.

Dust jacket: None.

Publication: 2,500 copies of the first printing. Published 28 August 1971. $12.50.

Locations: LC (deposited 2 October 1971); MJB; OKentU.

A 33 DEAR SCOTT/DEAR MAX
First edition, first printing [1971]

Dear Scott/Dear Max

THE FITZGERALD–PERKINS CORRESPONDENCE

Edited

by

JOHN KUEHL

and

JACKSON R. BRYER

CHARLES SCRIBNER'S SONS   NEW YORK

A 33: 9⁵⁄₁₆″ x 6¹⁄₁₆″

[i–iv] v–vi 1–15 [16] 17–282

[1–9]¹⁶

Contents: p. i: dedication; p. ii: blank; p. iii: title page; p. iv: copyright; pp. v–vi: 'Preface'; pp. 1–15: 'Introduction'; p. 16: blank; pp. 17–282: text.

Typography and paper: Forty-two lines per page. Running heads: rectos and versos, '*DEAR SCOTT* [slash] *DEAR MAX*'. Off-white wove paper.

Binding: Brown V cloth (fine linen-like grain). Spine: '[vertically] [white script] Dear Scott [slash] [green script] Dear Max | [horizontally] [white] *The Fitzgerald- | Perkins | Correspondence | Kuehl & Bryer | SCRIBNERS'*. Gray endpapers. All edges trimmed.

Dust jacket: Front has all the following on a brown panel, which is surrounded by off-white: '[off-white script] Dear Scott [slash] | [green script] Dear Max | [pale gray, left] *Dear Scott* [slash] *Dear Max | The Fitzgerald-Perkins | Correspondence | [right] Edited by | John Kuehl & | Jackson Bryer*'. Spine: '[vertically] [brown script] Dear Scott [slash] [pale gray script] Dear Max | [horizontally] [brown] *The Fitz-gerald- | Perkins | Correspondence | Kuehl & Bryer* | [green]

SCRIBNERS'. Back has signed photos of Fitzgerald and Perkins and '[green] SBN 684–12373–8'. Front flap has blurb for *Dear Scott/Dear Max;* back flap has biographical notes on the editors.

Publication: 6,000 copies of the first printing. Published 8 December 1971. $7.95.

Locations: MJB, NjP.

Note: A selection of these letters was published as "The Fitzgerald-Perkins Papers," *Esquire,* LXXV (June 1971), 107–111, 171, 174, 176, 178–180, 182–183. See C 322.

Dust jackets for (left-hand column, top to bottom) A 26.1.a, A 33, A 23, (right-hand column) A 32, A 34, and I 1

AS EVER,
SCOTT FITZ—

Letters Between
F. Scott Fitzgerald
and His Literary Agent
Howard Ober
1919-1940

Edited by
MATTHEW J. BRUCCOLI

With the Assistance of
JENNIFER McCABE ATKINSON
Foreword by
SCOTTIE FITZGERALD SMITH

J. B. LIPPINCOTT
COMPANY
Philadelphia and New York

A 34: 5¹⁵⁄₁₆″ x 8¹⁵⁄₁₆″

A 34 AS EVER, SCOTT FITZ—
First edition, first printing [1972]

[i–xi] xii–xvi [xvii] xviii–xxii [1–3] 4–55 [56–59] 60–122 [123–125] 126–212 [213–215] 216–288 [289–291] 292–425 [426–427] 428–441 [442]; 16 pp. of glossy illustrations inserted after p. 170.

[1–13]¹⁶ [14]⁸ [15]¹⁶; 8 leaves of photos inserted after the sixth gathering.

Contents: p. i: half title; p. ii: blank; p. iii: card page; pp. iv–v: title page; p. vi: copyright; p. vii: dedication; p. viii: blank; p. ix: 'Contents'; p. x: blank; pp. xi–xvi: 'Foreword' by Scottie Fitzgerald Smith; pp. xvii–xxii: 'Introduction'; p. 1: section title; p. 2: blank; pp. 3–441: text; p. 442: blank.

Typography and paper: Forty-two lines per page. Running heads: rectos, section titles; versos, *'AS EVER, SCOTT FITZ—'.* Wove paper.

Binding: Blue V cloth (fine linen-like grain). Front blind-stamped in facsimile of Fitzgerald's handwriting: 'As Ever | Scott Fitz—'. Spine goldstamped vertically: 'BRUCCOLI and ATKINSON   Lippincott | [swash] As Ever, Scott Fitz—'. Yellow endpapers with facsimiles of correspondence. All edges trimmed.

Dust jacket: Front printed against solid blue background: '[white] Edited by Matthew J. Bruccoli | [gold swash] As | Ever, | Scott | Fitz—| [white] Letters Between F. Scott Fitzgerald | and His Literary Agent, Harold Ober | 1919–1940'. Spine printed vertically against solid blue background: '[white] BRUCCOLI and ATKINSON   Lippincott | [gold swash] As Ever, Scott Fitz—'. Back has photo of the editors with biographical notes. Front and rear flaps have blurb for *As Ever, Scott Fitz—*.

Publication: 5,000 copies of the first printing. Published 12 June 1972. $15.

Locations: MJB, NjP.

Note: Twenty-two review copies bound in printed wrappers were printed by offset from the uncorrected galley proofs by The Country Press, Middleboro, Mass. Location: MJB.

                              *   *   *

Note

Fitzgerald's radio script "Let's Go Out And Play" for the Squibb *World Peaceways* program was broadcast on 3 October 1935 by WABC (CBS) in New York. This script may have been printed for distribution to listeners, but no copy has been located.

AA. Supplement

Collections

Note: None of these volumes includes first publication of material by Fitzgerald.

AA 1 PORTABLE FITZGERALD
1945

[within double-rule frame, decorated at sides] *The Portable* | F. SCOTT | FITZGERALD | [decoration] | *Selected by Dorothy Parker* | [decoration] | *Introduction by John O'Hara* | NEW YORK | THE VIKING PRESS | 1945

On copyright page: 'PUBLISHED BY THE VIKING PRESS IN SEPTEMBER 1945'

Contents: *The Great Gatsby, Tender is the Night,* "Absolution," "The Baby Party," "The Rich Boy," "May Day," "The Cut-Glass Bowl," "The Offshore Pirate," "The Freshest Boy," "Crazy Sunday," "Babylon Revisited." *No first book material.*

Publication: 20,000 copies of the first printing. Reprinted October 1945 (16,000 copies) and September 1949 (5,000 copies). Also issued as *The Indispensable F. Scott Fitzgerald* (New York: The Book Society, 1949); reprinted 1951.

AA 2 ARMED SERVICES DIAMOND
1946

[within double-rule frame] PUBLISHED BY ARRANGEMENT WITH CHARLES SCRIBNER'S SONS, NEW YORK | *The Diamond as Big as the Ritz* | *and other stories* | BY | F. SCOTT FITZGERALD | WITH AN INTRODUCTION BY LOUIS UNTERMEYER | *Editions for the Armed Services, Inc.* | A NON-PROFIT ORGANIZATION ESTABLISHED BY THE COUNCIL ON BOOKS IN WARTIME, NEW YORK | [outside of frame] 1043

4½ x 6½.

[1–6] 7–319 [320]. Saddle-stapled.

Contents: "The Diamond as Big as the Ritz," "Babylon Revisited," "May Day," "The Rich Boy," "Crazy Sunday," "Winter Dreams," "The Adjuster," "Hot and Cold Blood," " 'The Sensible Thing'," "Gretchen's Forty Winks." *No first book material.*

Typography and paper: Two columns; twenty-five lines per column. No running heads. Wove paper.

Binding: Printed paper wrappers. Front lettered in white, yellow, and black against green and red background. Spine lettered vertically in black and yellow against green and red background. Inside front cover has statement about Armed Services Editions. Inside back cover has list of other titles. Back cover has blurb for this collection.

Publication: Between 50,000 and 90,000 copies. Published April 1946.

Locations: LC (not deposit copy); MJB.

AA 3 BORROWED TIME
1951

F. SCOTT FITZGERALD | [star] | BORROWED | TIME | *Short Stories selected by* | *Alan and Jennifer Ross* | THE GREY WALLS PRESS

On copyright page: 'This edition first published in 1951. . . .'

London, 1951.

Contents: "The Cut-Glass Bowl," "May Day," "The Camel's Back," "The Diamond as Big as the Ritz," "The Rich Boy," "Absolution," "Crazy Sunday," "Two Wrongs," "Babylon Revisited." *No first book material.*

AA 4 THREE NOVELS
1953

MODERN STANDARD AUTHORS | [tapered rule] | *THREE NOVELS OF F. SCOTT FITZGERALD* | THE GREAT GATSBY | *With an Introduction by* MALCOLM COWLEY | TENDER IS THE NIGHT | (WITH THE AUTHOR'S FINAL REVISIONS) | *Edited by* MALCOLM COWLEY | THE LAST TYCOON | AN

UNFINISHED NOVEL | *Edited by* EDMUND WILSON | CHARLES SCRIBNER'S SONS | *New York*

1953. Reprints noted: C-4.56 [H]; D-7.57 [H]; E-4.58 [H]; H-5.62 [H]; I-9.63 [H].

No first book material.

AA 5 BODLEY HEAD FITZGERALD
1958–1963

The Bodley Head Scott Fitzgerald, 6 vols. London: Bodley Head, 1958–1963.

I (*1958*)

GG, LT, "May Day," "The Diamond as Big as the Ritz," "The Crack-Up," "Handle With Care," "Pasting It Together," "Crazy Sunday." *No first book material.* 5,000 copies published 6 October 1958; 3,000 copies, April 1960. Revised edition (*GG* and *LT* only): 3,000 copies, April 1963; 3,000 copies, March 1966; 3,000 copies, July 1970.

II (*1959*)

"Echoes of the Jazz Age," "My Lost City," "Ring," "Early Success," Letters to Frances Scott Fitzgerald, *TITN* (original version), "The Last of the Belles," "Pat Hobby Himself," "An Alcoholic Case," "Financing Finnegan." *No first book material.* 4,500 copies published 16 November 1959; 3,000 copies, July 1961. Revised edition (*TITN* only): 3,000 copies, January 1965; 2,000 copies, December 1969.

III (*1960*)

TSOP, "The Cut-Glass Bowl," "The Curious Case of Benjamin Button," "The Lees of Happiness," "The Rich Boy," "The Adjuster," "Gretchen's Forty Winks." *No first-book material.* 6,000 copies published 7 November 1960. Revised edition (*TSOP* and autobiographical writings): 3,000 copies, July 1965.

IV (*1961*)

B&D, "The Rough Crossing," "Babylon Revisited." *No first-book material.* 6,000 copies published 6 November 1961. Revised edition (*B&D* only): 2,000 copies, December 1967.

V & VI (1963)

Stories: same contents as Malcolm Cowley's *The Stories of F. Scott Fitzgerald* (1951). *No first book material.* 4,000 copies each published 24 October 1963; 2,000 copies each, December 1968.

AA 6 BABYLON REVISITED
1960

BABYLON REVISITED | and | OTHER STORIES | [type decoration] | by | F. Scott Fitzgerald | NEW YORK | CHARLES SCRIBNER'S SONS

On copyright page: 'A-8.60 [C]'.

1960. Scribner Library #SL22. Reprints noted: C-4.62 [C]; F-2.64 [Col]; H-12.65 [Col]; I-12.66 [Col]; J-8.68 [Col]; K-12.69 [C]—cloth.

Contents: "The Ice Palace," "May Day," "The Diamond as Big as the Ritz," "Winter Dreams," "Absolution," "The Rich Boy," "The Freshest Boy," "Babylon Revisited," "Crazy Sunday," "The Long Way Out." *No first book material.*

AA 7 PENGUIN DIAMOND
1962

F. SCOTT FITZGERALD | [decorated rule] | THE DIAMOND AS BIG | AS THE RITZ | AND OTHER STORIES | PENGUIN BOOKS

On copyright page: 'Published in Penguin Books 1962'.

Harmondsworth, Middlesex.

Penguin Modern Classics #1733. Reprinted 1963. See next entry.

Contents: "The Cut-Glass Bowl," "May Day," "The Diamond as Big as the Ritz," "The Rich Boy," "Crazy Sunday," "An Alcoholic Case," "The Lees of Happiness." *No first book material.*

AA 8 PENGUIN STORIES
1962–1968

The Stories of F. Scott Fitzgerald, 5 vols. (Harmondsworth, Middlesex: Penguin, 1962–68).

Volume 1

THE STORIES OF F. SCOTT FITZGERALD | VOLUME I | THE DIAMOND AS BIG | AS THE RITZ | AND OTHER STORIES | [penguin] | PENGUIN BOOKS

On copyright page: 'Published in Penguin Books 1962'.

Penguin #1733. Reprinted 1963, 1965, 1967, 1969.

Contents: "The Cut-Glass Bowl," "May Day," "The Diamond as Big as the Ritz," "The Rich Boy," "Crazy Sunday," "An Alcoholic Case," "The Lees of Happiness." *No first book material.*

Volume 2

F. Scott Fitzgerald | The Crack-Up | with other Pieces and Stories | Penguin Books

On copyright page: 'Published in Penguin Books 1965'.

Penguin #2326. Reprinted 1968.

Contents: "Echoes of the Jazz Age," "My Lost City," "Ring," "The Crack-Up," "Early Success," "Gretchen's Forty Winks," "The Last of the Belles," "Babylon Revisited," "Pat Hobby Himself," "Financing Finnegan." *No first book material.*

Volume 3

See *The Pat Hobby Stories,* A 24.

Volume 4

The Stories of F. Scott Fitzgerald | Volume 4 | Bernice Bobs Her Hair | and Other Stories | Penguin Books

On copyright page: 'Published in Penguin Books 1968'.

Penguin #2736.

Contents: "Bernice Bobs Her Hair," "Winter Dreams," " 'The Sensible Thing'," "Absolution," "The Baby Party," "A Short

Trip Home," "Magnetism," "The Rough Crossing." *No first book material.*

Volume 5

The Stories of F. Scott Fitzgerald | Volume 5 | The Lost Decade | and Other Stories | Penguin Books

On copyright page: 'Published in Penguin Books 1968'.

Penguin #2891.

Contents: "The Freshest Boy," "A Woman with a Past," "Two Wrongs," "The Bridal Party," "Crazy Sunday," "Three Hours Between Planes," "The Lost Decade." *No first book material.*

AA 9 FITZGERALD READER
1963

The | FITZGERALD | *Reader* | Edited by *ARTHUR MIZENER* | Charles Scribner's Sons *New York*

On copyright page: '3.63 [H]'.

1963. Issued simultaneously in Modern Standard Authors series: 3.63 [H]. Subsequently included in the Scribner Library (#SL 118). First Scribner Library printing not seen. Reprints noted: B-6.65 [Col]; E-12.68 (Col).

Contents: "May Day," "Winter Dreams," "Absolution," " 'The Sensible Thing'," *The Great Gatsby,* "The Rich Boy," "Basil and Cleopatra," "Outside the Cabinet-Maker's," "Babylon Revisited," "Echoes of the Jazz Age," "Crazy Sunday," "Family in the Wind," *Tender is the Night* (I–VI), "The Crack-Up," "Pasting it Together," "Handle with Care," "Afternoon of an Author," " 'I Didn't Get Over'," "The Long Way Out," "Financing Finnegan," "The Lost Decade," *The Last Tycoon* (I and IV). *No first book material.*

AA 10 LETTERS TO HIS DAUGHTER
1965

SCOTT FITZGERALD | [script] Letters to His Daughter | EDITED BY ANDREW TURNBULL | WITH AN INTRODUCTION | BY | [script] Frances Fitzgerald Lanahan | CHARLES SCRIBNER'S SONS, *NEW YORK*

On copyright page: 'A-8.65 (V)'.

1965. Reprint noted: B-12.65 [V].

From *Letters. No first book material.*

AA 11 SELECTED STORIES
1970

FRANCIS SCOTT FITZGERALD | *SELECTED STORIES* | *A cura di* | Biancamaria Tedeschini Lalli | U. MURSIA & C.

Milan, 1970.

Contents: "The Diamond as Big as the Ritz," "The Baby Party," "The Scandal Detectives," "The Freshest Boy," "The Captured Shadow," "Bablylon Revisited," "The Long Way Out," "Two Old–Timers," "The Lost Decade." *No first book material.*

B. First-Appearance Contributions to Books and Pamphlets

Titles in which material by Fitzgerald appears for the first time in a book or pamphlet, arranged chronologically. Previously unpublished items are so identified. The first printings only of these books are described, but the English editions are also noted. At the end of Section B there is a BB supplemental list of borderline items. Locations are provided only for scarce items.

B 1 PRINCETON VERSE
1919

A BOOK OF | PRINCETON VERSE II | 1919 | EDITED BY | HENRY VAN DYKE | MORRIS WILLIAM CROLL | MAXWELL STRUTHERS BURT | JAMES CREESE, JR. | PRINCETON UNIVERSITY PRESS | PRINCETON | LONDON: HUMPHREY MILFORD | OXFORD UNIVERSITY PRESS

Published 3 July 1919.

"Marching Streets," "The Pope at Confession," "My First Love," pp. 81–84. All signed *T. Scott Fitzgerald* '18. See C 71, C 72, C 73.

Locations: MJB; NjP.

B 2 O. HENRY PRIZE STORIES OF 1920
1921

[within frame of double black and single red rules] *O. HENRY MEMORIAL AWARD* | [red] PRIZE STORIES | [black] *of* 1920 | CHOSEN BY THE SOCIETY OF | ARTS AND SCIENCES | [red seal within blindstamped frame] | WITH AN INTRODUCTION | BY | BLANCHE COLTON WILLIAMS | GARDEN CITY, N.Y., AND TORONTO | DOUBLEDAY, PAGE & COMPANY | 1921

Published 27 May 1921.

"The Camel's Back," pp. 43–70. See C 84.

B 3 BEST SHORT STORIES OF 1922
1923

THE | BEST SHORT STORIES | OF 1922 | AND THE | YEAR-BOOK OF THE AMERICAN | SHORT STORY | EDITED BY |

EDWARD J. O'BRIEN | [eight lines of type] | [seal] | BOSTON | SMALL, MAYNARD & COMPANY | PUBLISHERS

Published 13 February 1923.

"Two for a Cent," pp. 115–131. See C 110.

Toronto: Goodchild, [1923].

B 4 ACES
1924

ACES | A COLLECTION OF SHORT STORIES | BY | [twelve names in two columns] | *COMPILED BY | THE COMMUNITY WORKERS | OF THE | NEW YORK GUILD FOR THE JEWISH BLIND* | G. P. Putnam's Sons | New York & London | [gothic] The Knickerbocker Press | [roman] 1924

Published 23 October 1924.

"Gretchen's Forty Winks," pp. 77–101. See C 136.

B 5 BARBER ENDORSEMENT
n.d.

[within single-rules frame] Constant Tras | Coiffeur | ANCIEN-NEMENT: | *95, Avenue des Champs-Elysées* | PARIS

Undated four-page advertising pamphlet for barber. Previously unpublished.

Fitzgerald's endorsement in facsimile, p. 4: 'For M. Contant Tras | The best barber in France. Who | cuts the hair of literary men—but | not as in the cartoons | F Scott Fitzgerald'. See A 32.

Location: NjP.

B 6 BEST SHORT STORIES OF 1926

The World's BEST | SHORT STORIES | OF 1926 | SIXTEEN TALES SELECTED BY | THE EDITORS OF THE | LEADING AMERICAN | MAGAZINES | WITH A FOREWORD BY | WILLIAM JOHNSTON | NEW [seal] YORK | GEORGE H. DORAN COMPANY

Published 23 September 1926. Copyright page of the first printing has the Doran seal. "One of My Oldest Friends," pp. 215–231. See C 154.

B 7 CREAM OF THE JUG
1927

[within frame of type ornaments] Cream *of* the Jug | An *Anthology of* | *Humorous Stories* | EDITED BY | GRANT OVERTON | [seal] | HARPER & BROTHERS | NEW YORK AND LONDON | 1927

Published 28 September 1927.

On copyright page: 'FIRST EDITION | H-B' (i.e., August 1927).

"The Pusher-in-the-Face," pp. 151–176. See C 150.

B 8 SAMPLES
1927

[within triple-rules frame] * Samples * | [three rules] *A Collection of Short Stories by* | [thirteen lines of type listing authors] | [ornament] | *Compiled for* | THE COMMUNITY WORKERS | *of the* | NEW YORK GUILD FOR THE JEWISH BLIND | *by* LILLIE RYTTENBERG & BEATRICE LANG | [three rules] | BONI & LIVERIGHT · NEW YORK

Published 5 October 1927.

"The Dance," pp. 203–222. See C 164.

Note

See B 81 for added entry.

B 9 YOU—AT TWENTY
1927

[script] You— | at twenty

Cover title only.

New York: *College Humor*, 1927.

Promotional book for *College Humor*.

First page of "My Old New England Homestead on the Erie,"
p. 33. See C 153.

Location: MJB.

B 10 TEN YEARS OF PRINCETON '17
1929

[double-rules orange frame within double-rules black frame]
[first two lines in orange, the rest in black] TEN YEARS | OF
PRINCETON '17 | *A Record of the Class of* 1917 | *of Princeton
University for the Decade* | 1917—1927 | EDITORIAL COM-
MITTEE | WELLS DRORBAUGH, *Chairman* | JAMES S. WAR-
REN | HARVEY H. SMITH | ILLUSTRATED BY PHOTO-
GRAPHS OF | INDIVIDUAL MEMBERS OF THE CLASS | AND
BY FAMILIAR PRINCETON SCENES | [Princeton seal in black
and orange] | PRINCETON NEW JERSEY | 1929

"Princeton," pp. 37–42. See C 168.

Locations: MJB; NjP.

B 11 FRANCES NEWMAN'S LETTERS
1929

FRANCES NEWMAN'S | LETTERS | *Edited by* | HANSELL
BAUGH | *With a* | *Prefatory Note* | *by James Branch Cabell* |
NEW YORK | HORACE LIVERIGHT: 1929

Published December 1929.

Letter from Fitzgerald, 26 February 1921, pp. 40–42. Previously
unpublished.

B 12 GREAT MODERN SHORT STORIES
1930

[within double-rules frame] GREAT MODERN | SHORT STO-
RIES | [rule] | EDITED BY | GRANT OVERTON | [rule] |
[Modern Library device] | [rule] | THE MODERN LIBRARY |
PUBLISHERS : NEW YORK

On copyright page: 'First Modern Library Edition | 1930'.

"At Your Age," pp. 293–311. See C 193.

B 13 BEST SHORT STORIES OF 1931

THE | BEST SHORT STORIES | OF 1931 | AND THE | YEARBOOK OF THE AMERICAN | SHORT STORY | ED-ITED BY | EDWARD J. O'BRIEN | [seal] | DODD, MEAD AND COMPANY | NEW YORK : : : 1931

Published 9 October 1931.

"Babylon Revisited," pp. 122–142. See C 212.

English edition: The Best Short Stories of 1931 II: American (London: Jonathan Cape, [1932]).

B 14 NEW YORKER SCRAPBOOK
1931

THE NEW YORKER | SCRAPBOOK | [seal] | DOUBLEDAY, DORAN & COMPANY, INC. | GARDEN CITY, NEW YORK, 1931

Published 23 November 1931.

On copyright page: 'FIRST EDITION'.

"A Short Autobiography (With Acknowledgements to Nathan)," pp. 318–321. See C 188.

B 15 THE TIGER'S FAMILY ALBUM
1931

THE TIGER'S | FAMILY ALBUM | [following three lines in gothic] Published on the Occasion | of the Fiftieth Anniversary of the Founding | of the Princeton Tiger | 1882 [tiger] 1932 | A Compendium of Half a Century | of Princeton Wit and Humor, | if any, in Prose, Picture | and Poesy. | PRINTED AT THE PRINCETON UNIVERSITY PRESS

On copyright page: 'FIRST EDITION, DECEMBER 1931 | ONE THOUSAND COPIES'.

"Yais," p. 68. Unsigned. See A 32, C 20.

Locations: MJB; NjP.

B 16 BEST AMERICAN LOVE STORIES
1932

The BEST | AMERICAN | LOVE | STORIES | *of the Year* |
[rule] | *Selected and with an Introduction by* | MARGARET
WIDDEMER | [rule] | *New York* | THE JOHN DAY COMPANY

Published 14 July 1932.

"A New Leaf," pp. 293–315. See C 214.

Reprinted by the Tudor Publishing Co.

B 17 BEST SHORT STORIES OF 1933

THE | BEST SHORT STORIES | 1933 | AND THE | YEARBOOK
OF THE AMERICAN | SHORT STORY | Edited by | EDWARD
J. O'BRIEN | [seal] | BOSTON AND NEW YORK | HOUGHTON
MIFFLIN COMPANY | [gothic] The Riverside Press Cambridge
| [roman] 1933

Published 21 June 1933.

"Crazy Sunday," pp. 115–132. See C 227.

B 18 O. HENRY PRIZE STORIES OF 1933

O. HENRY | MEMORIAL AWARD | [script] Prize Stories of
1933 | [roman] SELECTED AND EDITED BY | HARRY HAN-
SEN | *Literary Editor of the* | NEW YORK WORLD-TELEGRAM
| [red Doubleday, Doran seal] | DOUBLEDAY, DORAN & COM-
PANY, INC. | GARDEN CITY, NEW YORK | 1933

Published 1 November 1933.

On copyright page: 'FIRST EDITION'.

"Family in the Wind," pp. 139–161. See C 224. Statement by
Fitzgerald, p. 138—previously unpublished.

B 19 THE GREAT GATSBY
1934

[within double-rules frame] THE | GREAT GATSBY | [rule] |
BY | F. SCOTT FITZGERALD | [rule] | WITH A NEW INTRO-

DUCTION | BY | F. SCOTT FITZGERALD | [rule] | [four-line verse epigraph] | —Thomas Parke D'Invilliers. | [device] | [rule] | BENNETT A. CERF · DONALD S. KLOPPER | THE MODERN LIBRARY | NEW YORK

Published 13 September 1934.

On copyright page: 'First Modern Library Edition | 1934'.

Fitzgerald's previously unpublished "Introduction," pp. vii–xi. See A 11.1.e.

B 20 THESE STORIES WENT TO MARKET
1935

These Stories Went to Market | [five lines of type] | By | Vernon McKenzie | Head, Department of Journalism | University of Washington | [rule with seal in middle] | Robert M. McBride & Company, Publishers, New York

Published 10 May 1935.

On copyright page: 'FIRST EDITION'.

Previously unpublished notes on stories by Fitzgerald, p. xviii.

B 21 THE NEW REPUBLIC ANTHOLOGY
1936

[within double-rules frame] *The* | NEW REPUBLIC | *Anthology* | 1915 : 1935 | [dot] | Edited by | GROFF CONKLIN | Introduction by | BRUCE BLIVEN | [seal] | DODGE PUBLISHING COMPANY | New York

Published 5 October 1936.

On copyright page: 'FIRST EDITION'.

"Ring," pp. 456–461. See C 233.

B 22 COLONIAL AND HISTORIC HOMES
OF MARYLAND
Prospectus, 1939

COLONIAL AND HISTORIC | HOMES OF MARYLAND | IN TWO VOLUMES | ONE HUNDRED ORIGINAL ETCHINGS |

by | DON SWANN | WITH DESCRIPTIVE TEXT | *by* | DON
SWANN, JR. | [decoration] | Introduction | Herbert R.
O'Conor, *Governor of Maryland* | Foreword | Francis Scott
Key Fitzgerald | THE ETCHCRAFTERS ART GUILD | Balti-
more, Maryland | 1939

Eight-page prospectus for subscribers to the book printed from
the type pages for the book, but the pages of the prospectus are
not in the same order as the pages of the book. Priority of issue
undetermined. See B 23.

"Foreword" by Fitzgerald, p. [7]. Previously unpublished. See
A 32.

Locations: MJB; RLS.

B 23 COLONIAL AND HISTORIC HOMES
OF MARYLAND
Book, 1939

Same title page as the prospectus (B 22).

"Foreword," p. [9]. Previously unpublished. Limited to 200
numbered copies.

Locations: MJB; ViU.

B 24 BEST SHORT STORIES 1940

[black] THE | [red] *Best* | [black] SHORT STORIES | 1940 |
[decorated rule] | *and The Yearbook of the American Short
Story* | [rule] | *Edited by* | EDWARD J. O'BRIEN | 19 [red seal]
40 | [rule] | HOUGHTON MIFFLIN COMPANY · BOSTON |
[gothic] The Riverside Press Cambridge

Published 4 June 1940.

"Design in Plaster," pp. 82–88. See C 280.

B 25 INNOCENT MERRIMENT
1942

INNOCENT | MERRIMENT | *An Anthology of Light Verse* |
SELECTED BY | Franklin P. Adams | ("F.P.A.") | *Whittlesey*

House | McGRAW-HILL BOOK COMPANY, INC. | NEW YORK LONDON

Published 19 October 1942.

"Obit on Parnassus," pp. 345–346. See A 32, C 271.

B 26 MODERN READING NUMBER EIGHT
1944

MODERN | *READING* | *NUMBER EIGHT* | *EDITED BY* | *REGI-NALD MOORE* | [stag] | *LONDON:* | *WELLS GARDNER, DARTON & CO. LTD.*

Dated 1943 on copyright page, but published March 1944.

"Two Old-Timers," pp. 42–45. See A 20.1.a, A 24.1.a, C 299.

Location: MJB.

B 27 ESQUIRE'S 2nd SPORTS READER
1946

ESQUIRE'S | *2nd* | *Sports* | *Reader* | *Edited and with an Intro-duction by* | ARNOLD GINGRICH | [drawing of tennis players] | NEW YORK | A. S. BARNES & COMPANY

Published October 1946.

"Send Me In, Coach," pp. 34–44. See C 267.

B 28 OF MAKING MANY BOOKS
1946

OF MAKING | MANY BOOKS | [rule] | *A Hundred Years of Reading, Writing and Publishing* | [rule] | by | ROGER BURLIN-GAME | MDCCC XLVI [seal] MDCCCC XLVI | [rule] | *NEW YORK* | CHARLES SCRIBNER'S SONS | 1946

Published October 1946.

Copyright page of the first printing has 'A' and the Scribner Press seal.

Previously unpublished letters.

B 29 WE WERE INTERRUPTED
1947

BURTON RASCOE | *We Were Interrupted* | DOUBLEDAY &
COMPANY, INC. | *Garden City, N.Y.*

1947.

Three previously unpublished letters to Rascoe, pp. 22–24.

B 30 McGREGOR ROOM SEMINAR
1948

THE EIGHTH McGREGOR ROOM SEMINAR | IN | CONTEM-
PORARY PROSE AND POETRY | [two lines of type] | UNIVER-
SITY OF VIRGINIA | 7 *May 1948 8:00 P.M.* | THE WORK OF |
F. SCOTT FITZGERALD | *by* | Arthur Mizener | [seven lines
of type]

Excerpt from "General Plan" of *TITN*, passage from Francis
Melarky version of *TITN*, and letter to Frances Scott Fitzgerald
(31 October 1939). All previously unpublished.

Locations: MJB; ViU.

B 31 EDITOR TO AUTHOR
1950

EDITOR TO AUTHOR | THE LETTERS OF | MAXWELL E. PER-
KINS | *Selected and Edited, with Commentary* | *and an Introduc-
tion* | *by* | JOHN HALL WHEELOCK | [seal] | *CHARLES SCRIB-
NER'S SONS, NEW YORK* | *CHARLES SCRIBNER'S SONS,
LTD., LONDON* | 1950

Published March 1950.

Copyright page of the first printing has 'A' and the Scribner
Press seal.

Letter to Perkins, 19 April 1940, p. 158, and brief Fitzgerald
quote, p. 22. Previously unpublished.

B 32 THE FAR SIDE OF PARADISE
1951

THE FAR SIDE OF | Paradise | A BIOGRAPHY OF | F. SCOTT FITZGERALD | *by* | *Arthur Mizener* | ILLUSTRATED | 19 [device] 51 | HOUGHTON MIFFLIN COMPANY BOSTON | [gothic] The Riverside Press Cambridge

Published January 1951.

Previously unpublished quotes from letters, scrapbooks, and ledger—as well as from manuscripts and notes.

Revised edition, 1965.

London: Eyre & Spottiswoode, 1951.

B 33 IDEAS FOR WRITING
1951

[rule] | *Ideas* | *for* | *Writing* | *Readings for College Composition* | KENNETH L. KNICKERBOCKER | *Professor of English University of Tennessee* | HENRY HOLT AND COMPANY New York

Published March 1951.

"The Invasion of the Sanctuary," pp. 86–87. See C 132.

B 34 SHERWOOD ANDERSON
1951

JAMES SCHEVILL | SHERWOOD | ANDERSON | His Life and Work | THE UNIVERSITY OF DENVER PRESS

1951.

Previously unpublished letter to Anderson, p. 177.

B 35 THE GIRLS FROM ESQUIRE
1952

[two-page title on orange paper] [left page] *The Girls from* | [right page] [white script with drawing of Esky above] *Esquire* | [black] Introduction by | FREDERIC A. BIRMINGHAM | [white seal] | Random House · New York

1952.

On copyright page: 'First Printing'.

"The Woman from Twenty-one," pp. 101–102, 104. See C 302.

London: Arthur Barker, [1953].

B 36 THE FOURTH ROUND
1953

STORIES FOR MEN| [line of ornaments] | *The Fourth Round* |
An Anthology Edited by | CHARLES GRAYSON | *New York* :
HENRY HOLT AND COMPANY

Published April 1953.

On copyright page: 'FIRST EDITION'.

"The Bowl," pp. 28–47. See C 171.

B 37 THE FLOWERS OF FRIENDSHIP
1953

THE | FLOWERS of FRIENDSHIP | *Letters written to* | GER-
TRUDE STEIN | *Edited by* DONALD GALLUP | *Before the Flow-
ers of Friendship Faded Friendship Faded* | (TITLE OF A BOOK
BY GERTRUDE STEIN) | [Borzoi] 1953 | ALFRED A. KNOPF
NEW YORK

Published August 1953.

On copyright page: 'FIRST EDITION'.

Three previously unpublished letters: June 1925, p. 174; 28
April 1932, p. 257; 29 December 1934, p. 294.

B 38 ESQUIRE TREASURY
1953

[decorated rule] The | ESQUIRE | Treasury | [six lines of type] |
EDITED BY | ARNOLD GINGRICH | 19 [figure] 53 | [decorated
rule] | SIMON AND SCHUSTER : NEW YORK

Published November 1953.

On copyright page: 'FIRST PRINTING'.

"Pat Hobby's Christmas Wish," pp. 187–193. See A 24.1.a, C 283.

London: William Heinemann, [1954].

B 39 GREAT TALES OF CITY DWELLERS
1955

Great Tales | of | CITY DWELLERS | edited by | Alex Austin | [lion] | Lion Library Editions | 655 Madison Avenue | New York City

Published 15 November 1955. #LL53.

"A Millionaire's Girl," pp. 175–186. Mostly by Zelda Fitzgerald. See C 204.

Location: MJB.

Note

See B 80 for added entry.

B 40 THIRTEEN GREAT STORIES
1956

[two-page title] [left page has thirteen names in a column] 13 | [right page] great | stories | EDITED BY DANIEL TALBOT | a dell first edition

Published in New York, 16 February 1956. #D99.

"The Worlds Fair," pp. 90–101. See C 308.

Location: MJB.

B 41 GREAT TALES OF THE FAR WEST
1956

Great Tales | of the | FAR WEST | edited by | Alex Austin | [lion] | Lion Library Editions | 655 Madison Avenue | New York City

Published May 1956. #LL88.

"The Last Kiss," pp. 176–192. See C 309.

Location: MJB.

B 42 LETTERS OF THOMAS WOLFE
1956

THE LETTERS OF | THOMAS | WOLFE | *Collected and Edited,* | *with an Introduction and* | *Explanatory Text, by* | ELIZABETH NOWELL | *New York* | CHARLES SCRIBNER'S SONS

Published October 1956.

On copyright page: 'A-7.56 [V]'.

Blue and black binding probably precedes solid black binding.

Previously unpublished letter to Wolfe, 19 July 1937, p. 641.

B 43 LADIES' HOME JOURNAL TREASURY
1956

[two-page title surrounded by red, white, and black frames] [left page has three magazine covers] [right page] [red script] The Ladies' Home | [black roman] JOURNAL | [red script] Treasury | [following four lines in black roman] SELECTED FROM | THE COMPLETE FILES | BY JOHN MASON BROWN AND | THE EDITORS OF THE LADIES' HOME JOURNAL | [red] SIMON AND SCHUSTER · NEW YORK

Published December 1956.

On copyright page: 'FIRST PRINTING'.

"Imagination—and a Few Mothers," pp. 121–124. See C 127.

B 44 SCOTT FITZGERALD AT LA PAIX
1956

Scott Fitzgerald at La Paix | *by Andrew W. Turnbull* | *Publications in the Humanities Number* 22 | *from the* DEPARTMENT OF HUMANITIES | MASSACHUSETTS INSTITUTE OF TECHNOLOGY | CAMBRIDGE 39, MASSACHUSETTS 1956

Previously unpublished inscriptions, letters, and conversation. See F 80, F 81.

B 45 PAPERS OF CHRISTIAN GAUSS
1957

THE PAPERS | OF | Christian Gauss | EDITED BY | Katherine Gauss Jackson | AND | Hiram Haydn | [seal] | [tapered rule] | Random House New York

Published 14 January 1957.

On copyright page: 'FIRST PRINTING'.

Seven letters and one wire by Fitzgerald, all previously unpublished: 1 February 1928, 2 February 1933, 23 April 1934, 7 September 1934, 26 September 1934, 30 September 1935, 14 October 1935, pp. 213–223.

B 46 AUTHORS AT WORK
1957

Authors at Work | AN ADDRESS DELIVERED BY | Robert H. Taylor | [four lines of type] | CATALOGUE OF THE EXHIBITION BY | Herman W. Liebert | AND FACSIMILES OF MANY | OF THE EXHIBITS | [line of squares] | New York · The Grolier Club · 1957

Published 1 November 1957.

Facsimile of first page of revised typescript of "The Perfect Life," plate 63. Previously unpublished.

B 47 ARMCHAIR ESQUIRE
1958

THE ARMCHAIR | [script] Esquire | *Edited by* ARNOLD GINGRICH | *and* L. RUST HILLS | INTRODUCTION BY *Granville Hicks* | [seal] | G. P. PUTNAM'S SONS *New York*

Published 6 October 1958.

"Three Acts of Music," pp. 93–98. See C 260. Headnote quotes Fitzgerald, pp. 92–93. See C 260.

London: William Heinemann, [1959].

B 48 BELOVED INFIDEL
1958

BELOVED | INFIDEL | *The Education of a Woman* | *by* Sheilah Graham | *and* Gerold Frank | *Illustrated with Photographs* | HENRY HOLT AND COMPANY | NEW YORK

Published 24 November 1958.

On copyright page: 'FIRST EDITION'.

Facsimiles of Fitzgerald manuscripts on endpapers; facsimile of Fitzgerald reading list included with illustrations; also quotes from notes, letters, wires, and verses. All previously unpublished.

Condensed in *Cosmopolitan*, CLXVI (February 1959), 82–91.

London: Cassel, [1959].

B 49 JOY RIDE
1959

JOY RIDE | *Dwight Taylor* | [seal] *G. P. Putnam's Sons* | *New York*

Published 29 April 1959.

Conversation, pp. 234–250; verse, p. 244. See F 79.

B 50 STEPHEN LEACOCK
1959

STEPHEN LEACOCK | *Humorist and Humanist* | [double rules] | Ralph L. Curry | DOUBLEDAY & COMPANY, INC. | GARDEN CITY, NEW YORK | 1959

Published 23 June 1959.

On copyright page: 'First Edition'.

Previously unpublished letter to Leacock, pp. 119–120.

B 51 LES ANNÉES VINGT
1959

CENTRE CULTUREL AMÉRICAIN | 3, rue du Dragon, Paris 6° | LES ANNÉES VINGT | LES ÉCRIVAINS | AMÉRICAINS | A

PARIS | ET LEURS AMIS | 1920–1930 | EXPOSITION | du 11 Mars au 25 Avril 1959

Precedes *Shakespeare and Company* (New York: Harcourt Brace, 1959) and *Paris in the Twenties* (London: USIS, 1960).

Previously unpublished drawing by Fitzgerald commemorating "Festival of St. James," July 1928, facing p. 81.

Location: MJB.

B 52 ELLERY QUEEN'S 15th MYSTERY ANNUAL
          1960

ELLERY QUEEN'S | 15th MYSTERY | ANNUAL | The Year's Best | from *Ellery Queen's Mystery Magazine* | Edited by ELLERY QUEEN | [seal] | RANDOM HOUSE · NEW YORK

Published 30 September 1960. Preceded by Random House Keepsake. See A 23.

On copyright page: 'FIRST PRINTING'.

"The Mystery of the Raymond Mortgage," pp. 241–248. See C 1.

London: Victor Gollancz, 1961.

B 53 SCOTT FITZGERALD
          1962

SCOTT | FITZGERALD | [line of decorations] | *by* ANDREW TURNBULL | CHARLES SCRIBNER'S SONS | *New York*

Published 23 February 1962.

On copyright page: 'Copyright © 1962 . . . A-1.61 [V]'.

Previously unpublished material from letters, Ledger, scrapbooks, manuscripts, and notes.

London: Bodley Head, [1962].

B 54 BETWEEN FRIENDS
          1962

BETWEEN FRIENDS | LETTERS OF | JAMES BRANCH CABELL | AND OTHERS | EDITED BY | PADRAIC COLUM |

AND | MARGARET FREEMAN CABELL | WITH AN | INTRO-
DUCTION | BY | CARL VAN VECHTEN | [seal] | HARCOURT,
BRACE & WORLD, INC. NEW YORK

Published 28 March 1962.

On copyright page: 'first edition'.

Previously unpublished letters from Fitzgerald: 25 December
1920, pp. 212–213; 30 December 1920, p. 214; 23 December
1921, pp. 215–216; 4 March 1922, p. 251; n.d., p. 252; 27 March
1922, p. 255. Also letters to and from Zelda Fitzgerald. See I 29.

B 55 THAT SUMMER IN PARIS
1963

[two-page title] [left page] MORLEY CALLAGHAN [leaf] |
[right page] That Summer in Paris | MEMORIES OF TANGLED
FRIENDSHIPS | WITH HEMINGWAY, FITZGERALD, | AND
SOME OTHERS | NEW YORK *Coward-McCann, Inc.* [seal] 1963

Published 7 January 1963.

Previously unpublished letter, p. 12, and wire, p. 243.

London: MacGibbon & Kee, 1963.

B 56 F. SCOTT FITZGERALD
1963

F. SCOTT FITZGERALD | [rule] | by KENNETH EBLE | Univer-
sity of Utah | [within oval] TUSAS 36 | Twayne Publishers, Inc.
: : New York

Published 15 July 1963.

Material from unpublished preface to *TSOP*, p. 46; previously
unpublished material from *GG* galleys, pp. 92–93.

B 57 NEUROTICA
1963

[white lettering against black ink blot] NEUROTICA | [black]
*Editors: | Jay Irving Landesman | Gershon Legman | ST. LOUIS–
NEW YORK | 1948–51* | REPRINTED BY | Hacker Art Books
| New York | 1963

Facsimiles of the issues of the journal.

"The Boy Who Killed his Mother," #9, pp. 38–39. See C 312.

Unauthorized publication of the poem.

B 58 THE COMPOSITION OF *TENDER IS THE NIGHT*
   1963

THE COMPOSITION OF | *TENDER IS THE NIGHT* | A Study of the Manuscripts | *by* | Matthew J. Bruccoli | UNIVERSITY OF PITTSBURGH PRESS

Published 20 September 1963.

Previously unpublished material from the manuscripts, as well as letters and facsimiles.

Note: Two states of the first (only) printing. The first state has pp. 23–24 integral; the second state has a cancel to add the first line on p. 23.

B 59 THE ART OF F. SCOTT FITZGERALD
   1965

SERGIO PEROSA | [rule] | The Art | of | F. Scott | Fitzgerald | *Translated by Charles Matz and the author* | Ann Arbor | The University of Michigan Press

Published 28 May 1965.

Previously unpublished material from typescripts and manuscripts of *The Romantic Egotist*, *GG*, and *LT*.

Italian edition: Rome: Edizioni di Storia e Letteratura, 1961.

B 60 F. SCOTT FITZGERALD A CRITICAL PORTRAIT
   1965

HENRY DAN PIPER | F. | Scott | Fitzgerald | A Critical | Portrait | F$_S$F | HOLT, RINEHART AND WINSTON | New YORK CHICAGO SAN FRANCISCO

Published 28 July 1965.

On copyright page: 'First Edition'.

Previously unpublished material from letters, notes, and type-scripts.

London: Bodley Head, [1966].

B 61 A GIFT OF JOY
1965

[two-page title] [right page] HELEN HAYES | [left page] A GIFT [right page] OF JOY | [left page] WITH LEWIS FUNKE | [right page] *Published by* M. Evans and Company, Inc., *New York* | *and distributed in association with* | J. B. Lippincott Company, *Philadelphia and New York*

Published 1 September 1965.

Two previously unpublished poems: untitled and "For Mary's Eighth Birthday," pp. 193–195.

Excerpted in *McCall's*, XCII (September 1965), 73–75, 172–180.

B 62 SMART SET
1966

The | [a devil holding winged hearts by strings in the first S] SMART SET | [the next five lines within a decorated frame] A HISTORY | AND ANTHOLOGY BY | Carl R. Dolmetsch | WITH AN INTRODUCTORY REMINISCENCE BY | S. N. Behrman | THE DIAL PRESS | [device] | NEW YORK 1966

Published 21 November 1966.

On copyright page: 'FIRST PRINTING, 1966'.

"The Debutante," pp. 224–236. See C 75.

B 63 PENGUIN BOOK OF MODERN VERSE TRANSLATION
1966

THE PENGUIN BOOK OF | MODERN VERSE TRANSLATION | INTRODUCED AND EDITED BY | *George Steiner* | [penguin] | PENGUIN BOOKS

Published in Harmondsworth, Middlesex, November 1966. #D 91.

Fitzgerald's translation of Rimbaud's "Voyelles," p. 141. See F 38.

Subsequently published in America. Baltimore: Penguin, [1966(?)].

          B 64 COLLEGE OF ONE
              1967

College of One | [ornament] | *by Sheilah Graham* | [ornament] | THE VIKING PRESS [slash] *New York*

Published 28 February 1967.

Previously unpublished material from letters and notes; facsimiles of manuscripts and typescripts, pp. 203–245; also facsimiles on endpapers and dust jacket. See F 38.

London: Weidenfeld & Nicolson, [1967].

          B 65 THE LAST LAOCOÖN
              1967

F. SCOTT FITZGERALD | *The Last Laocoön* | ROBERT SKLAR | NEW YORK | OXFORD UNIVERSITY PRESS | 1967

Published 27 April 1967.

Previously unpublished material from letters, notes, inscriptions, and reviews.

          B 66 CREATIVE WRITING & REWRITING
              1967

John Kuehl | NEW YORK UNIVERSITY | *creative writing* | *&* *rewriting* | *contemporary American novelists at work* | [seal] | APPLETON-CENTURY-CROFTS [slash] New York | DIVISION OF MEREDITH PUBLISHING COMPANY

Published 13 September 1967.

Published simultaneously with B 67. Transcribes first chapter of *GG* manuscript, pp. 132–162.

B 67 WRITE AND REWRITE
1967

write and rewrite | *a study of the creative process* | by John
Kuehl | Also published under the title | *Creative Writing &*
Rewriting | by Appleton-Century-Crofts | *MEREDITH PRESS*
[slash] New York

Published 13 September 1967.

On copyright page: 'First edition'.

Published simultaneously with B 66. Transcribes first chapter of
GG manuscript, pp. 132–162.

B 68 CONNOISSEUR'S HAVEN
1968

Connoisseur's | *Haven* | THE PITTSBURGH BIBLIOPHILES'
JOURNEY TO BALTIMORE | 27–29 OCTOBER 1967 | Robert
C. Alberts

Published 27 January 1968.

Colophon: '250 COPIES OF THIS BOOKLET HAVE BEEN
PRINTED FOR THE MEMBERS OF THE BALTIMORE BIBLIO-
PHILES AND THE PITTSBURGH BIBLIOPHILES. . . .'

Previously unpublished Fitzgerald inscription to H. L. Mencken
in Hemingway's *Men Without Women*, p. 10.

Location: MJB.

B 69 THE MOVING IMAGE
1968

ROBERT GESSNER | *The Moving Image* | A GUIDE TO CINE-
MATIC LITERACY [decoration] | *New York E. P. Dutton & Co.,*
Inc. 1968

On copyright page: 'FIRST EDITION'.

Previously unpublished material from the screenplay "Cosmopolitan" ("Babylon Revisited"), pp. 240–248. See Appendix 5.

B 70 ERNEST HEMINGWAY
1969

Ernest | Hemingway | A LIFE STORY | [tapered rule] | *By* |
CARLOS BAKER | [two-line epigraph] | —JAMES JOYCE,
A Portrait of the Artist as a Young Man | *New York* | CHARLES
SCRIBNER'S SONS

Published April 1969.

On copyright page: 'A-3.69 [C]'.

Material from three previously unpublished telegrams, pp. 293,
316.

London: Collins, 1969.

B 71 FITZGERALD/HEMINGWAY ANNUAL, 1969

FITZGERALD [slash] HEMINGWAY | ANNUAL | 1969 | Edited
by Matthew J. Bruccoli | University of South Carolina |
N | C | R MICROCARD® EDITIONS | 901 TWENTY-SIXTH
STREET, N.W., WASHINGTON, D.C. 20037, 202 [slash] 333–
6393 | INDUSTRIAL PRODUCTS DIVISION, THE NATIONAL
CASH REGISTER COMPANY

Published September 1969.

Includes the following previously unpublished material:

"Dearly Beloved," pp. 1–3. See C 318.
Untitled poem, "Valentine was a Saint . . . ," p. 18. See
C 319, F 73.

B 72 FITZGERALD NEWSLETTER
1969

Fitzgerald Newsletter | Edited by Matthew J. Bruccoli | Uni-
versity of South Carolina | N | C | R MICROCARD® EDI-
TIONS | 901 TWENTY-SIXTH STREET, N.W., WASHINGTON,
D.C. 20037, 202 [slash] 333–6393 | INDUSTRIAL PRODUCTS
DIVISION, THE NATIONAL CASH REGISTER COMPANY

Published October 1969. Corrected and revised volume. Forty
numbers of the *Fitzgerald Newsletter* were published quarterly,
from Spring 1958 to Winter 1968.

See Sections C and F for first publication of material by Fitzgerald in the individual numbers of the *Fitzgerald Newsletter*.

B 73 THE MOVIES, MR. GRIFFITH, AND ME
1969

[decoration at each corner of the page] LILLIAN GISH | The
Movies | Mr. Griffith | and Me | *By* | *Lillian Gish* | *with Ann
Pinchot* | PRENTICE-HALL, INC., ENGLEWOOD CLIFFS, N.J.

1969.

Previously unpublished inscription, p. 283.

B 74 FITZGERALD/HEMINGWAY ANNUAL 1970

FITZGERALD [slash] HEMINGWAY | ANNUAL | 1970 | Edited
by Matthew J. Bruccoli | University of South Carolina | C. E.
Frazer Clark, Jr. | N | C | R | MICROCARD® EDITIONS |
901 TWENTY-SIXTH STREET, N.W., WASHINGTON, D.C.
20037, 202 [slash] 333–6393 | INDUSTRIAL PRODUCTS DI-
VISION, THE NATIONAL CASH REGISTER COMPANY

Published November 1970.

Includes the following previously unpublished material:

Letter to Ernest Hemingway, pp. 10–13. See C 320.
Jennifer E. Atkinson, "Fitzgerald's Marked Copy of *The Great
   Gatsby*," pp. 28–33. Fitzgerald's revisions. See F 7.
"Six Letters to the Menckens," pp. 102–104. See C 321.

B 75 ZELDA
1970

ZELDA | A BIOGRAPHY | [rule] | *by Nancy Milford* | Harper
& Row, Publishers | New York, Evanston, and London

Published 10 June 1970.

On copyright page: 'FIRST EDITION'.

Previously unpublished material from letters and notes, pp.
170–172, 181–183, 255–256, and passim. See F 57, I 30.

Zelda Fitzgerald (London: Bodley Head, [1970]).

B 76 PROFILE OF F. SCOTT FITZGERALD
1971

Profile | of | F. Scott Fitzgerald | *Compiled by* | Matthew J. Bruc-coli | *University of South Carolina* | Charles E. Merrill Publishing Company | *A Bell & Howell Company* | Columbus, Ohio

Published 7 January 1971.

On copyright page: '1 . . . 71'.

"My Generation," pp. 5–10. See C 317.

Also includes:

> John Kuehl, "Scott Fitzgerald's Critical Opinions," pp. 21–39. See F 43.
> John Kuehl, "Scott Fitzgerald's Reading," pp. 40–73. See F 42.

Note: Four sentences from "My Generation" appear in Andrew Turnbull, *Thomas Wolfe* (New York: Scribners, [1967]), p. 159.

B 77 CRAZY SUNDAYS
1971

[title within marquee] CRAZY | SUNDAYS | F. SCOTT FITZGERALD | IN HOLLYWOOD | Aaron Latham | NEW YORK [slash] THE VIKING PRESS

Published 19 March 1971.

Previously unpublished material from letters, notes, and scripts, throughout. See F 44.

B 78 EXILES FROM PARADISE
1971

[title page printed in gray] *Exiles from Paradise* | ZELDA AND SCOTT FITZGERALD | *by Sara Mayfield* | [portrait of the Fitzgeralds in oval frame] | *DELACORTE PRESS* [slash] *NEW YORK, N.Y.*

Published 12 July 1971.

On copyright page: 'First Printing'.

Previously unpublished material from letters, notebooks, manuscripts, and inscriptions. See F 55, F 56, I 31.

B 79 FITZGERALD/HEMINGWAY ANNUAL 1971

FITZGERALD [slash] HEMINGWAY | ANNUAL | 1971 | Edited by Matthew J. Bruccoli | University of South Carolina | C. E. Frazer Clark, Jr. | [N | C | R] Microcard Editions

Published in Washington, D.C., 11 November 1971.

Includes the following previously unpublished material:

Facsimile of Fitzgerald signatures, front endpaper.
"Preface to *This Side of Paradise*," pp. 1–2. See C 324.
"Fitzgerald's Ledger," pp. 3–31. See C 325.
Jennifer McCabe Atkinson, "The Lost and Unpublished Stories by F. Scott Fitzgerald," pp. 32–63. Includes facsimile of first page of "The I. O. U." manuscript. See F 8.
Matthew J. Bruccoli, "Fitzgerald's Marked Copy of *This Side of Paradise*," pp. 64–69. Includes list of corrections and facsimile of notes. See F 22.
Lawrence D. Stewart, "Fitzgerald's Film Scripts of 'Babylon Revisited'," pp. 81–104. Includes material from scripts. See F 78.
"Oh, Sister, Can You Spare Your Heart," pp. 114–116. Lyric. See C 326.
Daniel G. Siegel, "T. S. Eliot's Copy of *Gatsby*," pp. 291–293. Includes facsimile of inscription to Eliot. See F 75.
Jay Martin, "Fitzgerald Recommends Nathanael West for a Guggenheim," pp. 302–304. Includes letter (25 September 1934). See F 52.
Robert Emmet Long, "The Fitzgerald-Mencken Correspondence," pp. 319–321. Quotes letters. See F 46.

Note: This issue includes a recording of Fitzgerald reciting verse.

B 80 WITH LOVE FROM GRACIE 1955

WITH LOVE FROM [script] Gracie | [roman] SINCLAIR LEWIS: 1912–1925 | *BY GRACE HEGGER LEWIS* | HARCOURT, BRACE AND COMPANY, NEW YORK

1955.

Letter to Lewis, p. 186.

Note: This entry was added in proof, and chronologically comes after B 39.

B 81   THREE YEARS
         1927

THREE YEARS | 1924 to 1927 | *The Story of a New Idea* | And Its *Successful Adaptation* | With a Postscript by | H. L. MENCKEN | [seal] | NEW YORK | THE AMERICAN MERCURY | MCMXXVII
Note by Fitzgerald, p. 43.

Note: This entry was added in proof, and chronologically comes after B 8.

                              *   *   *

Note

C. Waller Barrett's "A Note on the Disenchanted, Francis Scott Key Fitzgerald 1896–1940," *Antiquarian Bookman*, VII (20 January 1951), 427–428, states that the 1917 Princeton *Bric-a-Brac* "contains poems by Fitzgerald." It includes nothing by Fitzgerald.

The following Princeton University yearbooks do, however, include photos and material about Fitzgerald's undergraduate activities: *The Bric-a-Brac*, XL (1914[?]); *The Bric-a-Brac*, XLI (1915); *The Bric-a-Brac*, XLII (1916[?]); *The Bric-a-Brac*, XLIII (1917); *The Nassau Herald Class of Nineteen Hundred and Seventeen* (1917).

BB. Supplement

Borderline Items

BB 1 WHO'S WHO IN AMERICA
1922–1923

WHO'S WHO | IN AMERICA | [rule] | A BIOGRAPHICAL DIC-
TIONARY OF NOTABLE LIVING | MEN AND WOMEN OF
THE UNITED STATES | VOL. 12 | 1922–1923 | EDITED BY |
ALBERT NELSON MARQUIS | FOUNDED 1899 | REVISED
AND REISSUED BIENNIALLY | CHICAGO: A. N. MARQUIS
& COMPANY

"Fitzgerald, Francis Scott Key," p. 1117. Fitzgerald's first appearance. Based on questionnaire. Revised and updated in later
volumes.

BB 2 MEN WHO MAKE OUR NOVELS
1924

[within single-rules frame] THE MEN WHO MAKE | OUR
NOVELS | BY | CHARLES C. BALDWIN | REVISED EDITION |
[seal] | NEW YORK | DODD, MEAD AND COMPANY | 1924

Published 26 December 1924.

"F. Scott Fitzgerald" pp. 166–173. Based on letter or interview.
Previously unpublished.

BB 3 THE LOW-DOWN
1928

[within triple-rules frame] THE | Low-Down | BY | Charles G.
Shaw | [seal] | NEW YORK | HENRY HOLT AND COMPANY

Published 13 March 1928.

On copyright page: 'Printed, March, 1928'.

"F. Scott Fitzgerald," pp. 163–169. Based on interview. Previously unpublished.

BB 4 LIVING AUTHORS
1931

LIVING | AUTHORS | *A Book of Biographies* | Edited by DILLY TANTE | and Illustrated with 371 Photographs and Drawings | [seal] | THE H. W. WILSON COMPANY | NEW YORK 1931

Published 5 May 1931.

"F. Scott Fitzgerald," pp. 127–128. Probably based on letter. Previously unpublished.

BB 5 CONTEMPORARY AMERICAN AUTHORS
1940

CONTEMPORARY | American Authors | *A Critical Survey and* 219 *Bio-Bibliographies* | FRED B. MILLETT | *New York* | HARCOURT, BRACE AND COMPANY | 1940

Published 8 February 1940.

"F(rancis) Scott (Key) Fitzgerald, 1896–," pp. 354–355. Probably based on letter. Previously unpublished.

BB 6 THE LIVES OF 18 FROM PRINCETON
1946

[within double-rules frame] The Lives of | Eighteen from | Princeton | Edited by Willard Thorp | [cut of archway] | PRINCETON NEW JERSEY | PRINCETON UNIVERSITY PRESS | 1946

Arthur Mizener, "F. Scott Fitzgerald The Poet of Borrowed Time," pp. 333–363. Includes first publication of material from letters.

BB 7 CHARLIE
1957

[letters of 'CHARLIE' separated by stars] CHARLIE | *The improbable life and times of* | CHARLES MacARTHUR | *by Ben*

Hecht | ILLUSTRATED | [torch] HARPER & BROTHERS | *Publishers, New York*

Published 17 June 1957

On copyright page: 'FIRST EDITION'.

Previously unpublished letter, p. 161.

BB 8 THE SUN WITHIN US
1963

THE SUN | WITHIN US | [ornamental rule] | JAMES DRAW-BELL | *Life is a pure flame, and we live* | *by an invisible sun within us* | —*Sir Thomas Browne, 1605–82* | *Collins* | ST. JAMES'S PLACE, LONDON | 1963

Published 30 September 1963.

Conversation, pp. 170–179.

An Autobiography. New York: Pantheon, 1964.

BB 9 HEMINGWAY AN OLD FRIEND REMEMBERS
1965

HEMINGWAY | AN OLD FRIEND REMEMBERS | Jed Kiley | HAWTHORN BOOKS, INC. | *Publishers* New York City

Published 10 May 1965.

On copyright page: 'First Edition, April, 1965'.

Conversation, pp. 57–58. See F 41.

London: Methuen, [1965].

BB 10 AN UNFINISHED WOMAN
1969

AN UNFINISHED | WOMAN—*a memoir* | *by* Lillian Hellman | LITTLE, BROWN AND COMPANY · BOSTON · TORONTO | [seal] *with illustrations*

1969.

On copyright page: 'FIRST EDITION'.

Conversation, pp. 68–69.

C. Appearances in Magazines and Newspapers

First publication in magazines and newspapers of material by Fitzgerald, arranged chronologically. A few reprintings are noted in cases where the fact of republication seems especially important—for example, syndication of a story or article. The first English publication of stories is noted, but none of these English appearances has been seen by the compiler.

C 1
"The Mystery of the Raymond Mortgage," *The St. Paul Academy Now and Then*, II (October 1909), 4–8.

Fiction. See A 23, A 27, B 52.[1]

C 2
"Reade, Substitute Right Half," *The St. Paul Academy Now and Then*, II (February 1910), 10–11.

Fiction. See A 27.

C 3
"A Debt of Honor," *The St. Paul Academy Now and Then*, II (March 1910), 9–11.

Fiction. See A 27.

C 4
"S. P. A. Men in College Athletics," *The St. Paul Academy Now and Then*, III (December 1910), 7.

News article.

C 5
"The Room with the Green Blinds," *The St. Paul Academy Now and Then*, III (June 1911), 6–9.

Fiction. See A 27.

C 6
" 'Football'," *Newman News*, IX (Christmas 1911[?]), 19.

Verse. See A 32.

---

1. The only located file of *The St. Paul Academy Now and Then* for the Fitzgerald years is at the academy library.

C 7

Untitled news feature about school election, *Newman News* (1912), 18.[2]

Signed 'F. S. F.'

C 8

"A Luckless Santa Claus," *Newman News*, IX (Christmas 1912), 1–7.

Fiction. See A 27.

C 9

"Pain and the Scientist," *Newman News* (1913), 5–10.

Fiction. See A 27.

C 10

"The Trail of the Duke," *Newman News*, IX (June 1913), 5–9.

Fiction. See A 27.

C 11

Untitled news feature about school dance, *Newman News* (1913), 18.

Signed 'F. S. F.'

Note

In "A Few Early Years Recollections of F. Scott Fitzgerald and Princeton's Literary Past" (*The Princeton Tiger*, LXVIII [January 1957], 14, 21) John Biggs, Jr., wrote: "One brilliant thing which Bishop, Wilson and Fitzgerald did get together was the creation of a mythical *belle lettres* writer whose name was Edward Moore Gresham. . . . It is also my recollection that Gresham did some work for the Tiger, probably his very best." However, Edmund Wilson has informed the compiler (19 April 1968) that "I never wrote a word for the *Tiger*, nor did Scott have anything to do with Edward Moore Gresham. That was something I wrote for the *Lit.* . . . Afterwards, we published

---

2. There is no known file of the *Newman News*. The entries for Fitzgerald's contribution to the *Newman News* are taken from his scrapbook, "Published Juvenilia of F. Scott Fitzgerald, 1909–1917," at the Princeton University Library. See Henry Dan Piper, "Scott Fitzgerald's Prep-School Writings," *The Princeton University Library Chronicle*, XVII (Autumn 1955), 1–10.

some of his literary remains, written by John Bishop, Alfred Bellinger of Yale and me." See "Lost Remains of Edward Moore Gresham," *The Nassau Literary Magazine*, LXXI (March 1916), 408–418.

C 12
Untitled humor article, beginning "There was once a second group student . . . ," *The Princeton Tiger*, XXV (December 1914), 5.

Unsigned—attributed to Fitzgerald on basis of clipping in the Princeton Fitzgerald Papers. See A 32.

C 13
"Shadow Laurels," *The Nassau Literary Magazine*, LXXI (April 1915), 1–10.

Play. See A 27.

C 14
"May Small Talk," *The Princeton Tiger*, XXVI (June 1915), 10.

Verse. Unsigned—attributed to Fitzgerald on basis of clipping in Princeton Fitzgerald Papers. See A 32.

C 15
"The Ordeal," *The Nassau Literary Magazine*, LXXI (June 1915), 153–159.

Fiction. Incorporated in "Benediction," C 78. See A 27.

C 16
"How They Head the Chapters," *The Princeton Tiger*, XXVI (September 1915), 10.

Humor article. Unsigned—attributed to Fitzgerald on basis of clipping in Princeton Fitzgerald Papers. See A 32.

C 17
"Mass Meeting To-Night To Practice New Song," *The Daily Princetonian* (28 October 1915), 1.

News story (not written by Fitzgerald) includes Fitzgerald's lyrics for "A Cheer for Princeton." See A 32.

C 18
"The Conquest of America (as some writers would have it),"
The Princeton Tiger, XXVI (Thanksgiving 1915), 6.

Humor article. Unsigned—tentatively attributed to Fitzgerald on the basis of headnote attributing the article to "Mr. Fitzcheesecake." No clipping in Princeton Fitzgerald Papers. See A 32.

C 19
"Three Days at Yale," *The Princeton Tiger*, XXVI (December 1915), 8–10.

Humor article. Unsigned. Landon T. Raymond, '17, has written the compiler that Alan Jackman, '17, told him that this item was "conceived" by Fitzgerald.

C 20
"Yais," *The Princeton Tiger*, XXVII (June 1916), 13.

Verse. Unsigned—attributed to Fitzgerald by John McMaster, '19, who supplied the title (see *Fitzgerald Newsletter*, no. 40).[3] No clipping in Princeton Fitzgerald Papers. See A 32 and B 15.

C 21
"To My Unused Greek Book (*Acknowledgments to Keats*)," *The Nassau Literary Magazine*, LXXII (June 1916), 137.

Verse. See A 32.

C 22
"Our Next Issue," *The Nassau Literary Magazine*, LXXII (December 1916), unpaged.

Prose parody. Unsigned—attributed to Fitzgerald on basis of clipping in Princeton Fitzgerald Papers. See A 32.

C 23
"Jemina A Story of the Blue Ridge Mountains By John Phlox, Jr.," *The Nassau Literary Magazine*, LXXII (December 1916), 210–215.

---

3. Mr. McMaster has also suggested to the compiler that the following *Princeton Tiger* items may have been by Fitzgerald: "Our Society Column," XXVI (February 1916), 6; "What Happened to Susie," XXVI (February 1916), 15; "The Awful Optic," XXVI (March 1916), 7; "The Lost Lover," XXVII (18 December 1916), 8; and "Bohemia," XXVII (18 December 1916), 15. Fitzgerald did not save the clippings, and there is no other evidence for these attributions.

Most of Fitzgerald's contributions to the *Tiger* were unsigned, and the attributions here are based on the clippings he pasted in a scrapbook which is now in the Princeton University Library—see note 2 above. It is possible that there are more *Tiger* items.

Prose Parody. Unsigned.[4] Reprinted in *Vanity Fair*. In *TJA*. See A 32, C 90.

C 24
"The Usual Thing By Robert W. Shameless," *The Nassau Literary Magazine*, LXXII (December 1916), 223–228.

Prose Parody. Unsigned—attributed to Fitzgerald in the index to volume LXXII. See A 32.

C 25
"Little Minnie McCloskey A Story for Girls," *The Princeton Tiger*, XXVII (1 December 1916), 6–7.

Humor article. Unsigned—attributed to Fitzgerald on basis of clipping in Princeton Fitzgerald Papers. See A 32.

C 26
"One from Penn's Neck," *The Princeton Tiger*, XXVII (10 December 1916), 7.

Verse. Unsigned—attributed to Fitzgerald on basis of clipping in the Princeton Fitzgerald Papers. See A 32.

C 27
"A Litany of Slang," *The Princeton Tiger*, XXVII (18 December 1916), 7.

Humor sketch. Unsigned—attributed to Fitzgerald on basis of clipping in Princeton Fitzgerald Papers. See A 32.

C 28
" 'Triangle Scenery by Bakst'," *The Princeton Tiger*, XXVII (18 December 1916), 7.

Humor sketch. Unsigned—attributed to Fitzgerald on basis of clipping in Princeton Fitzgerald Papers. See A 32.

---

4. Doubtful attribution: "The Vampiest of the Vampires," *The Nassau Literary Magazine*, LXXII (December 1916), 216. Prose parody. Unsigned—credited to Fitzgerald by Piper (*The Princeton University Library Chronicle*, XII [Summer 1951]) on basis of clipping in Princeton Fitzgerald Papers. But "The Vampiest of the Vampires" is on the verso of the last page of "Jemina," which makes this attribution shaky. Fitzgerald did not save a clipping of "The Apotheosis of the Amateur," which is a companion piece to "The Vampiest of the Vampires," p. 217. Neither item is listed in the index to volume LXXII.

C 29
"Futuristic Impressions of the Editorial Boards," *The Princeton Tiger*, XXVII (18 December 1916), 7.

Humor sketch. Unsigned—attributed to Fitzgerald on basis of clipping in Princeton Fitzgerald Papers. See A 32.

C 30
" 'A glass of beer kills him'," *The Princeton Tiger*, XXVII (18 December 1916), 7.

Joke. Unsigned—attributed to Fitzgerald on basis of clipping in Princeton Fitzgerald Papers. See A 32.

C 31
Untitled verse, beginning "Oui, le backfield est from Paris . . . ," *The Princeton Tiger*, XXVII (18 December 1916), 7.

Unsigned—attributed to Fitzgerald on basis of clipping in Princeton Fitzgerald Papers. See A 32.

C 32
Untitled joke, beginning " 'When you find a man doing a little more . . . ,' " *The Princeton Tiger*, XXVII (18 December 1916), 7.

Unsigned—attributed to Fitzgerald on the basis of clipping in Princeton Fitzgerald Papers. See A 32.

C 33
"Things That Never Change! Number 3333," *The Princeton Tiger*, XXVII (18 December 1916), 7.

Humor sketch. Unsigned—attributed to Fitzgerald on basis of clipping in Princeton Fitzgerald Papers. See A 32.

C 34
"The Old Frontiersman A Story of the Frontier," *The Princeton Tiger*, XXVII (18 December 1916), 11.

Humor article. Unsigned—attributed to Fitzgerald on basis of clipping in Princeton Fitzgerald Papers. See A 32.

C 35
"The Debutante," *The Nassau Literary Magazine*, LXXII (January 1917), 241–252.

Play. Revised for *The Smart Set.* Incorporated into *TSOP.* See A 27.

C 36
Untitled book review of *Penrod and Sam* by Booth Tarkington, *The Nassau Literary Magazine,* LXXII (January 1917), 291–292.

See A 32.

C 37
Untitled joke, beginning "Boy Kills Self Rather Than Pet . . . ," *The Princeton Tiger,* XXVII (3 February 1917), 12.

Unsigned—attributed to Fitzgerald on basis of clipping in Princeton Fitzgerald Papers. See A 32.

C 38
"Things That Never Change. No. 3982," *The Princeton Tiger,* XXVII (3 February 1917), 12.

Joke. Unsigned—attributed to Fitzgerald on basis of clipping in Princeton Fitzgerald Papers. See A 32.

C 39
"Precaution Primarily," *The Princeton Tiger,* XXVII (3 February 1917), 13–14.

Burlesque musical comedy. Signed 'F.S.F.' See A 32.

C 40
"The Spire and the Gargoyle," *The Nassau Literary Magazine,* LXXII (February 1917), 297–307.

Fiction. See A 27.

C 41
"Rain Before Dawn," *The Nassau Literary Magazine,* LXII (February 1917), 321.

Verse. See A 32.

C 42
Untitled book review of *David Blaize* by E. F. Benson, *The Nassau Literary Magazine,* LXXII (February 1917), 343–344.

See A 32.

Note

The index to volume LXXII of *The Nassau Literary Magazine* lists an article, "Indicators," by Fitzgerald in the March 1917 issue. But nothing with this title was published. "Indicators" is the only item in the index without a page reference.

C 43
"A Few Well-Known Club Types And Their Futures," *The Princeton Tiger*, XXVII (17 March 1917), 7.

Cartoon. Signed 'LB' (Lawrence Boardman), but possibly Fitzgerald supplied the idea. Attributed to Fitzgerald on basis of clipping in Princeton Fitzgerald Papers. See A 32.

C 44
Untitled joke, beginning "McCaulay Mission—Water Street . . . ," *The Princeton Tiger*, XXVII (17 March 1917), 10.

Unsigned—attributed to Fitzgerald on basis of clipping in Princeton Fitzgerald Papers. See A 32.

C 45
"Popular Parodies—No. 1," *The Princeton Tiger*, XXVII (17 March 1917), 10.

Verse. Unsigned—attributed to Fitzgerald on basis of clipping in Princeton Fitzgerald Papers. See A 32.

C 46
"The Diary of a Sophomore," *The Princeton Tiger*, XXVII (17 March 1917), 11.

Humor article. Signed 'F.S.F.' See A 32.

C 47
"True Democracy," *The Princeton Tiger*, XXVII (17 March 1917), 18.

Cartoon. Signed 'Jackman' (Alan Jackman), but Fitzgerald supplied the idea. Attributed to Fitzgerald on basis of clipping in Princeton Fitzgerald Papers and corroborated by Mr. Jackman. See A 32.

C 48
"Undulations of an Undergraduate," *The Princeton Tiger*, XXVII (17 March 1917), 20.

Verse. Unsigned—attributed to Fitzgerald on basis of clipping in Princeton Fitzgerald Papers. See A 32.

C 49
"Kenilworth Socialism," *The Princeton Tiger*, XXVII (17 March 1917), 22.

Cartoon. Signed 'Fitzgerald 18 + Jackman 17)'. See A 32.

C 50
"Tarquin of Cheepside," *The Nassau Literary Magazine*, LXXIII (April 1917), 13–18.

Fiction. Revised and expanded for *The Smart Set*. In *TJA*. See A 27, C 100.

C 51
"The Prince of Pests A Story of the War," *The Princeton Tiger*, XXVII (28 April 1917), 7

Humor article. Signed 'F.S.F.' See A 32.

C 52
Untitled joke, beginning " 'These rifles *** will probably not be used . . . ,' " *The Princeton Tiger*, XXVII (28 April 1917), 8.

Unsigned—attributed to Fitzgerald on basis of clipping in Princeton Fitzgerald Papers. See A 32.

C 53
Untitled joke, beginning " 'It is assumed that the absence of submarines . . . ,' " *The Princeton Tiger*, XXVII (28 April 1917), 8.

Unsigned—attributed to Fitzgerald on basis of clipping in Princeton Fitzgerald Papers. See A 32.

C 54
Untitled verse beginning "Ethel had her shot of brandy . . . ," *The Princeton Tiger*, XXVII (28 April 1917), 8.

Unsigned—attributed to Fitzgerald on basis of clipping in Princeton Fitzgerald Papers. See A 32.

C 55
Untitled joke, beginning "Yale's swimming team will take its maiden plunge to-night," *The Princeton Tiger*, XXVII (28 April 1917), 8.

Unsigned—attributed to Fitzgerald on basis of clipping in Princeton Fitzgerald Papers. See A 32.

C 56
"Babes in the Woods," *The Nassau Literary Magazine*, LXXIII (May 1917), 55–64.

Fiction. Revised in *The Smart Set*. Incorporated in *TSOP*. See A 27, C 74.

C 57
"Princeton—The Last Day," *The Nassau Literary Magazine*, LXXIII (May 1917), 95.

Verse. See A 32.

C 58
Untitled book review of *The Celt and the World* by Shane Leslie, *The Nassau Literary Magazine*, LXXIII (May 1917), 104–105.

See A 32.

C 59
"Sentiment—And the Use of Rouge," *The Nassau Literary Magazine*, LXXIII (June 1917), 107–123.

Fiction. See A 27.

C 60
"On a Play Twice Seen," *The Nassau Literary Magazine*, LXXIII (June 1917), 149.

Verse. See A 32.

C 61
Untitled book review of *Verses in Peace and War* by Shane Leslie, *The Nassau Literary Magazine*, LXXIII (June 1917), 152–153.

See A 32.

C 62
Untitled book review of *God, The Invisible King* by H. G. Wells, *The Nassau Literary Magazine*, LXXIII (June 1917), 153.

See A 32.

C 63
"The Dream and the Awakening," *The Princeton Tiger*, XXVIII (15 June 1917), 16.

Cartoon. Signed 'F. S. S. 18   A J 17'. Fitzgerald supplied the idea. Attribution corroborated by Alan Jackman, who drew the cartoon.

Note

In September 1917 Fitzgerald noted in his Ledger (p. 172): "Poet Lore accepts a poem." This poem was "The Way of Purgation," but was not published. It is the untitled poem printed on p. 273 of *TSOP*. See *CU*, pp. 248–249.

C 64
"The Camco Frame," *The Nassau Literary Magazine*, LXXIII (October 1917), 169–172.

Verse. See A 32.

C 65
"The Pierian Springs and the Last Straw," *The Nassau Literary Magazine*, LXXIII (October 1917), 173–185.

Fiction. See A 27.

C 66
"The Staying Up All Night," *The Princeton Tiger*, XXVIII (10 November 1917), 6.

Humor article. Signed 'F. S. F.' See A 32.

C 67
"Intercollegiate Petting-Cues," *The Princeton Tiger*, XXVIII (10 November 1917), 8.

Joke. Unsigned—attributed to Fitzgerald on basis of clipping in Princeton Fitzgerald Papers. See A 32.

C 68
"Our American Poets," *The Princeton Tiger*, XXVIII (10 November 1917), 11.

Verse parodies. Signed 'F. S. F.' See A 32.

C 69
"Cedric the Stoker (The True Story of the Battle of the Baltic),"
The Princeton Tiger, XXVIII (10 November 1917), 12.

Humor article. Signed 'F. S. F. and J. B.' (John Biggs, Jr.).
See A 32.

C 70
"City Dusk," *The Nassau Literary Magazine*, LXXIII (April
1918), 315.

Verse. See A 32.

C 71
"My First Love," *The Nassau Literary Magazine*, LXXIV (February 1919), 102.

Verse. See A 32, B 1.

C 72
"Marching Streets," *The Nassau Literary Magazine*, LXXIV
(February 1919), 103–104.

Verse. See A 32, B 1.

C 73
"The Pope at Confession," *The Nassau Literary Magazine*,
LXXIV (February 1919), 105.

Verse. See A 32, B 1.

C 74
"Babes in the Woods," *The Smart Set*, LX (September 1919),
67–71.

Fiction. See A 27, C 56.

C 75
"The Débutanté," *The Smart Set*, LX (November 1919), 85–96.

Play. See A 27, B 62.

C 76
"A Dirge (Apologies to Wordsworth)," *Judge*, LXXVII (20 December 1919), 30.

Humorous verse. See A 32.

C 77
"Porcelain and Pink (A One-Act Play)," *The Smart Set*, LXI
(January 1920), 77–85.

In *TJA*.

C 78
"Benediction," *The Smart Set*, LXI (February 1920), 35–44.

Fiction. In *F&P*. See "The Ordeal," C 15.

C 79
"Dalyrimple Goes Wrong," *The Smart Set*, LXI (February 1920),
107–116.

Fiction. In *F&P*.

C 80
"Head and Shoulders," *The Saturday Evening Post*, CXCII
(21 February 1920), 16–17, 81 82, 85–90.

Fiction. In *F&P*. Reprinted in England as "Topsy Turvy," *Yellow Magazine* (March 1922).

C 81
"Mister Icky The Quintessence of Quaintness in One Act," *The Smart Set*, LXI (March 1920), 93–98.

Humorous play. In *TJA*.

C 82
"The Claims of the *Lit.*," *The Princeton Alumni Weekly*, XX
(10 March 1920), 514.

Public letter.

C 83
"Myra Meets his Family," *The Saturday Evening Post*, CXCII
(20 March 1920), 40, 42, 44, 46, 49–50, 53.

Fiction. Reprinted in England in *Sovereign* (July 1921).

C 84
"The Camel's Back," *The Saturday Evening Post*, CXCII
(24 April 1920), 16–17, 157, 161, 165.

Fiction. In *TJA*. See B 2. Reprinted in England in *Pearson's* (July 1921).

C 85
"The Cut-Glass Bowl," *Scribner's Magazine*, LXVII (May 1920), 582–592.

Fiction. In *F&P*.

C 86
"Bernice Bobs Her Hair," *The Saturday Evening Post*, CXCII (1 May 1920), 14–15, 159, 163, 167.

Fiction. In *F&P*. Reprinted in England in *Pan* or *20 Story* (?) (August 1921).

C 87
"The Ice Palace," *The Saturday Evening Post*, CXCII (22 May 1920), 18–19, 163, 167, 170.

Fiction. In *F&P*.

C 88
"The Offshore Pirate," *The Saturday Evening Post*, CXCII (29 May 1920), 10–11, 99, 101–102, 106, 109.

Fiction. In *F&P*. Reprinted in England in *Sovereign* (February 1922).

C 89
"The Four Fists," *Scribner's Magazine*, LXVII (June 1920), 669–680.

Fiction. In *F&P*.

C 90
"The Smilers," *The Smart Set*, LXII (June 1920), 107–111.

Fiction.

C 91
"May Day," *The Smart Set*, LXII (July 1920), 3–32.

Fiction. In *TJA*. See Colin Cass, "Fitzgerald's Second Thoughts About 'May Day,'" *Fitzgerald/Hemingway Annual 1970*, pp. 69–95.

C 92
"Contemporary Writers and Their Work, A Series of Autobiographical Letters—F. Scott Fitzgerald," *The Editor*, LIII (Second July Number, 1920), 121–122.

Account of writing "The Ice Palace."

C 93
"Who's Who—and Why," *The Saturday Evening Post*, CXCIII (18 September 1920), 42, 61.

Autobiographical essay. See A 22.1.a.

C 94
"The Jelly-Bean," *Metropolitan Magazine*, LII (October 1920), 15–16, 63–67.

Fiction. Fitzgerald's Ledger indicates that this story was possibly syndicated by Metropolitan Newspaper Service, but no appearance has been located. In *TJA*.

C 95
"Sleep of a University," *The Nassau Literary Magazine*, LXXVI (November 1920), 161.

Verse. See A 32.

C 96
"This is a Magazine," *Vanity Fair*, XV (December 1920), 71.

Humorous article.

C 97
"The Lees of Happiness," *Chicago Sunday Tribune* (12 December 1920), blue ribbon fiction section, 1, 3, 7.

Fiction. In *TJA*.

C 98
"Jemina, the Mountain Girl (One of Those Family Feud Stories of the Blue Ridge Mountains with Apologies to Stephen Leacock)," *Vanity Fair*, XV (January 1921), 44.

In *TJA*. See A 32, C 23.

C 99
"His Russet Witch," *Metropolitan Magazine*, LIII (February 1921), 11–13, 46–51.

Fiction. In *TJA* as "O Russet Witch!"

C 100
"Tarquin of Cheapside," *The Smart Set*, LXIV (February 1921), 43–46.

Fiction. In *TJA*. See C 50.

C 101
Public letter to Thomas Boyd, *St. Paul Daily News* (20 February
1921), feature section, 8.

Reprinted as "The Credo of F. Scott Fitzgerald," *Chicago Daily
News* (9 March 1921), and as "How the Upper Class Is Being
Saved by 'Men Like Mencken'," *Baltimore Sun* (22 March
1921), section C, 2. See A 32.

C 102
"The Baltimore Anti-Christ," *The Bookman*, LIII (March 1921),
79–81.

Review of H. L. Mencken's *Prejudices. Second Series*. See A 32.

C 103
"Three Soldiers," *St. Paul Daily News* (25 September 1921),
feature section, 6.

Review of John Dos Passos' *Three Soldiers*. See A 32.

C 104
"Three Cities," *Brentano's Book Chat*, I (September–October
1921), 15, 28.

Essay. See A 32.

C 105
"Poor Old Marriage," *The Bookman*, LIV (November 1921),
253–254.

Review of Charles Norris's *Brass*. See A 32.

C 106
"Reminiscences of Donald Stewart by F. Scott Fitzgerald (in the
Manner of . . . .)," *St. Paul Daily News* (11 December
1921), city life section, 6.

Parody. See A 32.

C 107
"The Far-seeing Skeptics," *The Smart Set*, LXVII (February
1922), 48.

Excerpt from *B&D*.

C *108*
"The Popular Girl," *The Saturday Evening Post*, CXCIV (11 February and 18 February 1922), 3–5, 82, 84, 86, 89; 18–19, 105–106, 109–110.

Fiction.

C *109*
"Aldous Huxley's 'Crome Yellow'," *St. Paul Daily News* (26 February 1922), feature section, 6.

Book review. See A 32.

C *110*
"Two For a Cent," *Metropolitan Magazine*, LV (April 1922), 23–26, 93–95.

Fiction. Syndicated by Metropolitan Newspaper Service (not seen, but located in *Brooklyn Standard Union*, 12 August 1923). See B 3. Reprinted in England in *Argosy* (April 1933).

C *111*
"What I Was Advised To Do—And Didn't," *Philadelphia Public Ledger* (22 April 1922), 11.

Autobiographical note. See A 32.

C *112*
" 'Margey Wins the Game'," *New York Tribune* (7 May 1922), section IV, 7.

Review of John V. A. Weaver's *Margey Wins the Game*. See A 32.

C *113*
"Tarkington's 'Gentle Julia'," *St. Paul Daily News* (7 May 1922), feature section, 6.

Book review. See A 32.

C *114*
"Homage to the Victorians," *New York Tribune* (14 May 1922), section IV, 6.

Review of Shane Leslie's *The Oppidan*. See A 32.

C *115*
"The Curious Case of Benjamin Button," *Collier's*, LXIX (27 May 1922), 5–6, 22–28.

Fiction. Possibly syndicated by Metropolitan Newspaper Service, but no appearance has been located. In *TJA*.

C 116
"The Diamond as Big as the Ritz," *The Smart Set,* LXVIII (June 1922), 5–29.

Fiction. In *TJA*. See David J. F. Kelley, "The Polishing of 'Diamond'," *Fitzgerald Newsletter,* no. 40 (Winter 1968).

C 117
"What I think and Feel at Twenty-Five," *The American Magazine,* XCIV (September 1922), 16, 17, 136–140.

Autobiographical article. See A 32.

C 118
"A Rugged Novel," *New York Evening Post* (28 October 1922), 143–144.

Review of Woodward Boyd's *The Love Legend*. See A 32.

C 119
"Winter Dreams," *Metropolitan Magazine,* LVI (December 1922), 11–15, 98, 100–102, 104–107.

Fiction. In *ASYM*. Reprinted in Canada in *McLean's* (15 November 1922). Reprinted in England as "Dream Girl of Spring," *The Royal Magazine,* XLIX (February 1923).

C 120
"How I Would Sell My Book If I Were a Bookseller," *Bookseller and Stationer,* XVIII (15 January 1923), 8.

Article. See A 32.

C 121
"Minnesota's Capital in the Role of Main Street," *The Literary Digest International Book Review,* I (March 1923), 35–36.

Review of Grace Flandrau's *Being Respectable*. See A 32.

C 122
"Sherwood Anderson on the Marriage Question," *New York Herald* (4 March 1923), section 9, 5.

Review of Sherwood Anderson's *Many Marriages*. See A 32.

C 123
"10 Best Books I Have Read," *Jersey City Evening Journal* (24 April 1923), 9.

Article. Syndicated under various titles by the North American Newspaper Alliance.

C 124
"Dice, Brass Knuckles & Guitar," *Hearst's International,* XLIII (May 1923), 8–13, 145–149.

Fiction.

C 125
"Confessions," *Chicago Daily Tribune* (19 May 1923), 9.

Public letter to Fanny Butcher. See A 32.

C 126
"Under Fire," *New York Evening Post* (26 May 1923), 715.

Review of Thomas Boyd's *Through the Wheat.* See A 32.

C 127
"Imagination—and a Few Mothers," *The Ladies' Home Journal,* XL (June 1923), 21, 80–81.

Essay. See B 43.

C 128
Letter to A. Philip Randolph (Great Neck, Long Island, 25 May 1923), *The Messenger,* V (June 1923), 749.

C 129
"Censorship or Not," *The Literary Digest,* LXXVII (23 June 1923), 31, 61.

Includes statements by Fitzgerald. See A 32.

C 130
"Hot & Cold Blood," *Hearst's International,* LXIV (August 1923), 80–84, 150–151.

Fiction. In *ASYM.* Syndicated by Metropolitan Newspaper Service (not seen, but located in *Kansas City Monthly Star,* 28 September 1924; *Brooklyn Standard Union,* 9 November 1924). Also reprinted as "A Story of Generosity," *The Household Magazine,* XXV (September 1925), 5, 16–17.

C 131
Entry cancelled.

C 132
"The Most Disgraceful Thing I Ever Did: 2. The Invasion of the Sanctuary," *Vanity Fair*, XXI (October 1923), 53.

Humor article. Unsigned—identified as by Fitzgerald in vol. XXI (January 1924), 30. See A 32, B 33.

C 133
"The Cruise of the Rolling Junk," *Motor*, XLI (February, March, April 1924), 24–25, 58, 62, 64, 66; 42–43, 58, 72, 74, 76; 40–41, 58, 66, 68, 70.

Humorous narrative.

C 134
" 'Why Blame It on the Poor Kiss if the Girl Veteran of Many Petting Parties Is Prone to Affairs After Marriage?' " *New York American* (24 February 1924), LII-3.

Article. Syndicated by Metropolitan Newspaper Service and published under variant titles. Listed by Piper as "Love, Marriage and the Modern Woman." In his Ledger (p. 104) Fitzgerald listed "Making Monogamy Work Article Metropolitan Sydicate Jan. 1924," which is almost certainly " 'Why Blame It on the Poor Kiss . . . .' " See A 32.

C 135
"Does a Moment of Revolt Come Sometime to Every Married Man?" *McCall's*, LI (March 1924), 21, 36.

Article. See A 32, I 10.

C 136
"Gretchen's Forty Winks," *The Saturday Evening Post*, CXCVI (15 March 1924), 14–15, 128, 130, 132.

Fiction. In *ASYM*. See B 4. Reprinted in England in *Home Magazine* (March 1924).

C 137
"What Kind of Husbands Do 'Jimmies' Make?" *Baltimore American* (30 March 1924), ME-7.

Article. Syndicated by Metropolitan Newspaper Service and published under variant titles. Also located in *Philadelphia Evening*

Bulletin (29 March 1924), 14. In his Ledger (p. 104) Fitzgerald listed "Our Irresponsible Rich Article Metropolitan Syndicate Feb. 1924," which is almost certainly "What Kind of Husbands Do 'Jimmies' Make?" See A 32.

C *138*
"Diamond Dick and the First Law of Woman," *Hearst's International*, XLV (April 1924), 58–63, 134, 136.

Fiction.

C *139*
"How to Live on $36,000 a Year," *The Saturday Evening Post*, CXCVI (5 April 1924), 22, 94, 97.

Essay. See A 22.1.a.

C *140*
"The Third Casket," *The Saturday Evening Post*, CXCVI (31 May 1924), 8–9, 78.

Fiction. Reprinted in England in *Pearson's* (December 1924).

C *141*
"Absolution," *The American Mercury*, II (June 1924), 141–149.

Fiction. In *ASYM*.

C *142*
" 'Wait Till You Have Children of Your Own!' " *Woman's Home Companion*, LI (July 1924), 13, 105.

Essay. An ad for *Woman's Home Companion* in the *New York Times* (20 June 1924), p. 20, quotes from this article. See A 32.

Note

Mizener (*The Far Side of Paradise*) and Bryer (*The Critical Reputation of F. Scott Fitzgerald*) list an article by Fitzgerald, "What Do We Wild Young People Want for Our Children?," in *Woman's Home Companion*, LI (July 1924). This article is not in that issue and has not been located. Fitzgerald did not list it in his Ledger.

C *143*
"Who's Who in this Issue," *Woman's Home Companion*, LI (July 1924), 110.

Letter to editor.

C 144
"Rags Martin-Jones and the Pr-nce of W-les," *McCall's*, LI (July 1924), 6–7, 32, 48, 50.

Fiction. In *ASYM*. Syndicated by Metropolitan Newspaper Service (noted in *Cincinnati Enquirer*, 4 January 1925). Reprinted in England in *Woman's Pictorial* (December 1924 [?]).

C 145
" 'The Sensible Thing,' " *Liberty*, I (5 July 1924)' 10–14.

Fiction. In *ASYM*. Reprinted in England in *Woman's Pictorial* (December 1924 [?]).

C 146
"The Unspeakable Egg," *The Saturday Evening Post*, CXCVII (12 July 1924), 12–13, 125–126, 129.

Fiction.

C 147
"John Jackson's Arcady," *The Saturday Evening Post*, CXCVII (26 July 1924), 8–9, 100, 102, 105.

Fiction. See A 13.

C 148
"How to Live on Practically Nothing a Year," *The Saturday Evening Post*, CXCVII (20 September 1924), 17, 165–166, 169–170.

Essay. See A 22.1.a.

Note

Fitzgerald's Ledger (p. 103) lists under "Published Miscelanis (including movies) for which I was Paid" "The Little Brother of the Flapper Article *McCalls* Dec 1924." Mizener (*The Far Side of Paradise*) and Bryer (*The Critical Reputation of F. Scott Fitzgerald*) both list "The Flapper's Little Brother" in the December 1924 *McCall's*. This article is not in that issue and has not been located.

C 149
"The Baby Party," *Hearst's International*, XLVII (February 1925), 32–37.

Fiction. In *ASYM*.

C *150*
"The Pusher-in-the-Face," *Woman's Home Companion*, LII (February 1925), 27–28, 143–144.

Fiction. Syndicated by Metropolitan Newspaper Service (noted in *Washington Sunday Star*, 28 June 1925). See B 7.

C *151*
"Love in the Night," *The Saturday Evening Post*, CXCVII (14 March 1925), 18–19, 68, 70.

Fiction. Reprinted in England in *Woman's Pictorial* (December 1925).

C *152*
"Our Own Movie Queen," *Chicago Sunday Tribune* (7 June 1925), magazine section, 1–4.

Fiction. Signed only by Fitzgerald, but Ledger notes: "Two thirds written by Zelda. Only my climax and revision." See I 12.

C *153*
"My Old New England Homestead on the Erie," *College Humor*, VI (August 1925), 18–19.

Parody. See B 9.

C *154*
"One of My Oldest Friends," *Woman's Home Companion*, LII (September 1925), 7–8, 120, 122.

Fiction. Possibly syndicated by Metropolitan Newspaper Service or by New York World Syndicate (1926 [?]), but no appearance has been located. See B 6. Reprinted in England in *Red Magazine* (July 1926).

C *155*
"The Adjuster," *The Red Book Magazine*, XLV (September 1925), 47–51, 144–148.

Fiction. In *ASYM*. Syndicated by Metropolitan Newspaper Service (located in *Philadelphia Record*, 13 December 1925).

C *156*
"What Became of Our Flappers and Sheiks?" *McCall's*, LIII (October 1925), 12, 30, 42, 66, 69.

Article. See A 32, I 13.

C 157
"A Penny Spent," *The Saturday Evening Post*, CXCVIII (10 October 1925), 8–9, 160, 164, 166.

Fiction. Reprinted in England in *Modern Woman* (July 1926).

C 158
"Not in the Guidebook," *Woman's Home Companion*, LII (November 1925), 9–11, 135–136.

Fiction.

C 159
"The Rich Boy," *The Red Book Magazine*, XLVI (January and February 1926), 27–32, 144, 146; 75–79, 122, 124–126.

Fiction. In *ASYM*.

C 160
"Presumption," *The Saturday Evening Post*, CXCVIII (9 January 1926), 3–5, 226, 228–229, 233–234.

Fiction. Reprinted in England in *Woman's Pictorial* (June 1926).

C 161
"The Adolescent Marriage," *The Saturday Evening Post*, CXCVIII (6 March 1926), 6–7, 229–230, 233–234.

Fiction. Reprinted in England in *Woman's Pictorial* (July 1926).

C 162
Letter to Class Secretary, *The Princeton Alumni Weekly*, XXVI (14 April 1926), 718.

C 163
"How to Waste Material A Note on My Generation," *The Bookman*, LXIII (May 1926), 262–265.

Essay-review of Ernest Hemingway's *In Our Time*. See A 22.1.a.

C 164
"The Dance," *The Red Book Magazine*, XLVII (June 1926), 39–43, 134, 136, 138.

Fiction. See B 8.

C 165
"Your Way and Mine," *Woman's Home Companion*, LIV (May 1927), 7–8, 61, 64, 67, 68.

Fiction. Syndicated by Metropolitan Newspaper Service (located in *Cincinnati Enquirer*, 28 August 1927).

C 166
"Jacob's Ladder," *The Saturday Evening Post*, CC (20 August 1927), 3–5, 57–58, 63–64.

Fiction.

C 167
"The Love Boat," *The Saturday Evening Post*, CC (8 October 1927), 8–9, 134, 139, 141.

Fiction.

C 168
"Princeton," *College Humor*, XIII (December 2927), 28–29, 130–131.

Essay. See B 10.

C 169
"A Short Trip Home," *The Saturday Evening Post*, CC (17 December 1927), 6–7, 55, 57–58.

Fiction. In *TAR*.

C 170
"The Changing Beauty of Park Avenue," *Harper's Bazar*, LXII (January 1928), 61–63.

Article. By-lined "Zelda and F. Scott Fitzgerald," but credited to Zelda in Ledger (p. 143). See I 14.

C 171
"The Bowl," *The Saturday Evening Post*, CC (21 January 1928), 6–7, 93–94, 97, 100.

Fiction. See B 36.

C 172
"Magnetism," *The Saturday Evening Post*, CC (3 March 1928), 5–7, 74, 76, 78.

Fiction. See A 20. Reprinted in England in *Grand Magazine* (1928).

C *173*
"F. Scott Fitzgerald Is Bored by Efforts At Realism In 'Lit'," *The Daily Princetonian* (16 March 1928), 1, 3.

Review of March issue of *The Nassau Literary Magazine*. See A 32.

C *174*
"The Scandal Detectives," *The Saturday Evening Post*, CC (28 April 1928), 3–4, 178, 181–182, 185.

Fiction—Basil story. In *TAR*.

C *175*
"Looking Back Eight Years," *College Humor*, XIV (June 1928), 36–37.

Article. By-lined "F. Scott and Zelda Fitzgerald," but credited to Zelda in Ledger (p. 143). See I 15.

C *176*
"A Night at the Fair," *The Saturday Evening Post*, CCI (21 July 1928), 8–9, 129–130, 133.

Fiction—Basil story. See A 22.1.a.

C *177*
"The Freshest Boy," *The Saturday Evening Post*, CCI (28 July 1928), 6–7, 68, 70, 73.

Fiction—Basil story. In *TAR*.

C *178*
"He Thinks He's Wonderful," *The Saturday Evening Post*, CCI (29 September 1928), 6–7, 117–118, 121.

Fiction—Basil story. In *TAR*.

C *179*
"Who Can Fall in Love After Thirty?" *College Humor*, XV (October 1928), 9, 92.

Article. By-lined "F. Scott and Zelda Fitzgerald," but credited to Zelda in Ledger (p. 143). See I 16.

C 180
"Outside the Cabinet-Maker's," *The Century Magazine*, CXVII (December 1928), 241–244.

Fiction. See A 22.1.a.

C 181
"The Captured Shadow," *The Saturday Evening Post*, CCI (29 December 1928), 12–13, 48, 51.

Fiction—Basil story. In *TAR*.

C 182
"The Perfect Life," *The Saturday Evening Post*, CCI (5 January 1929), 8–9, 113, 115, 118.

Fiction—Basil story. In *TAR*.

C 183
"Ten Years in the Advertising Business," *The Princeton Alumni Weekly*, XXIX (22 February 1929), 585.

Satirical article. See A 22.1.a.

Note

According to Fitzgerald's Ledger (pp. 64–65), he was paid $1,000 in 1928 and $500 in 1929 for "Advertisement." These entries refer to the Woodbury Soap Beauty Contest that Fitzgerald judged with Cornelius Vanderbilt, Jr., and John Barrymore. For these ads see *Woman's Home Companion* (February and June 1929), *The Saturday Evening Post* (2 March 1929), and *McCall's* (October 1929). The ads use Fitzgerald's photo, but they print nothing written by him. See also *New York Evening Post* (28 May 1929), 17.

C 184
"The Last of the Belles," *The Saturday Evening Post*, CCI (2 March 1929), 18–19, 75, 78.

Fiction. In *TAR*.

C 185
"Forging Ahead," *The Saturday Evening Post*, CCI (30 March 1929), 12–13, 101, 105.

Fiction—Basil story. See A 22.1.a.

C 186
"Basil and Cleopatra," *The Saturday Evening Post*, CCI (27 April 1929), 14–15, 166, 170, 173.

Fiction—Basil story. See A 22.1.a.

C 187
"Paint and Powder," *The Smart Set, LXXXIV* (May 1929), 68.

Article. By-lined "F. Scott Fitzgerald" only but written by Zelda Fitzgerald as "Editorial on Youth" for *Photoplay* in 1927; credited to Zelda in Ledger (p. 143). Not published by *Photoplay*. See I 17.

C 188
"A Short Autobiography (With Acknowledgments to Nathan)," *The New Yorker*, V (25 May 1929), 22–23.

Prose sketch. See B 14.

C 189
"The Rough Crossing," *The Saturday Evening Post*, CCI (8 June 1929), 12–13, 66, 70, 75.

Fiction. See A 20.1.a.

C 190
"Fitzgerald Sets Things Right About His College," *Washington Herald* (28 June 1929), II-1.

Letter to Stanley Olmsted. See A 32.

C 191
"The Original Follies Girl," *College Humor*, XVII (July 1929), 40–41, 110.

Fiction. By-lined "Zelda and F. Scott Fitzgerald," but credited to Zelda in Ledger (p. 143). See I 18.

C 192
"Majesty," *The Saturday Evening Post*, CCII (13 July 1929), 6–7, 57–58, 61–62.

Fiction. In *TAR*.

C 193
"At Your Age," *The Saturday Evening Post*, CCII (17 August 1929), 6–7, 79–80.

Fiction. See B 12.

C 194
"Southern Girl," *College Humor*, XVIII (October 1929), 27–28, 94, 96.

Fiction. By-lined "F. Scott and Zelda Fitzgerald," but credited to Zelda in Ledger (p. 143). See I 19.

C 195
"The Swimmers," *The Saturday Evening Post*, CCII (19 October 1929), 12–13, 150, 152, 154.

Fiction.

C 196
"Two Wrongs," *The Saturday Evening Post*, CCII (18 January 1930), 8–9, 107, 109, 113.

Fiction. In *TAR*.

C 197
"The Girl the Prince Liked," *College Humor*, no. 74 (February 1930), 46–48, 121–122.

Fiction. By-lined "F. Scott and Zelda Fitzgerald," but credited to Zelda in Ledger (p. 143). See I 20.

C 198
"Girls Believe in Girls," *Liberty*, VII (8 February 1930), 22–24.

Essay. See A 32.

C 199
"Salesmanship in the Champs-Élysées," *The New Yorker*, V (15 February 1930), 20.

Humor article. See A 32.

C 200
"False and Extremely Unwise Tradition," *The Daily Princetonian* (27 February 1930), 2.

Letter signed "Seventeen," dated "Paris, January 24, 1930." Fitzgerald pasted clipping in his scrapbook. See A 32.

C 201
"The Girl With Talent," *College Humor*, no. 76 (April 1930), 50–52, 125–127.

Fiction. By-lined "F. Scott and Zelda Fitzgerald," but credited to Zelda in Ledger (p. 143). See I 21.

C 202
Letter to H. N. Swanson, *College Humor*, no. 76 (April 1930), 134.

C 203
"First Blood," *The Saturday Evening Post*, CCII (5 April 1930), 8–9, 81, 84.

Fiction—Josephine story. In *TAR*.

C 204
"A Millionaire's Girl," *The Saturday Evening Post*, CCII (17 May 1930), 8–9, 118, 121.

Fiction. By-lined "F. Scott Fitzgerald" only, but credited to Zelda in Ledger (p. 143).[5] See B 39, I 22.

C 205
"A Nice Quiet Place," *The Saturday Evening Post*, CCII (31 May 1930), 8–9, 96, 101, 103.

Fiction—Josephine story. In *TAR*.

C 206
"The Bridal Party," *The Saturday Evening Post*, CCIII (9 August 1930), 10–11, 109–110, 112, 114.

Fiction. See A 20.1.a.

C 207
"A Woman with a Past," *The Saturday Evening Post*, CCIII (6 September 1930), 8–9, 133–134, 137.

Fiction—Josephine story. In *TAR*.

C 208
"One Trip Abroad," *The Saturday Evening Post*, CCIII (11 October 1930), 6–7, 48, 51, 53–54, 56.

Fiction. See A 22.1.a.

C 209
"A Snobbish Story," *The Saturday Evening Post*, CCIII (29 November 1930), 6–7, 36, 38, 40, 42.

Fiction.

5. The publication of this story under Fitzgerald's name was the error of his agent, Harold Ober. See *As Ever, Scott Fitz—*, p. 166.

C 210
"Poor Working Girl," *College Humor,* no. 85 (January 1931), 72–73, 122.

Fiction. By-lined "F. Scott and Zelda Fitzgerald," but credited to Zelda in Ledger (p. 143). See I 23.

C 211
"The Hotel Child," *The Saturday Evening Post,* CCIII (31 January 1931), 8–9, 69, 72, 75.

Fiction.

C 212
"Babylon Revisited," *The Saturday Evening Post,* CCIII (21 February 1931), 3–5, 82–84.

Fiction. In *TAR.* See B 13. See William White, "The Text of 'Babylon Revisited'," *Fitzgerald Newsletter,* no. 28 (Winter 1965); and "Two Versions of Fitzgerald's 'Babylon Revisited'," *Papers of the Bibliographical Society of America,* LX (Fourth Quarter 1966), 439–452. See also Kenneth McCollum, " 'Babylon Revisited' Revisited," *Fitzgerald/Hemingway Annual 1971,* pp. 314–316.

C 213
"Indecision," *The Saturday Evening Post,* CCIII (16 May 1931), 12–13, 56, 59, 62.

Fiction.

C 214
"A New Leaf," *The Saturday Evening Post,* CCIV (4 July 1931), 12–13, 90–91.

Fiction. See B 16. Reprinted in England in *Homemaking* (August 1933).

C 215
"Emotional Bankruptcy," *The Saturday Evening Post,* CCIV (15 August 1931), 8–9, 60, 65.

Fiction—Josephine story.

C 216
"Between Three and Four," *The Saturday Evening Post,* CCIV (5 September 1931), 8–9, 69, 72.

Fiction.

C 217
"A Change of Class," *The Saturday Evening Post*, CCIV (26 September 1931), 6–7, 37–38, 41.

Fiction.

C 218
"Echoes of the Jazz Age," *Scribner's Magazine*, XC (November 1931), 459–465.

Essay. In *CU*.

C 219
"A Freeze-Out," *The Saturday Evening Post*, CCIV (19 December 1931), 6–7, 84–85, 88–89.

Fiction.

C 220
"Six of One—," *Redbook Magazine*, LVIII (February 1932), 22–25, 84, 86, 88.

Fiction.

C 221
"Diagnosis," *The Saturday Evening Post*, CCIV (20 February 1932), 18–19, 90, 92.

Fiction.

C 222
"Confused Romanticism," *The Princeton Alumni Weekly*, XXXII (22 April 1932), 647–648.

Public letter. See A 32.

C 223
"Flight and Pursuit," *The Saturday Evening Post*, CCIV (14 May 1932), 16–17, 53, 57.

Fiction. Reprinted in England in *Britannia and Eve* (June 1932).

C 224
"Family in the Wind," *The Saturday Evening Post*, CCIV (4 June 1932), 3–5, 71–73.

Fiction. In *TAR*. See B 18.

C 225
"The Rubber Check," *The Saturday Evening Post*, CCV (6 August 1932), 6–7, 41–42, 44–45.

Fiction.

C 226
"What a Handsome Pair!," *The Saturday Evening Post*, CCV (27 August 1932), 16–17, 61, 63–64.

Fiction.

C 227
"Crazy Sunday," *The American Mercury*, XXVII (October 1932), 209–220.

Fiction. In *TAR*. See B 17.

C 228
"One Interne," *The Saturday Evening Post*, CCV (5 November 1932), 6–7, 86, 88–90.

Fiction. In *TAR*.

C 229
"One Hundred False Starts," *The Saturday Evening Post*, CCV (4 March 1933), 13, 65–66.

Essay. See A 22.1.a.

C 230
"On Schedule," *The Saturday Evening Post*, CCV (18 March 1933), 16–17, 71, 74, 77, 79.

Fiction.

C 231
"More Than Just a House," *The Saturday Evening Post*, CCV (24 June 1933), 8–9, 27, 30, 34.

Fiction.

C 232
"I Got Shoes," *The Saturday Evening Post*, CCVI (23 September 1933), 14–15, 56, 58.

Fiction.

C 233
"Ring," *The New Republic,* LXXVI (11 October 1933), 254–255.

Essay. In *CU.* See B 21.

C 234
"The Family Bus," *The Saturday Evening Post,* CCVI (4 November 1933), 8–9, 57, 61–62, 65–66.

Fiction.

C 235
Entry cancelled.

C 236
" 'Show Mr. and Mrs. F. to Number ——'," *Esquire,* I–II (May and June 1934), 19, 154B; 23, 120.

Autobiographical article. By-lined "F. Scott and Zelda Fitzgerald," but credited to Zelda in Ledger (p. 143). In *CU.* See I 27.

C 237
"An Open Letter to Fritz Crisler," *Princeton Athletic News,* II (16 June 1934), 3.

See A 32.

C 238
"Anonymous '17," *The Nassau Literary Magazine,* XCV (June 1934), 9.

Statement about *The Lit.* Unsigned, but editorial note identifies it as by the author of *TSOP.* See A 32.

C 239
"Auction—Model 1934," *Esquire,* II (July 1934), 20, 153, 155.

Autobiographical article. By-lined "F. Scott and Zelda Fitzgerald," but credited to Zelda in Ledger (p. 143). In *CU.* See I 28.

C 240
"No Flowers," *The Saturday Evening Post,* CCVII (21 July 1934), 10–11, 57–58, 60.

Fiction.

C 241
"New Types," *The Saturday Evening Post*, CCVII (22 September 1934), 16–17, 74, 76, 78–79, 81.

Fiction.

C 242
"In the Darkest Hour," *Redbook Magazine*, LXIII (October 1934), 15–19, 94–98.

Fiction—Philippe story.

C 243
"Her Last Case," *The Saturday Evening Post*, CCVII (3 November 1934), 10–11, 59, 61–62, 64.

Fiction.

C 244
"Sleeping and Waking," *Esquire*, II (December 1934), 34, 159–160.

Essay. In *CU*.

C 245
"The Fiend," *Esquire*, III (January 1935), 23, 173–174.

Fiction. In *TAR*. Reprinted in England in *London Evening Standard* (29 March 1935).

C 246
"The Night before Chancellorsville" *Esquire*, III (February 1935), 24, 165.

Fiction. In *TAR*.

C 247
"Lamp in a Window," *The New Yorker*, XI (23 March 1935), 18.

Verse. In *CU*.

C 248
"Shaggy's Morning," *Esquire*, III (May 1935), 26, 160.

Fiction. Reprinted in England in *London Daily Express* (1 June 1935).

C 249
"The Count of Darkness," *Redbook Magazine*, LXV (June 1935), 20–23, 68, 70, 72.

Fiction—Philippe story.

C 250
"The Intimate Strangers," *McCall's*, LXII (June 1935), 12–14, 36, 38, 40, 42, 44.

Fiction.

C 251
"The Passionate Eskimo," *Liberty*, XII (8 June 1935), 10–14, 17–18.

Fiction.

C 252
"Zone of Accident," *The Saturday Evening Post*, CCVIII (13 July 1935), 8–9, 47, 49, 51–52.

Fiction. Reprinted in England as "Except to Bill," *Woman's Journal* (April 1936).

C 253
"The Kingdom in the Dark," *Redbook Magazine*, LXV (August 1935), 58–62, 64, 66–68.

Fiction—Philippe story.

Note

The September 1935 *Redbook Magazine* lists Fitzgerald as a contributor on the front cover, but this issue includes nothing by him.

C 254
"The Crack-Up," *Esquire*, V (February 1936), 41, 164.

Essay. In *CU*.

C 255
"Pasting It Together," *Esquire*, V (March 1936), 35, 182–183.

Essay. In *CU*.[6]

---

6. The titles for "Pasting It Together" and "Handle with Care" were transposed in *The Crack-Up*.

C 256
"Handle with Care," *Esquire*, V (April 1936), 39, 202.

Essay. In *CU*.[6]

C 257
"Fate in her Hands," *The American Magazine*, CXXI (April 1936), 56–59, 168–172.

Fiction.

C 258
"Image on the Heart," *McCall's*, LXIII (April 1936), 7–9, 52, 54, 57–58, 62.

Fiction. Reprinted in England as "Goodbye to Provence," *Woman's Journal* (November 1936).

C 259
"Too Cute for Words," *The Saturday Evening Post*, CCVIII (18 April 1936), 16–18, 87, 90, 93.

Fiction—Gwen story.

C 260
"Three Acts of Music," *Esquire*, V (May 1936), 39, 210.

Fiction. See B 47.

C 261
"The Ants at Princeton," *Esquire*, V (June 1936), 35, 201.

Satire.

C 262
"Inside the House," *The Saturday Evening Post*, CCVIII (13 June 1936), 18–19, 32, 34, 36.

Fiction—Gwen story.

C 263
"Author's House," *Esquire*, VI (July 1936), 40, 108.

Autobiographical essay. See A 22.1.a.

C 264
"Afternoon of an Author," *Esquire,* VI (August 1936), 35, 170.

Autobiographical essay. See A 22.1.a.

C 265
"An Author's Mother," *Esquire,* VI (September 1936), 36.

Fiction.

C 266
" 'I Didn't Get Over'," *Esquire,* VI (October 1936), 45, 194–195.

Fiction. See A 22.1.a.

C 267
" 'Send Me In, Coach'," *Esquire,* VI (November 1936), 55, 218–221.

Fiction. See B 27.

C 268
"An Alcoholic Case," *Esquire,* VI [VII] (February 1937), 32, 109.

Fiction. See A 20.1.a.

C 269
" 'Trouble'," *The Saturday Evening Post,* CCIX (6 March 1937), 14–15, 81, 84, 86, 88–89.

Fiction.

C 270
"The Honor of the Goon," *Esquire,* VII (June 1937), 53, 216.

Fiction.

C 271
"Obit on Parnassus," *The New Yorker,* XIII (5 June 1937), 27.

Verse. See A 32, B 25.

C 272
"A Book of One's Own," *The New Yorker,* XIII (21 August 1937), 19.

Humor article. See A 32.

C 273
"The Long Way Out," *Esquire*, VIII (September 1937), 45, 193.

Fiction. See A 20.1.a.

C 274
"Early Success," *American Cavalcade*, I (October 1937), 74–79.

Essay. In *CU*.

C 275
"The Guest in Room Nineteen," *Esquire*, VIII (October 1937),
56, 209.

Fiction.

C 276
"In the Holidays," *Esquire*, VIII (December 1937), 82, 184, 186.

Fiction.

C 277
"Financing Finnegan," *Esquire*, IX (January 1938), 41, 180,
182, 184.

Fiction. See A 20.1.a.

C 278
Letter to Harvey H. Smith, *The Princeton Alumni Weekly*,
XXXVIII (28 January 1938), 372.

Letter to class secretary.

C 279
Letter to Harvey H. Smith (MGM, 3 January 1939), *The Princeton Alumni Weekly*, XXXIX (3 February 1939), 369–370.

Letter to class secretary, facsimiled and quoted. See A 32.

C 280
"Design in Plaster," *Esquire*, XII (November 1939), 51, 169.

Fiction. See B 24.

C 281
"The Lost Decade," *Esquire*, XII (December 1939), 113, 228.

Fiction. See A 20.1.a.

C 282
"Strange Sanctuary," *Liberty*, XVI (9 December 1939), 15–20.

Fiction.

C 283
"Pat Hobby's Christmas Wish," *Esquire*, XIII (January 1940), 45, 170–172.

Fiction. See A 24.1.a, and B 38.

C 284
"A Man in the Way," *Esquire*, XIII (February 1940), 40, 109.

Fiction—Hobby story. See A 24.1.a.

C 285
" 'Boil Some Water—Lots of It'," *Esquire*, XIII (March 1940), 30, 145, 147.

Fiction—Hobby story. See A 22.1.a, A 24.1.a.

C 286
"Teamed with Genius," *Esquire*, XIII (April 1940), 44, 195–197.

Fiction—Hobby story. See A 22.1.a, A 24.1.a.

C 287
"Pat Hobby and Orson Welles," *Esquire*, XIII (May 1940), 38, 198–199.

Fiction. See A 24.1.a.

C 288
"Pat Hobby's Secret," *Esquire*, XIII (June 1940), 30, 107.

Fiction. See A 24.1.a.

C 289
"The End of Hate," *Collier's*, CV (22 June 1940), 9–10, 63–64.

Fiction.

C 290
"Pat Hobby, Putative Father," *Esquire*, XIV (July 1940), 36, 172–174.

Fiction. See A 24.1.a.

C 291
"The Homes of the Stars," *Esquire*, XIV (August 1940), 28, 120–121.

Fiction—Hobby story. See A 24.1.a.

C 292
"Pat Hobby Does His Bit," *Esquire*, XIV (September 1940), 41, 104.

Fiction. See A 24.1.a.

C 293
"Pat Hobby's Preview," *Esquire*, XIV (October 1940), 30, 118, 120.

Fiction. See A 24.1.a.

C 294
"No Harm Trying," *Esquire*, XIV (November 1940), 30, 151–153.

Fiction—Hobby Story. See A 22.1.a, A 24.1.a

C 295
"A Patriotic Short," *Esquire*, XIV (December 1940), 62, 269.

Fiction—Hobby story. See A 20.1.a, A 24.1.a.

C 296
"On the Trail of Pat Hobby," *Esquire*, XV (January 1941), 36, 126.

Fiction. See A 24.1.a.

C 297
"Fun in an Artist's Studio," *Esquire*, XV (February 1941), 64, 112.

Fiction—Hobby story. See A 24.1.a.

C 298
Elgin, Paul [pseud.]. "On an Ocean Wave," *Esquire*, XV (February 1941), 59, 141.

Fiction.

C 299
"Two Old-Timers," *Esquire*, XV (March 1941), 53, 143.

Fiction—Hobby story. See A 20.1.a, A 24.1.a, B 26.

C 300
"Mightier than the Sword," *Esquire*, XV (April 1941), 36, 183.

Fiction—Hobby story. See A 24.1.a.

C 301
"Pat Hobby's College Days," *Esquire*, XV (May 1941), 55, 168–169.

Fiction. See A 24.1.a.

C 302
"The Woman from Twenty-One," *Esquire*, XV (June 1941), 29, 164.

Fiction. See B 35.

C 303
"Three Hours Between Planes," *Esquire*, XVI (July 1941), 41, 138–139.

Fiction. See A 20.1.a.

C 304
"Gods of Darkness," *Redbook Magazine*, LXXVIII (November 1941), 30–33, 88–91.

Fiction—Philippe story.

C 305
"The Broadcast We Almost Heard Last September," *Furioso*, III (Fall 1947), 8–10.

Satire.

C 306
"News of Paris—Fifteen Years Ago," *Furioso*, III (Winter 1947), 5–10.

Fiction. See A 22.1.a.

C 307
"Discard," *Harper's Bazaar*, LXXXII (January 1948), 103, 143–144, 146, 148–149.

Fiction. Fitzgerald's title for this story was "Director's Special."

C 308
"The World's Fair," *The Kenyon Review*, X (Autumn 1948), 567–578.

Fiction. Section from early version of *TITN*. See B 40.

C 309
"Last Kiss," *Collier's*, CXXIII (16 April 1949), 16–17, 34, 38, 41, 43–44.

Fiction. See B 41. Reprinted in England in *London Evening Standard* (1 August 1949).

C 310
"That Kind of Party," *The Princeton University Library Chronicle*, XII (Summer 1951), 167–180.

Fiction—Basil story.

C 311
"The Death of My Father," *The Princeton University Library Chronicle*, XII (Summer 1951), 187–189.

Essay. See A 27.

C 312
"The Boy Who Killed His Mother," *Neurotica*, IX (Winter 1952), 38–39.

Verse. Unauthorized publication. See B 57.

C 313
"The High Cost of Macaroni," *Interim*, IV, nos. 1 and 2 (1954), 6–15.

Article.

C 314
"Martin's Thoughts," *Fitzgerald Newsletter*, no. 13 (Spring 1961), 1.

Poem. See B 72.

C *315*
"Love to All of You, of All Generations," *Esquire*, LX (July 1963), 87–90, 111–112.

Nine letters.

C *316*
"Scott Fitzgerald's 'Thoughtbook'" (Introduction by John Kuehl), *The Princeton University Library Chronicle*, XXVI (Winter 1965), 102–108 and unpaged plates.

Facsimile. See A 28.

C *317*
"My Generation," *Esquire*, LXX (October 1968), 119, 121.

Essay. See B 76.

C *318*
"Dearly Beloved," *Fitzgerald/Hemingway Annual 1969*, pp. 1–3.

Fiction. See A 31, B 71.

C *319*
Untitled poem, "Valentine was a Saint . . . ," *Fitzgerald/ Hemingway Annual 1969*, p. 18.

See B 71.

C *320*
Letter to Ernest Hemingway (1925), *Fitzgerald/Hemingway Annual 1970*, pp. 10–13.

See B 74.

C *321*
"Six Letters to the Menckens," *Fitzgerald/Hemingway Annual 1970*, pp. 102–104.

See B 74.

C *322*
"The Fitzgerald-Perkins Papers," *Esquire*, LXXV (June 1971), 107–111, 171, 174, 176, 178–180, 182–183.

Letters. Precedes A 33.

C 323
"Lo, the Poor Peacock," *Esquire*, LXXVI (September 1971), 154–
158.

Fiction.[7]

C 324
"Preface to *This Side of Paradise*," *Fitzgerald/Hemingway
Annual 1971*, pp. 1–2.

See B 79.

C 325
"Fitzgerald's Ledger," *Fitzgerald/Hemingway Annual 1971*, pp.
3–31.

See B 79.

C 326
"Oh, Sister, Can You Spare Your Heart," *Fitzgerald/Hemingway
Annual 1971*, pp. 114–116.

Lyric. See B 79.
                                    *   *   *

Note

See Jennifer McCabe Atkinson, "Lost and Unpublished Stories
by F. Scott Fitzgerald," *Fitzgerald/Hemingway Annual 1971* for
information about:

   "The I. O. U."—1920
   "Recklessness"—1922
   "On Your Own" ("Home to Maryland")—1931
   "Nightmare" ("Fantasy in Black")—1932
   "What to Do About It"—1933
   "Daddy Was Perfect"—1934
   "Travel Together"—1935
   "I'd Die For You" ("The Legend of Lake Lure")—1935–36
   "Lo, The Poor Peacock!"—1935
   "Make Yourself at Home"—1935
   "The Pearl and the Fur"—1936
   "Cyclone in Silent Land"—1936
   "Thank You for the Light"—1936

---

7. The text as printed here is drastically abridged from Fitzgerald's typescript. See "Indeed, 'Lo, The Poor Peacock,'" *Fitzgerald/
Hemingway Annual 1972*.

"They Never Grow Older"—1937
"The Vanished Girl"—1937
"Offside Play" ("Athletic Interview," "Athletic Interval")—
     1937
"Temperature" ("The Women in the House")—1939
"The Couple"—n.d.

D. Material Quoted in Catalogues

Manuscript and typescript material by Fitzgerald quoted in auction, bookdealer, and library-exhibition catalogues. This section does not include books listed in these catalogues unless the book is inscribed by Fitzgerald. These entries are arranged chronologically, with the undatable catalogues at the end of the section.

D 1

SCRIBNER FIRSTS 1846–1936 . . . THE SCRIBNER BOOK
STORE . . . NEW YORK [catalogue 108, c. 1936]

#*125:* *GG*, with ANS laid in: 'Dear Sinclair Lewis: I've just
sent for Arrowsmith. My hope is that The Great Gatsby will be
the second best American book of the spring. F. Scott Fitzgerald.'

D 2

"AUTOGRAPHED By THE AUTHOR" . . . CATALOGUE 303
GOODSPEED'S BOOK SHOP . . . BOSTON, MASSACHUSETTS
[1938]

#*61:* *B&D*, inscribed: 'For Charles T. from F. Scott Fitzgerald.
This lowsy, uneven, rambling, stumbling, tumbling, rattling,
groaning, coughing novel—from the author, who once considered it the best book ever written. "Ellerslie" Edgemoor,
Delaware. April 18, 1927.'

#*62:* *GG*, inscribed: 'For Charles T. Scott. Gatsby was never
quite real to me. His original served for a good enough ex-
terior until about the middle of the book he grew thin and I began to fill him with my own emotional life. So he's synthetic—
and that's one of the flaws in this book. F. Scott Fitzgerald,
Ellerslie, Edgemoor, Delaware, 1927.'

D 3

SALE NUMBER 1207 . . . *December 11 . . . and . . . December 12* . . . PARKE-BERNET GALLERIES · INC . . . NEW
YORK . . . 1950

#*58:* *TSOP*, inscribed and with note on M. O. Green's book-
plate: 'F. Scott Fitzgerald crowds to the nice fireplace'.

#*59:* *B&D*, inscribed: 'The phrase: "Beautiful but dumb" was
this book's contribution to its time. F. Scott Fitzgerald. It has
awful spots but some good ones. I was trying to learn'.

255

#62:   *ASYM*, signed: 'F. Scott Fitzgerald. April 14, 1936'.

#63:   *TAR*, signed: 'F. Scott Fitzgerald. Baltimore, April 13th 1936'.

D 4

. . . CITY BOOK AUCTION SALE No. 513 . . . SALE No. 514 . . . FEBRUARY 10th & 17th, 1951 . . . NEW YORK . . .

#612:   ALS to Milton Boger, Edgemoor, Del., 31 March 1928: 'The Vegetable won't play. Its been tried by Sam Harris & by dozens of amateurs & always been a failure. So I must deny you permission to use it & in doing so I am really being kind. It is cursed & brings only bad luck. Yrs. Sincerely. F. Scott Fitzgerald.'

D 5

AUTUMN 1952 Modern RARE BOOKS and FIRST EDITIONS *Offered for sale by* JACK POTTER . . . Chicago . . .

#50:   Five TLSs to Samuel Marx (script director of MGM), Spring 1934.

First letter.   Asks Marx to transmit something to George Cukor.

Second letter.   'The letter to Cukor dealt with the idea of Gable playing "Gatsby." . . . "Tender is the Night" is still an unknown quantity . . . Would rather like to come out there now that the main chore is finished. It seems to be that or the Saturday Evening Post and I long for variety—but at any price (and I am cherishing none of the illusions of 1931 about money) I wouldn't come out there with any such line-up as I had to face last time. Who is this Joan Crawford? Is she the one who preaches in the Los Angeles temple, or is that Greta Mc-Arthur?'

Third letter.   'It's just occurred to me, in regard to a letter I have from Carl Laemmle asking if I had any old silent productions that I thought could be done over into a talkie, that you own the first two stories I ever sold to pictures. They were Saturday Evening Post stories that appeared in 1920 and later in a book called "Flappers and Philosophers." The first one, "Head and Shoulders" you made with Viola Dana and Garret Hughes (it was the start of his short-lived career) under the title of "The Chorus Girls Romance." I believe it was a big hit at the time. The second was called "The Offshore Pirate" and was made with Viola Dana and I have forgotten what man. If you still have the originals in your library it might be worth while to look them up.'

Fourth letter. Transmits a treatment of *TITN* and states he has 'abandoned the idea of coming to the coast even if urged.'

Fifth letter. 'Apropos of a proposed treatment of my book (Tender Is the Night) which went to you (by the way Publishers Weekly lists it third best seller this week) you will remember that I collaborated on that first treatment with a kid named Charles Warren who has shown a remarkable talent for the theatre in writing, composing and directing two shows which have packed them in and had repeat weeks here in Baltimore and in Princeton. My intention, if Tender Is the Night was sold immediately, was to back him in going out there and seeing if he could help round it into shape. So far the offers have been unsatisfactory considering the work put on it—nevertheless Warren has planned to brave Hollywood even without the permit to enter which a definite connection would be to him. He will be without acquaintance there save for such letters as I can give him. I would be much in your debt if you will see him, give him what advice you can about finding an opening. His talents are amazingly varied—he writes, composes, draws and has this afore-said general gift for the theatre—and I have a feeling that he should fit in there somewhere within a short time and should go close to the top, in fact I haven't believed in anybody so strongly since Ernest Hemingway. Incidentally, he is not a highbrow, his instincts are toward practical showmanship which is why I engaged him, as a sort of complement to me. Perhaps you could arrange to let him look around the lot for a few hours, lend him a few sample treatments that he could take back to his hotel and study and also some story that he could work on without salary . . . Ever your friend, Scott Fitzgerald.'

#51: *VEG*, inscribed: 'For Edna Hooper from F. Scott Fitzgerald—On the eve of the first performance of this great moral document. Atlantic City, Nov. 20th, 1923.' See Parke-Bernet Galleries Catalogue No. 2184 (1963).

#52: *TSOP*, inscribed: 'For Sam Marx, who has just arranged my future for me—very different from the future of Amory Blaine. From his friend, F. Scott Fitzgerald, Hollywood 1931.' See Charles S. Boesen Catalogue No. 27.

Location: MJB.

D 6

RARE BOOKS FIRST EDITIONS . . . CHARLES S. BOESEN
. . . DETROIT 26, MICHIGAN . . . [catalogue 24, c. 1952]

#139:   *B&D,* inscribed: 'To a bookseller Who declares himself
to·be ⅜ tight and promises the other ⅝ before night and says
he wouldn't try to be too damn clever if he was me—after
compromising with you on this description. A. L. Sugarman, I
officially declare myself to be—F. Scott Fitzgerald and swear
from this day forward to take all books to be autographed into
the next room.' With ALS laid in: 'Your letter makes me feel
guilty—as if I had enviegled you into my book under false pre-
tenses. The title is bad but I regret you only reached p. 71, for
on p. 72 . . . however . . . I am struggling over some Boden-
heim verse as you suggest. I think I have a great future at it.
Faithfully F. Scott Fitzgerald.' On the bottom of the page are
two drawings by Fitzgerald headed 'Advertisement ! ! !' The one
sketch shows a man with a happy smile on his face. The caption
below reads: 'The man who read beyond p. 71 of the B&D.' The
other sketch is that of a frowning man. Below it Fitzgerald has
written: 'The man who abandoned the B&D at p. 71.' Below
the drawings Fitzgerald has written: 'The Beautiful & Damned!
A tale for red-blooded he-men! Read it here! See it in the movies!
Play it on the phonograph! Run it on the sewing machine! To
A. J. Sugarman. esq. Northwest Bk. Co. 625 Boston Block.
Minneapolis.'

D 7

FIRST EDITIONS . . . From the Estate of the late HAROLD
DAVIS . . . PART TWO . . . SEPTEMBER 16th, 1954 . . .
SALE No. 384 SWANN AUTION GALLERIES . . . NEW
YORK CITY . . .

#121:   *TSOP,* inscribed: 'For Harold Davis, with Best Wishes
from F. Scott Fitzgerald. July 2nd, 1920.'

D 8

OLD AND RARE BOOKS . . . *Catalogue 491* . . . GOOD-
SPEED'S . . . BOSTON 8, MASSACHUSETTS [1960]

#138:   *VEG,* inscribed to Ernest Truex: 'The best postman in
the world'. Dated 'Nov 19th. 1923, Atlantic City' and signed by
Fitzgerald and Truex.

D 9
AUTOGRAPHS . . . BOOKS—PRINTS—MAPS . . . THURS-
DAY, MAY 25th, 1961 . . . SALE NO. 568 . . . SWANN
GALLERIES, INC. . . . NEW YORK . . .

#148: *TSOP* inscribed: 'To Spencer Jones '14 from F. Scott
Fitzgerald '17.'

D 10
ROBERT A. WILSON RARE BOOKS . . . A SECOND SE-
LECTION . . . NEW YORK . . . [December 1962]

#35: John W. Thomason's *Jeb Stuart* inscribed: 'For A----G----
from F. Scott Fitzgerald (who didn't get to Seven Pines) Aug
13th (unlucky day?) 1934'.

Location: MJB.

D 11
SALE NUMBER 2168 . . . *February* 19 . . . PARKE-BERNET
GALLERIES · INC . . . NEW YORK . . . 1963

#75: Two ALSs to George Norton Northrop, Juan-les-Pins,
France, n.d. In the first letter Fitzgerald says he wants to see
Northrop as soon as Fitzgerald finishes a chapter of his new
novel, in about a fortnight. In the second letter Fitzgerald
apologizes for not having seen Northrop, refers to a tennis game
played fifteen years before, and reports he is suffering from
hives.

D 12
SALE NUMBER 2207 . . . *October* 1 . . . PARKE-BERNET
GALLERIES · INC . . . NEW YORK . . . 1963

#95: *TSOP*, inscribed: 'Dear Uncle & Aunt—The Great
American Novel at Last. Scott.'

D 13
. . . Charles Hamilton AUCTION Number Two . . . OCTO-
BER 17th . . . [New York, 1963]

#86: ANS at bottom of letter from Lenox Hill Players, New
York, 14 June 1928, requesting permission to perform *VEG:* 'All
right—but against my better advice. It simply doesn't play
. . . it is psychologicly wrong—the writing conceals it in the
reading but on the stage from the beginning of Act II—My God

—watch them die. Yrs. ect. F. Scott Fitzgerald (and very pessimisticly).'

D 14
CATALOGUE NUMBER SIX . . . *Henry W. Wenning* . . .
NEW HAVEN 11, CONN. [1963]

#*370:*   Revised TS, "The Count of Darkness."

#*371:*   Revised TS, "A Kingdom in the Dark."

#*372:*   Revised TS, "Her Last Case."

#*373:*   Wire to Alice Richardson, 28 November 1934: 'I got up out of more sickness than you ever saw in this house and you saw plenty to crawl down to the B and O to send this. . . . with dearest love Scott'.

#*374:*   TLS to Mary Brown, 8 December 1934. Letter of recommendation requesting a place for Alice Richardson in 'your paternal store' [Wanamaker's]. 'Both Zelda and I are very fond of her and would appreciate anything you could do for her . . . starting out on her own in New York.'

#*375:*   TLS to Horace F. Simon, 20 January 1935. Letter of recommendation for Alice Richardson: 'I boasted to her of having been a classmate of yours at Princeton.'

#*376:*   TLS to Charles MacArthur, 2 March 1935. Letter of recommendation for Alice Richardson.

#*376A:*   TLS to Maxwell Perkins, 2 March 1935. Letter of recommendation for Alice Richardson.

#*377:*   TLS to Alice Richardson, 28 February 1935: 'It won't do, Alyce. It is in part too personal and in part not personal enough. It is not really English to write such a sentence as "Her tonsils were in terrible shape," which gives a rather revolting picture of the lady's throat. I appreciate your sparing me on the alcoholic side, at the same time the picture of a writer living in a dressing gown isn't sufficiently new or startling to give personality interest. Due to the fact that my books no longer have the national circulation they used to have, but sell chiefly in big cities, the interest in such articles would be limited to magazines such as THE NEW YORKER, whose readers would not consider the company of an author very exciting after all. This is sad but true. . . .'

#*378:*   TLS to Alice Richardson, 14 May 1935: 'The establishment here is breaking up and I am going south to recuperate.

I don't drink anymore (4 mos) and you would like me better. No possible news. Mrs. Owens and I often think of you riding in the park on your roan stallion. I have put a "tail" on your husband and find he is running around with a lovely high yellow girl named Sally Washington. No other news really. Scottie has leprosy. Mrs. Owens is in prison for assault and battery.'

#379: TLS to Alice Richardson, 29 July 1940: '. . . working on a story for little Miss Temple. Santa Barbara is supposed to have some escape magic like Palm Springs but no matter how hard you look it's still California. . . . Gertrude Stein's passage through Baltimore. It was a solemn winter but there were worse to come and in retrospect those months have an air of early April. . . . Your old friend . . . Scott'. Postscript: 'Isn't Hollywood a dump—in the human sense of the word. A hideous town, pointed up by the insulting gardens of its rich, full of the human spirit at a new low of debasement.'

#380: *ASYM*, inscribed to Alice Richardson: 'God speed thee FSF'.

#381: *TITN*, inscribed: 'For Alyce Wooten with high regards and many thanks from that old & experienced bully F. Scott Fitzgerald Nov 5th 1934 Baltimore, Md'.

D 15
Treasures of The Library A SAMPLING *by Howard C. Rice Jr.* [Princeton University Library, Princeton, N.J. 1963]

Includes facsimiles of title page and p. 128 of *TSOP* manuscript. Reprinted from *The Princeton Alumni Weekly*, LXIV (3 December 1963), 6–11.

D 16
RARE BOOKS & AUTOGRAPHS . . . JANUARY 16, 1964 . . . SALE NO. 639 . . . SWANN GALLERIES, INC. . . . New York . . .

#160: *TSOP*, with tipped-in ALS: 'Dear Mr. Hill—If my book was half as good as your cover I'd sell a million copies . . . Very gratefully one of your many admirers. F. Scott Fitzgerald.'

D 17
CATALOGUE 11 AUTOGRAPHS . . . PAUL C. RICHARDS . . . BROOKLINE, MASS. . . . [1964]

#118: *VEG*, inscribed: 'For Fanny Hurst from hers admiringly F. Scott Fitzgerald May 4th 1923'. Facsimile. See Paul C. Richards Catalogues Nos. 13 and 14. Also see The Phoenix Book Shop Catalogue No. 75 (1965) and Argosy Bookshop Catalogue No. 506.

D 18
Catalogue No. 3 [double rules] *First Editions Autographs & Manuscripts* [Heritage Book Shop, Long Grove, Ill. Winter 1964–65]

#A-19: ALS to Mr. Emmerich, Great Neck, L.I., n.d.: 'Only last week I tried making a speech and almost collapsed from sheer terror. I guess we'd better call off the idea.' See Lew David Feldman Catalogue No. 66A.

D 19
. . . Charles Hamilton AUCTION Number VIII . . . MAY 20th 1965 [New York]

#45: ALS to Ashley Trimble Cole: 'I never can think of anything clever to write to people. I keep trying to think of something clever to write to people but I never can think of anything clever to write to people Dolefully,'

D 20
. . . Charles Hamilton AUCTION Number IX . . . SEPT. 30th 1965 . . . [New York]

#55a: ALS to Zella R. Kimball, St. Paul, Minn., 10 June 1922: 'You mention pages 276 & 391. But—look on page 192 and see the worst! August! God! How come, indeed!' Refers to errors in *B&D*. See Charles Hamilton Catalogue No. 16 (13 December 1966).

D 21
Catalog Seventy-five MODERN FIRST EDITIONS *The Phoenix Book Shop* . . . NEW YORK . . . [1965]

#129: *VEG*, inscribed: 'Amand Tarleton Winchester from hers faithfully F. Scott Fitzgerald'. See The Phoenix Book Shop Catalogue No. 83 (1967) and Robert K. Black Catalogue No. 113 (1967).

D 22
. . . Charles Hamilton AUCTION Number 15 . . . Nov. 3rd, 1966 [New York]

#311: *B&D,* inscribed: 'To Mary Craven, who doesn't think it's fun to be rich—from one who's one idea is GOLD, from a sincere admirer of Mary & Frank Craven (& what's more—an imitator of the latter) Nov 17th 1(9)22.' See Eleventh Co-operative Catalogue of Middle Atlantic ABAA.

D 23
Catalog Eighty MODERN FIRST-EDITIONS *The Phoenix Book Shop* . . . NEW YORK . . . [1966]

On inside rear cover: ALS to Tom [Thomas Smith of Boni & Liveright], Great Neck, L.I., n.d. Catalogue quotes from letter. Fuller text in Paul C. Richards Catalogue No. 28, #260—see D 48.

D 24
. . . Charles Hamilton AUCTION Number 19 . . . MAY 24th, 1967 [New York]

#282: ALS to Mrs. Hammond, The Plaza, New York, n.d.: 'In the matter of the stories I will have to refer you to Scribners as the rights have passed out of my hands.' See Robert K. Black Catalogue No. 113 (1967).

D 25
. . . Charles Hamilton AUCTION Number 21 . . . SEPT. 28th, 1967 [New York]

#275: ALS to Mackies, n.d.: 'Sorry I missed you. Saw your progeny who appear flourishing . . .'

#276: Holograph poem, July 1933: 'Don't expect me | I've gone fancy | I'm all set | With Bryan Dancy. | Scotty's Windbag | Michell's Berries | Back at midnight | Out with Fairies | F. Scott Fitzgerald'. Reproduced in facsimile.

D 26
Catalog Eighty-three MODERN FIRST-EDITIONS *The Phoenix Book Shop* . . . NEW YORK . . . [1967]

On inside rear cover: TSOP, inscribed: 'For Aiken Reichner Hoping that you'll find your literary stride within the next year —and with a great deal of confidence that you will—F. Scott Fitzgerald March 28, 1920 Princeton, N.J.'

D 27
PAUL C. RICHARDS . . . BROOKLINE, MASS. . . . THE
BEACON BULLETIN Catalogue No. 23 Issue No. 14. . . .
[1967]

#963: Holograph poem, Paris, 26 June 1926: 'Of wonders is
Silas M. Hanson the champ | He asked for an aut'graph and
sent me a stamp | But none of his pleadings would go on a
shelf | If he'd added an envelope 'dressed to himself.' Facsimiled
in Paul C. Richards Catalogue No. 46, which also describes
envelope.

D 28
Catalogue 113 . . . ROBERT K. BLACK . . . Upper Mont-
clair New Jersey . . . [1967]

#49: *VEG,* inscribed: 'Maud Tarleton Winchester from hers
faithfully, F. Scott Fitzgerald.' See The Phoenix Book Shop
Catalogues Nos. 75 (1965) and 83 (1967).

D 29
SALE   NUMBER   2763 . . . *November*   13 . . . PARKE-
BERNET GALLERIES · INC . . . NEW YORK . . . 1968

#67: One-page MS and ALS. MS reproduced in facsimile: 'For
Harry W. Winslow [Winston(?)]. A.B; M.D; P.H.D from The
Very Reverend F. Scott Fitzgerald Archbishop of the Church
of St. Voltaire Patterson, New Jersey. "Now is the time for all
good men to come to the aid of the party." Ezeliel III V.2 May
31st, 1922 [drawing] A Self portrait of Mr. Fitzgerald just after
the battle of Gettysburg'. The letter reads: 'Dear Mr. Winslow:
Be glad to autograph your book. I know Farrar slightly. Sin-
cerely F. Scott Fitzgerald 626 Goodrich Avenue. St. Paul, Minn.
May 21st 1922.' Literary Heritage Catalogue No. 11 (Sharon,
Mass., 1969), #278, adds note on postcard: 'Look at this and
think of me if you want to be cool'. See also Literary Heritage
Catalogue No. 14 (1970) and Heritage Book Shop Catalogue
No. 114 (1971).

D 30
DOUGLAS M. JACOBS . . . RIDGEFIELD, CONN. . . . Catalogue No. 18 [1968]

#103: ALS to an editor of *Vanity Fair,* n.d.: 'Memory had
blotted out the experience but the faded ink recalled the also
vanished liquor I drank that day. I am now full of cham-
pagne . . .'

D 31
SWANN GALLERIES, INC · . . . NOVEMBER 20, 1969 · . .
SALE NUMBER 803 . . . *NEW YORK* . . .

#153: *TSOP,* inscribed: 'For Kermit Roosevelt, from F. Scott Fitzgerald.'

D 32
CATALOGUE TWELVE SUMMER 1969 MODERN FIRST EDI-
TIONS . . . Literary Heritage, Inc. . . . Sharon, Mass. . . .

#216: *TLS* to Southgate Morison, Baltimore, Md., 9 Nov. 1934. Refers to Booth Tarkington's "Blue Milk." See Literary Heritage Catalogue No. 14 (1970).

D 33
SALE NUMBER 3088 . . . *OCTOBER* 13 . . . PARKE-
BERNET GALLERIES INC . . . *New York* . . . 1970

#198: Proof of biography from *Standard American Encyclo-pedia,* with form letter signed 'O.K. F. Scott Fitzgerald.'

D 34
An Auction of Literary and Artistic Materials for the benefit of antiwar Congressional candidates . . . 8 October 1970 . . . New York . . .

#44: ALS to Marya Mannes, Paris, 21 October 1925: 'Thank you for writing me about *Gatsby*—I especially appreciate your letter because women, and even intelligent women, haven't generally cared much for it. . . . America's greatest promise is that something is going to happen, and after a while you get tired of waiting because nothing happens to American people except that they grow old, and nothing happens to American art because America is the story of the moon that never rose. . . . My new novel is marvellous. I'm in the first chapter. . . . Can you name a single American artist except James & Whistler (who lived in England) who didn't die of drink? . . .'

D 35
. . . Charles Hamilton AUCTION Number 45 . . . October 22, 1970 . . . [New York]

#119: *TITN,* inscribed: 'Tom Rennie from his friend Scott.'

D 36
SALE NUMBER 3130 . . . *December* 8 . . . PARKE-BERNET
GALLERIES · INC . . . NEW YORK . . . 1970

#39:   *TSOP,* inscribed to Bert Cohn, 25 March 1920.

D 37
BENNETT & MARSHALL Catalogue No. 9 . . . Los Angeles . . .
[1970]

#55:   *TAR,* inscribed: 'For Sylvia Lewis in memory of those
days when she translated *A Rebours* for me in my cork-lined
converted Pullman F. Scott ("Huysmans") Fitzgerald The
Flood—1938'.

D 38
CATALOGUE NO. 49 . . . PAUL C. RICHARDS, AUTO-
GRAPHS . . . Brookline, Mass. . . . [1970]

#239:   *ASYM,* inscribed: 'For Dorothy Hale Litchfield from
hers faithfully F. Scott Fitzgerald. Villa St. Louis. Juan-les Pins,
France. June 1926.' See Paul C. Richards Catalogue No. 56
(1971).

D 39
SALE NUMBER 3209 . . . ENGLISH & AMERICAN FIRST EDI-
TIONS . . . Uncorrected galleys of *The Great Gatsby* . . . *May*
18 . . . PARKE-BERNET GALLERIES · INC . . . 980 *Madi-
son Avenue · New York* . . . 1971 . . .

#22:   Unrevised original galleys of *GG* ("Trimalchio"); first
galley facsimiled on p. 3.

D 40
Printed Books . . . and a collection relating to the Motion Pic-
ture Industry . . . Christie, Manson & Woods . . . London,
S.W. 1 . . . June 2, 1971 . . .

#278:   *TITN,* inscribed to David O. Selznick: 'Dear Dave,
Highballs to you, Scott. David Selznick c/o M.G.M., Hollywood'.

D 41
FIRST EDITIONS . . . CATALOGUE TWO [Joseph the Pro-
vider, San Francisco, Cal., July 1971]

#181: *TSOP,* inscribed: 'For——This immature product of which, did I not feel an unnatural affection for it, I would be somewhat ashamed. F. Scott Fitzgerald, April 22nd 1922, St. Paul, Minn.'

D 42
MODERN LITERATURE . . . BLACK SUN BOOKS . . .
BROOKLYN, NEW YORK 11202 [catalogue 10, n.d.]

#110: *B&D,* inscribed: 'For _____ with best wishes from F. Scott Fitzgerald This was a book about things I knew nothing about, a drawing upon experiences that I had not had. Much more than my first book this was a piece of insolence.'

D 43
CATALOGUE No. 9 FIRST EDITIONS 1643–1943 . . .
CHARLES S. BOESEN . . . New York . . . [n.d.]

#100: The dedication copy of *TJA,* inscribed: 'For Mamma from Her Angel Child Scott'. An unlocated later catalogue issued by Boesen in Detroit listed a *TJA* inscribed to W. B. Corcoran.

Location: MJB.

D 44
CATALOGUE · SIXTY · SIX · A · . . . . LEW DAVID FELDMAN
[New York, n.d.]

#288: *B&D,* inscribed: 'For Rosalind Smith, Wanderer on the face of the earth—from F. Scott Fitzgerald, St. Paul, Minn. This is *not* autobiography.'

#290: *TITN,* inscribed: 'For Nell: as we (lie) sit here on the old (bed) swing we often think of you. Miss Garbo realizes that you *had* no past & feels no real jealousy when I speak of our *"platonic"* friendship (You remember our encounter in the family wastebasket?) But all is over between us (Nell Mary) Nell, and Greta feels the same way I do—we wish you the best of happiness (and Marlene joins us), even if you weren't (sic) able to make F. Scott Fitzgerald'. On title page after "A Romance" Fitzgerald wrote 'about Nell Brooks' and signed his name again.

#540: *TSOP,* inscribed for Harold Davis, 2 July 1920.

#543: *B&D,* signed.

D 45
FIRST EDITIONS . . . HOUSE of BOOKS, Ltd. . . . NEW
YORK . . . [no catalogue number, n.d.]

#207:   *B&D*, signed: 'Sincerely F. Scott Fitzgerald'.

D 46
FIRST EDITIONS . . . HOUSE of BOOKS, Ltd. . . . NEW
YORK . . . [no catalogue number, n.d.]

#167:   *TSOP*, inscribed: 'This book is a history of mistakes—
something never retracted yet, in a way, to be ashamed of, by a
conscientious worker . . . Scott Fitzgerald.'

D 47
CHARLES HAMILTON Autographs . . . NEW YORK . . .
Catalog No. 45 SPECIAL WORLD'S FAIR EDITION . . . [n.d.]

#343:   Holograph note with accolades for St. John Ervine.

D 48
PAUL C. RICHARDS . . . BROOKLINE, MASS. . . . THE
BEACON BULLETIN Catalogue No. 28 Issue No. 19 . . . [n.d.]

#260:   ALS to Tom [Thomas Smith of Boni & Liveright], Great
Neck, L.I., n.d.: 'The books arrived and I'm looking forward
eagerly to reading the coon volume & the English book. The
Waldo Frank novel is I'm afraid just his usual canned rubbish.
He seems to me to be an ambitious but totally uninspired person
under the delusion that by filching the most advanced methods
from the writers who originated them . . . he can supply a
substitute for his own lack of feeling and cover up the bogus
arty-ness of his work. He strains for a simile until his belly
aches . . . I'm afraid Horace has made a bad guess on him. I
wish to God you'd republish Gertrude Stein's *Three Lives* and
expose some of these fakers. Her book is utterly real. Its in her
early manner before the attempt to transfer the technique of
Matisse & Picasso to prose made her coo-coo . . .' See D 23.

* * *

Note

Publisher's Weekly, CXCVI (27 October 1969), 51, notes a c.
1935 Schulte catalogue that offered a Fitzgerald letter. Not seen.

E. Interviews

Interviews with Fitzgerald, arranged chronologically.

E 1
Broun, Heywood. "Books," *New York Tribune* (7 May 1920), 14.

Quotes from unpublished interview with Carleton R. Davis. See E 32.

E 2
"More Than Hundred Notes Of Rejection Failed to Halt Scott Fitzgerald's Pen," *St. Paul Pioneer Press* (12 September 1920), and section, 8

Based on interview.

E 3
H. H. [Harry Hansen]. "Have Faith in Fitzgerald," *Chicago Daily News* (27 October 1920), 12.

E 4
Smith, Frederick James. "Fitzgerald, Flappers and Fame," *Shadowland*, III (January 1921), 39, 75.

See A 32.

E 5
Boyd, Thomas Alexander. "Scott Fitzgerald Here on Vacation; 'Rests' by Outlining New Novels," *St. Paul Daily News* (28 August 1921), city life section, 6.

E 6
Boyd, Thomas Alexander. "Scott Fitzgerald Speaks At Home," *St. Paul Daily News* (4 December 1921), city life section, 6.

Quotes from Fitzgerald's talk to the St. Paul Women's City Club.

E 7
Boyd, Thomas Alexander. "Literary Libels—Francis Scott Key Fitzgerald," *St. Paul Daily News* (5, 12, 19 March 1922), city life section, 6.

See A 32.

E 8
J. V. A. W. [John V. A. Weaver]. "The Lion's Cage," *Brooklyn Daily Eagle* (25 March 1922), 5.

E 9
Marshall, Marguerite Mooers. "F. Scott Fitzgerald, Novelist, Shocked by 'Younger Marrieds' and Prohibition," *New York Evening World* (1 April 1922), 3.

See A 32.

E 10
O'Donnell, John. "Fitzgerald Condemns St. Paul Flappers," *St. Paul Daily News* (16 April 1922), section 1, 1, 5.

Printed in other newspapers.

E 11
"The Gossip Shop," *The Bookman*, LV (May 1922), 333–334.

E 12
McCardell, Roy L. "F. Scott Fitzgerald—Juvenile Juvenal of the Jeunesse Jazz," *New York Morning Telegraph* (12 November 1922), magazine section, 3.

E 13
"Novelist Flays Drys, Exalting Our Flappers," *New York Daily News* (24 January 1923), 18.

Interview statement.

E 14
"Prediction Is Made About James Novel F. S. Fitzgerald Believes 'Ulysses' Is Great Book of Future," *Richmond Times-Dispatch* (24 June 1923), II, 5.

E 15
"What a 'Flapper Novelist' Thinks of His Wife," *Detroit News* (30 September 1923), Metropolitan Section, 3. Reprinted: *Baltimore Sun* (7 October 1923), magazine section, 2.

See A 32.

E 16
Wilson, B. F. "F. Scott Fitzgerald Says: 'All Women Over Thirty-Five Should Be Murdered,'" *Metropolitan Magazine*, LVIII (November 1923), 34, 75–76.

See A 32.

E 17
Wilson, B. F. "Notes on Personalities, IV—F. Scott Fitzgerald," *The Smart Set,* LXXIII (April 1924), 29–33.

E 18
Wales, Henry. "N.Y. '400' Apes Chicago Manner; Fails; So Dull," *Chicago Daily Tribune* (7 December 1925), 12.

E 19
"Novelist Admires French," *Baltimore Evening Sun* (21 December 1926), 11.

E 20
Salpeter, Harry. "Fitzgerald, Spenglerian," *New York World* (3 April 1927), 12M.

See A 32.

E 21
Reid, Margaret. "Has the Flapper Changed?" *Motion Picture Magazine,* XXXIII (July 1927), 28–29, 104.

See A 32.

E 22
Whitman, William. "They Write Books—The Gin and Jazz Age," *Boston Globe* (13 April 1929), 14.

Possibly based on interview.

E 23
Keith, Walling. "Scott Fitzgeralds to Spend Winter Here Writing Books," *Montgomery Advertiser* (8 October 1931), 1, 7.

See A 32.

E 24
"Scott Fitzgerald Seeking Home Here," *Baltimore Sun* (8 May 1932), 18, 12.

See A 32.

E 25
" 'No, Not Cellar-Door!' Baltimore Writers Cry," *Baltimore Post* (13 December 1932), 2.

E 26
"F. Scott Fitzgerald Is Visitor In City; New Book Appears Soon," *Charlottesville Daily Progress* (25 May 1933), 1.

E 27
"Holds 'Flappers' Fail As Parents," *New York Times* (18 September 1933), 17.

Syndicated.

E 28
Malcolm Cowley. "Ivory Towers To Let," *The New Republic* LXXVIII (18 April 1934), 260–263.

Quote.

E 29
"F. Scott Fitzgerald Staying At Hotel Here," *Asheville Citizen-Times* (21 July 1935), 1–2. Reprinted: Thomas, Ed. G. "Our 'Oh, Yeah' Generation," *Atlanta Journal* (25 August 1935), magazine section, 8.

See A 32.

E 30
Buttitta, Anthony. "Fitzgerald's Six Generations," *Raleigh News and Observer* (1 September 1935), 3.

See A 32.

E 31
Mok, Michel. "The Other Side of Paradise, Scott Fitzgerald, 40, Engulfed in Despair," *New York Post* (25 September 1936), 1, 15.

See A 32.

E 32
"An Interview with F. Scott Fitzgerald," *Saturday Review,* XLIII (5 November 1960), 26, 56.

Self-interview by Fitzgerald, written for Carleton R. Davis. See A 32 and E 1.

E 33
Buttitta, Anthony. "An Encounter With Fitzgerald In a North Carolina Bookshop," *San Francisco Chronicle, "This World"* (26 August 1962), supplement, 38.

F. Articles That Include Fitzgerald Material

Articles that include material by Fitzgerald, arranged alphabetically by author.

F 1
Anon. " 'Cheapest Funeral' Asked in F. Scott Fitzgerald's Will,"
St. Paul Dispatch (22 January 1941).

AP dispatch.

F 2
Anon. "New & Notable," *The Princeton University Library Chronicle*, XXIII (Autumn 1961), 31–32.

Inscription to Julian Street.

F 3
Anon. "The Literary Sampler," *Saturday Review*, XLVI (5 October 1963), 28.

Includes letter to Perkins (18 September 1919). Precedes *Letters*. See A 25, A 26.1.a.

F 4
Anon. "The Spell of Scott Fitzgerald Grows Stronger," *Life*, XLVI
(16 February 1959), 85–86, 88.

Includes letters and material from "Thoughtbook." Precedes
Thoughtbook (1965). See A 28.

F 5
Anon. "F. Scott Fitzgerald and the Roaring Twenties! After the
whoopee came sadness, then these letters to an only daughter,"
McCall's, XCI (October 1963), 100–101, 201–202, 204–206.

Includes nineteen letters. Precedes *Letters*. See A 26.1.a.

F 6
Arthur, Chester A. "The Sublime Governess," *New Statesman*,
LXV (12 April 1963), 520.

Reply to F 40; also quotes Fitzgerald.

277

F 7

Atkinson, Jennifer E. "Fitzgerald's Marked Copy of *The Great Gatsby*," *Fitzgerald/Hemingway Annual 1970*, pp. 28–33.

Includes Fitzgerald's revisions. See B 74.

F 8

Atkinson, Jennifer McCabe, "The Lost and Unpublished Stories by F. Scott Fitzgerald," *Fitzgerald/Hemingway Annual 1971*, pp. 32–63.

Includes facsimile of first page of "The I. O. U." manuscript and quotes from Fitzgerald/Ober correspondence. See B 79.

F 9

Azrael, Louis. "F. S. Fitzgerald's Critical Years," *Baltimore American* (28 July 1963), section C, 1.

Quotes from conversation with Fitzgerald.

F 10

Bishop, John Peale. "The Missing All," *Virginia Quarterly Review*, XIII (Winter 1937), 106–121.

Quotes Fitzgerald conversation.

F 11

Block, Ralph. "A Recollection of F," *Fitzgerald Newsletter*, no. 35 (Fall 1966), 4–5.

Includes letter to Block (1921). See B 72.

F 12

[Bruccoli, Matthew J.] "F Highlights from the Barrett Library," *Fitzgerald Newsletter*, no. 11 (Fall 1960), 1–4.

Includes lyric for "It Is Art"; inscriptions to Fitzgerald's mother, Joseph Hergesheimer, W. R. K. Taylor, Jr., and Ruth Sturtevant. See B 72.

F 13

[Bruccoli, Matthew J.] "Still More F at Yale," *Fitzgerald Newsletter*, no. 13 (Spring 1961), 3.

Quotes from letter to Fred Millet (27 February 1937). See B 72.

F 14

[Bruccoli, Matthew J.] "F Inscriptions," *Fitzgerald Newsletter*, no. 16 (Winter 1962), 3.

Inscriptions to Juliana Armour Lincoln and Dr. Nardini. See B 72.

F 15
[Bruccoli, Matthew J.] "Inscription," *Fitzgerald Newsletter,* no. 22 (Summer 1963), 4.

Inscription to Shirley Britt. See B 72.

F 16
[Bruccoli, Matthew J.] "F Parodies F," *Fitzgerald Newsletter,* no. 25 (Spring 1964), 8.

Parody ending for "Magnetism." See B 72.

F 17
[Bruccoli, Matthew J.] "Inscription," *Fitzgerald Newsletter,* no. 28 (Spring 1964), 8.

Inscription to Carmel Myers. See B 72.

F 18
Bruccoli, Matthew J. "Material for a Centenary Edition of *Tender is the Night,*" *Studies in Bibliography,* XVII (1964), 177–193. Also paperbound offprints.

Lists Fitzgerald's revisions.

F 19
[Bruccoli, Matthew J.] "F, Brooks, Hemingway, and James: A New F Letter," *Fitzgerald Newsletter,* no. 29 (Spring 1965), 1–3.

Includes letter to Van Wyck Brooks (June 1925). See B 72.

F 20
[Bruccoli, Matthew J.] "Inscribed TITN," *Fitzgerald Newsletter,* no. 31 (Fall 1965), 4.

Inscription to Laura Guthrie. See B 72.

F 21
[Bruccoli, Matthew J.] "F as Autobibliographer," *Fitzgerald Newsletter,* no. 32 (Winter 1966), 5.

Quotes from letters to Argus Bookshop (17 March and 7 April 1936) and Mrs. Newman Smith (4 March 1938). See B 72.

F 22
Bruccoli, Matthew J. "Fitzgerald's Marked Copy of *This Side of Paradise*," *Fitzgerald/Hemingway Annual 1971*, pp. 64–69.

Includes Fitzgerald's revisions. See B 79.

F 23
Christian, Henry A. "F and 'Superman': An Unpublished Letter to Louis Adamic," *Fitzgerald Newsletter*, no. 31 (Fall 1965), 1–3.

Includes letter (2 April 1929). See B 72.

F 24
Cowley, Malcolm. "Good Books That Almost Nobody Has Read," *The New Republic*, LXXVIII (18 April 1934), 281–283. Includes Fitzgerald's list of neglected books. Reprinted in B 74.

F 25
Cowley, Malcolm. "Third Act and Epilogue," *The New Yorker*, XXI (30 June 1945), 53–54, 57–58.

Quotes conversation and statements.

F 26
Cowley, Malcolm. "Fitzgerald: The Double Man," *Saturday Review*, XXXIV (24 February 1951), 9–10, 42–44.

Quotes conversations.

F 27
Cowley, Malcolm. "A Ghost Story of the Jazz Age," *Saturday Review*, XLVII (25 January 1964), 20–21.

"Reminiscences of Twenty-Four Hours with F. Scott Fitzgerald."

F 28
Davis, Curtis Carroll. "A Life of Scott Fitzgerald," *Baltimore Evening Sun* (27 January 1951), 4.

Review of *The Far Side of Paradise*. Quotes 1936 note from Fitzgerald; also *TAR* inscription.

F 29
Dolbier, Maurice. "Some Memories of F. Scott Fitzgerald," *New York Herald-Tribune Book Review* (30 November 1958), 2.

Interview with Sheilah Graham. Quotes Fitzgerald letter with career summary.

F 30
Doyno, Victor. "F as Poet," *Fitzgerald Newsletter*, no. 35 (Fall 1966), 6–8.

"A god-intoxicated fly . . ." and "Thousand-and-First Ship." See B 72.

F 31
Eble, Kenneth. "The Craft of Revision: *The Great Gatsby*," *American Literature*, XXXVI (November 1964), 315–326.

Includes material from Gatsby manuscript.

F 32
[Farrington, Janet.] "Scribners Archives Presented to Princeton," *APGA Bulletin*, no. 10 (June 1967), inserted in *University*, no. 33 (Summer 1967).

Facsimiles a 1924 letter to Perkins

F 33
Fitzgerald, Frances Scott. "Princeton and F. Scott Fitzgerald," *The Nassau Lit*, C (100th Anniversary Issue, 1942), 45–48.

Includes excerpts from letters.

F 34
Gilroy, Harry. "Scribner's Is Giving Archives to Princeton," *New York Times* (31 March 1967), late city edition, 33.

Facsimiles 1924 letter to Perkins recommending Hemingway. Also "Scribner Papers Go to Princeton," city edition, 37.

F 35
[Gingrich, Arnold.] "Editorial: Salute and Farewell to F. Scott Fitzgerald," *Esquire*, XV (March 1941), 6.

Quotes from letter.

F 36
A. G. [Arnold Gingrich]. "Will the real Scott Fitzgerald please stand up and be counted?" *Esquire*, LXII (December 1964), 8, 10, 12, 16.

Quotes Fitzgerald.

F 37
Gingrich, Arnold. "Scott, Ernest and Whoever," *Esquire*, LXVI (December 1966), 186–189, 322–325.

Includes inscription, conversations, and verse.

Note: See F 87 for entry by Donald W. Goodwin.

F 38
Graham, Sheilah. "The Education of Lily Sheil," *The Sunday Times Weekly Review* (30 January and 6 February 1966), 41–42; 42–43.

Facsimiles and quotes notes. First publication of Fitzgerald's translation of Rimbaud's "Voyelles." See B 63, B 64.

F 39
Hearne, Laura Guthrie. "A Summer With F. Scott Fitzgerald," *Esquire*, LXII (December 1964), 160–165, 232, 236–237, 240, 242, 246, 250, 252, 254–258, 260.

Diary includes Fitzgerald conversations.

F 40
Hodgson, Simon. "Sublime Governess," *New Statesman*, LXV (22 February 1963), 268.

Gives account of Fitzgerald-Wharton encounter; quotes Fitzgerald. See F 6.

F 41
Kiley, Jed. "Hemingway a title bout in ten rounds," *Playboy*, III (October 1956), 55–56.

Quotes conversation. See BB 9.

F 42
Kuehl, John. "Scott Fitzgerald's Reading." *The Princeton University Library Chronicle*, XXII (Winter 1961), 58–89.

Quotes from letters, notes, and reading lists. See B 76.

F 43
Kuehl, John. "Scott Fitzgerald's Critical Opinions," *Modern Fiction Studies*, VII (Spring 1961), 3–18.

Quotes from letters and notes. See B 76.

F 44
Latham, John Aaron. "A Day at the Studio—Scott Fitzgerald in Hollywood," *Harper's Magazine*, CCXLI (November 1970), 38–39, 41–42, 46, 48, 50.

Prepublication of first chapter of *Crazy Sundays*. Includes two poems. See B 77.

F 45
Leslie, Shane. "Scott Fitzgerald's First Novel" (letter to editor), *The Times Literary Supplement* (6 November 1959), 643.

Includes five letters to Leslie (22 December 1917, 13 January 1918, two undated, 8 May 1918).

F 46
Long, Robert Emmet. "The Fitzgerald-Mencken Correspondence," *Fitzgerald/Hemingway Annual 1971*, pp. 319–321.

Quotes from letters. See B 79.

F 47
Margolies, Alan. "F. Scott Fitzgerald's Work in the Film Studios," *The Princeton University Library Chronicle*, XXXII (Winter 1971), 81–110.

Two pages of facsimiles inserted; also quotes from scripts, letters, and memos.

F 48
Marsden, Donald. "F and The Princeton Triangle Club (I)," *Fitzgerald Newsletter*, no. 35 (Fall 1966), 1–4.

Lyric for "Rag-time Melodrama." See B 72.

F 49
Marsden, Donald. "F and the Triangle Club (III)," *Fitzgerald Newsletter*, no. 38 (Summer 1967), 1–3.

Lyric for "On My Ragtime Family Tree." See B 72.

F 50
Marsden, Donald. "F and the Princeton Triangle Club (IV)," *Fitzgerald Newsletter*, no. 39. (Fall 1967), 8–11.

Material from *The Captured Shadow* and *The Coward*. See B 72.

F 51
Marsden, Donald. "F and the Princeton Triangle Club, V," *Fitzgerald Newsletter*, no. 40 (Winter 1968), 11–13.

Material from *Assorted Spirits*. See B 72.

F 52
Martin, Jay. "Fitzgerald Recommends Nathanael West for a Guggenheim," *Fitzgerald/Hemingway Annual 1971*, pp. 302–304.

Includes letter (25 September 1934). See B 79.

F 53
Mayfield, John S. "A Jazz Ager Confesses a Crime," *Autograph Collectors' Journal*, III (Summer 1951), 55.

Includes letter to Mayfield, 6 February 1924.

F 54
[Mayfield, John S.] "Three Stars Charioted," *The Courier*, III (June 1963), 4–7.

Facsimiles *TITN* inscription to Sinclair Lewis.

F 55
Mayfield, Sara. "The Fitzgeralds: Exiles from Paradise," *Comment*, IV (Winter 1965), 43–50.

Reports conversations. See B 78.

F 56
Mayfield, Sara. "Exiles from Paradise," *McCall's*, XCVIII (July 1971), 64–65, 127–129, 131–132, 140.

Prepublication excerpt from book. See B 78.

F 57
Milford, Nancy. "Zelda," *The Ladies' Home Journal*, LXXXVII (June 1970), 117–121.

Prepublication excerpt from book. See B 75.

F 58
Mitchell, Peggy. "Novelist Loved Atlanta Girl's Picture," *Atlanta Journal* (30 September 1923), 5.

Includes two poems: "To Anne" and untitled. See A 32.

F 59
Mizener, Arthur. "Scott Fitzgerald and the Imaginative Possession of American Life," *Sewanee Review*, LIV (Winter 1946), 66–86.

Quotes from Ledger and letters.

F 60
Mizener, Arthur. *The Work of F. Scott Fitzgerald.* McGregor
Room Seminars in Contemporary Poetry and Prose, University
of Virginia, 7 May 1948.

Mimeographed lecture. Quotes from letters and notebooks.

F 61
Mizener, Arthur. "Fitzgerald in the Twenties," *Partisan Review,*
XVII (January 1950), 7–38.

Quotes letters.

F 62
Mizener, Arthur. "F. Scott Fitzgerald's Tormented Paradise,"
Life, XXX (15 January 1951), 82–88, 91–94, 96–98, 101.

Quotes letters and illustrates memorabilia.

F 63
Mosher, John Chapin. "That Sad Young Man," *The New Yorker,*
II (17 April 1926), 20–21.

Includes statements.

F 64
Myers, Carmel. "Scott and Zelda," *Park East,* II (May 1951),
18, 32–33.

Includes two untitled poems and quotes conversation.

F 65
Northup, Helen. "Fitzgerald in Wolfe's Clothing," *University of
Wisconsin Library News,* VI (November 1961), 2–3.

Quotes conversation

F 66
Piper, Henry Dan. "F. Scott Fitzgerald and the Image of his
Father," *The Princeton University Library Chronicle,* XII (Sum-
mer 1951), 181–186.

Quotes letter.

F 67
Piper, Henry Dan. "F, Mark Twain and Thomas Hardy," *Fitzgerald Newsletter,* no. 8 (Winter 1960), 1–2.

Includes Fitzgerald's statement on Huck Finn written for the
Mark Twain Society's banquet marking the centenary of Clem-
ens's birth, 30 November 1935. See A 29, A 32. Reprinted in
Mark Twain Journal, XII (Summer 1965), front cover. Also re-
printed in *Twentieth Century Interpretations of Huckleberry
Finn*, ed. Claude M. Simpson (Englewood Cliffs, N.J.: Prentice-
Hall, [1968]). See B 72.

F 68
[Rice, Howard C., Jr.] "Americans in Paris," *The Princeton University Library Chronicle*, XVII (Summer 1956), 191–259.

Includes facsimile of revised typescript of "Babylon Revisited."

F 69
Entry cancelled.

F 70
Ring, Frances Kroll. "Footnotes on Fitzgerald," *Esquire*, LII
(December 1959), 149–150.

Includes notes, inscriptions, letters and wires.

F 71
Ring, Frances. "My Boss, Scott Fitzgerald," *Los Angeles Magazine* (January 1964), 34–36.

Includes wire.

F 72
Robbins, J. Albert. "Fitzgerald and the Simple, Inarticulate
Farmer," *Modern Fiction Studies*, VII (Winter 1961–62), 365–
369.

Quotes letter to Perkins (14 Rue de Tilsitt, Paris, c. 1 June
1925).

F 73
Samsell, R. L. "Hollywood—It Wasn't All That Bad," *Fitzgerald/
Hemingway Annual 1969*, pp. 15–19.

Includes untitled poem, "Valentine was a Saint . . ." See B 71.

F 74
Schulberg, Budd. "Old Scott: the Mask, the Myth, and the Man,"
Esquire, LV (January 1961), 96–101.

Quotes conversation and prints inscription.

F 75
Siegel, Daniel G. "T. S. Eliot's Copy of *Gatsby,*" *Fitzgerald/Hem-ingway Annual 1971*, pp. 291–293.

Includes facsimile of inscription. See B 79.

F 76
Stallings, Laurence. "The Youth in the Abyss," *Esquire*, XXXVI (October 1951), 47, 107–111.

Quotes conversations.

F 77
Stallman, R. W. "Two New Scott Fitzgerald Letters," *Modern Fiction Studies*, XI (Summer 1965), 189 191.

F 78
Stewart, Lawrence D. "Fitzgerald's Film Scripts of 'Babylon Revisited'," *Fitzgerald/Hemingway Annual 1971*, pp. 81–104.

Includes material from scripts. See B 79.

F 79
Taylor, Dwight. "Scott Fitzgerald in Hollywood," *Harper's Magazine*, CCXVIII (March 1959), 67–71.

Includes verse and quotes conversation. See B 49.

F 80
Turnbull, Andrew W. "Scott Fitzgerald at La Paix," *The New Yorker*, XXXII (7 April 1956), 92, 94–96, 99–103.

Includes letters. See B 44.

F 81
Turnbull, Andrew W. "Further Notes on Fitzgerald at La Paix," *The New Yorker*, XXXII (17 November 1956), 153–165.

Includes letters. See B 44.

F 82
[Turnbull, Andrew.] "Advice to a Young Writer," *Esquire*, L (October 1958), 158–159.

Includes three letters.

F 83
Turnbull, Andrew. "Scott Fitzgerald & Ernest Hemingway,"
Esquire, LVII (March 1962), 110–124.

Quotes letters and conversation.

F 84
Warren, Dale. "(Signed) F.S.F.," *The Princeton University
Library Chronicle,* XXV (Winter 1964), 129–136.

Quotes letters.

F 85
Wilkinson, Burke. "Scott Fitzgerald: Ten Years After," *New
York Times Book Review* (24 December 1950), 7, 10.

Quotes letter to Marya Mannes and facsimiles manuscripts.

F 86
Winston, Carl. "My Night with the Scott Fitzgeralds," *Saturday
Review,* XLVI (16 November 1963), 12, 14.

Includes letters to Winston (November 1925).

F 87
Goodwin, Donald W., "The Alcoholism of F. Scott Fitzgerald,"
Journal of the American Medical Association, CCXII (6 April
1970), 86–90.

Includes letter.

Note: This entry was added in proof and belongs alphabetically after F 37.

G. Dust-Jacket Blurbs

Blurbs (statements by Fitzgerald on dust jackets of books by other authors), arranged chronologically.

G 1
Cournos, John. *Babel.* New York: Boni & Liveright, [1922].

Statement by Fitzgerald on front or back of dust jacket. An unlocated ad for *Babel* has a fuller version of Fitzgerald's statement. See A 32.

Location: MJB.

G 2
Biggs, Mary. *Lily-Iron.* New York:McBride, 1927.

Statement by Fitzgerald on front of dust jacket. See A 32.

Location: MJB.

G 3
Gingrich, Arnold. *Cast Down the Laurel.* New York: Knopf, 1935.

Statement by Fitzgerald on back of dust jacket. See A 32.

Location: MJB.

G 4
Schulberg, Budd. *What Makes Sammy Run?.* New York: Random House, 1941

Letter to Bennett Cerf, 13 December 1940, on back of dust jacket. The letter appears on the wrappers of advance copies and on the dust jacket for early printings; however, in later printings Fitzgerald's letter was removed. See A 32.

Location: MJB (wrappers and dj).

G 5
West, Nathanael. *The Day of the Locust.* New York: New Directions, [1950]. New Classics #29.

Quote from letter to S. J. Perelman, 7 June 1939, on back of dust jacket. Reprinted in revised form in New Directions paper-book 125. See A 32.

Location: MJB (both).

*   *   *

Note

Books | FALL 1940 | DUELL, SLOAN & PEARCE, INC. | 270 MADISON AVENUE, NEW YORK

Page 6 of this catalogue has Fitzgerald's blurb for *Flight Surgeon* by Herman E. Halland and Cameron Rogers. The statement does not appear on the dust jacket.

Location: MJB.

H. Keepsakes

Keepsakes, arranged chronologically.

H 1 MARTIN'S THOUGHTS
1962

Title page: 'F. Scott Fitzgerald'

Colophon: 'Four Copies Printed At The TAUSER HEAD PRESS, 1962.'

"Martin's Thoughts." Poem. See C 314.

French fold. Printing exercise by Arlyn and Matthew J. Bruccoli, Columbus, Ohio.

Locations: MJB; ViU (proof copy).

H 2 CRAZY SUNDAY KEEPSAKE
1963

On title page: . . . *Sunday, December 8, 1963* | *may well be remembered* | *as the Sunday upon which* | *NBC's Sunday show visited* | *The Cycling Frog Press.* | *The following passage,* | *from the opening of part V* | *of Crazy Sunday, by* |*F. Scott Fitzgerald* | *is reprinted to honor* | *this occasion.* . . .'

[Pound Ridge, N.Y.: Cycling Frog Press, 1963].

Single leaf folded once to make four pages; printed by Samuel N. Antupit.

Location: MJB.

H 3 MEMORIAL DAY KEEPSAKE
1963

On title page: '. . . They watched as he got out and went over to the girl, who stood uncertainly by the gate with a wreath in her hand . . . come from Knoxville to lay | a memorial on her brother's grave. . . .'

[Pound Ridge, N.Y.: Cycling Frog Press, (1963)].

Single leaf folded once to make four pages. 'A Memorial Day memento printed at the sign of the Cycling Frog Press, Samuel N. Antupit, prop.' The passage is from the visit to the trenches in *TITN*.

Location: MBJ.

H 4 AUTHOR'S APOLOGY, PRINTED
1970

On title page: 'This Side of Paradise | 26 March 1920 | 26 March 1970'

Colophon: 'Fifty Copies Privately Printed for Friends of the *Fitzgerald/Hemingway Annual* Copy No. _____.'

Columbia, S.C.:   Matthew J. Bruccoli, 1970.

Single leaf folded once to make four pages. Facsimiles "The Author's Apology" printed in *TSOP*. See A 5.1.c, A 32, H 6.

Locations: Lilly; MJB.

H 5 CEAA KEEPSAKE
1970

On title page: '[brown] "—and | a | few | missing words would destroy so much" | [black signature] F. Scott Fitzgerald'

Colophon: '200 Copies Privately Printed For Distribution At The Conference On Editing And American Literature, Embassy Of The United States Of America, London, 1 July 1970. Copy #_____.'

Bloomfield Hills, Mich.:   M. S. Clark, 1970.

Single leaf folded twice to make six pages. Includes facsimile of first page of revised typescript for "My Generation," with Fitzgerald's holograph note to secretary.

Locations: Lilly; MJB.

II 6 AUTHOR'S APOLOGY, HOLOGRAPH
1971

On title page: '[sketch] The Authors Apology'

Colophon: 'Two hundred copies of the holograph have been printed on the occasion of the publication of F. SCOTT FITZGERALD IN HIS OWN TIME: A MISCELLANY, Matthew J. Bruccoli and Jackson R. Bryer, eds., by The Kent State University Press. . . .'

Kent, Ohio: Kent State University Press, 1971.

Single leaf, printed on both sides. Facsimile of Fitzgerald's holograph draft of "The Author's Apology" for *TSOP*. See A 5.1.c, H 4.

Location: MJB; OKentC.

I. Zelda Fitzgerald's Publications

Publications of Zelda Fitzgerald, arranged chronologically.

SAVE ME THE WALTZ

I I
First edition, only printing

SAVE ME THE WALTZ

By ZELDA FITZGERALD

NEW YORK

CHARLES SCRIBNER'S SONS
1932

I I: three lines of type decoration in blue; the rest in black;
7¼″ x 5¼″

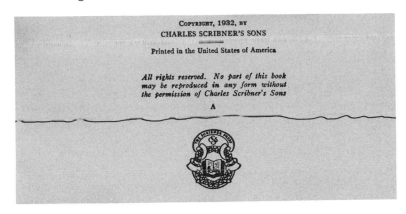

[i–viii] 1–285 [286–288]

[1–17]⁸ [18]⁴ [19]⁸

Contents: p. i: half title; p. ii: blank; p. iii: title; p. iv: copyright; p. v: 'TO | MILDRED SQUIRES'; p. vi: blank; p. vii: half title; p. viii: epigraph, 'We saw of old blue skies and summer seas | [four lines of italic type] | OEDIPUS, KING OF THEBES'; pp. 1–285: text, headed 'Chapter One | [decoration] | I'; pp. 286–288: blank.

Typography and paper: 5⅝″ (6⅛″) x 3½″; thirty-one lines per page. Running heads: rectos and versos, '[decoration] *Save Me the Waltz* [decoration]'. Wove paper.

Binding: Light green V cloth (fine linen-like grain). Front bluestamped: '[three rules broken by decoration in center] | *Save Me the Waltz* | *Zelda Fitzgerald* | [three rules broken by decoration in center].' Spine bluestamped: '[three rules broken by decoration in center] | *Save Me* | *the* | *Waltz* | [small circle] | *Fitzgerald* | [three rules broken by decoration in center] | *Scribners.*' White wove endpapers of heavier stock than text paper.

Dust jacket: Front has drawing of wraith-like dancing man and woman among flowers against pink sky, signed by 'Cleomin': '[at top in white lettering against solid black background] SAVE ME | THE WALTZ | [at bottom in white lettering against solid red background] ZELDA FITZGERALD'. Spine: '[white lettering against solid black background] SAVE ME | THE | WALTZ | [red lettering against pink background] ZELDA | FITZGERALD | [white lettering against red background] SCRIBNERS'. Back has photo of Zelda Fitzgerald. Front flap has blurb for *SMTW;* back flap has blurb and order blank for *Scribner's Magazine.*

Publication: 3,010 copies. Published 7 October 1932. $2.00.

Locations: LC; MJB (dj).

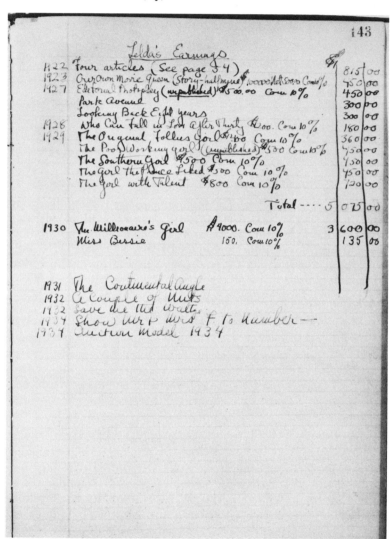

Page from Fitzgerald's Ledger

I 2
First English edition, only printing

ZELDA FITZGERALD

SAVE ME
THE WALTZ

LONDON

THE GREY WALLS PRESS

I 2: 7¼" x 4¾"

[1–8] 9–272

[A] B-I K-R⁸

Contents: p. 1: half title; p. 2: blank; p. 3: title; p. 4: copyright; p. 5: epigraph; p. 6: blank; p. 7: dedication; p. 8: blank; pp. 9–272: text, headed 'Chapter One | I.'

Typography and paper: Thirty-four lines per page. No running heads. Wove paper.

Binding: Blue V cloth (fine linen-like grain). Spine goldstamped: '[five lines in frame] Zelda | Fitzgerald | [decoration] | SAVE ME | THE WALTZ | GREY | WALLS | PRESS.' White wove endpapers.

Dust jacket: Front has drawing of artist and ballet dancer in white against pink background: '[blue script] save | me | the | waltz | [white roman] ZELDA FITZGERALD.' Spine: '[blue lettering against pink background] ZELDA | FITZ | GERALD | [white] save | me | the | waltz | [blue] GREY | WALLS | PRESS.' Back has note on F. Scott Fitzgerald and his books. Front flap has blurb for *SMTW;* back flap has advertisement for Grey Walls Press and 'Catalogue No. R. 6713'.

Publication: Unknown number of copies. Published in 1953. 10s. 6d.

Locations: Bodleian (deposited 2 April 1953); MJB (dj).

I 3
Third edition, American printing

Zelda Fitzgerald | SAVE ME | THE WALTZ | [three fleurons] | SOUTHERN ILLINOIS UNIVERSITY PRESS | CARBONDALE AND EDWARDSVILLE | FEFFER & SIMONS, INC. | LONDON AND AMSTERDAM

1967. Preface by Harry T. Moore and textual note by Matthew J. Bruccoli. Crosscurrents/Modern Fiction series (clothbound), published April 1967 (2,868 copies). Second printing December 1967 (1,979 copies). Also published in Arcturus series (paperbound) in April 1967 (4,838 copies). Second printing November 1967 (4,970 copies).

I 4
Third edition, English printing

ZELDA FITZGERALD | *Save Me the Waltz* | *Preface by* HARRY T. MOORE | *A Note on the Text by* | MATTHEW J. BRUCCOLI | [Cape seal] | JONATHAN CAPE | THIRTY BEDFORD SQUARE | LONDON

1968.

I 5
Fourth edition

[wavy line] | *Zelda Fitzgerald* | SAVE | ME | THE | WALTZ | [wavy line] | With a Preface by | HARRY T. MOORE | and an Afterword by | MATTHEW J. BRUCCOLI | [Signet seal] | A SIGNET BOOK | Published by The New American Library

1968. #Q3485.

On copyright page: 'FIRST PRINTING, JUNE, 1968'. Three printings between 1968 and 1971.

I 6
Fifth edition

Zelda Fitzgerald | Save Me the Waltz | Penguin Books

Harmondsworth, Middlesex, 1971. #140032592.

Preface by Harry T. Moore and textual note by Matthew J. Bruccoli.

MATERIAL IN BOOKS AND MAGAZINES

I 7
"The Super-Flapper," sold in 1922 (Ledger, p. 54), but apparently unpublished.

I 8
"Friend Husband's Latest," *New York Tribune* (2 April 1922), magazine section, 11.

Review of *B&D*.

I 9
"Eulogy on the Flapper," *Metropolitan Magazine*, LV (June 1922), 38–39.

Article.

I 10
"Does a Moment of Revolt Come Sometime to Every Married Man?" *McCall's*, LI (March 1924), 82.

Article accompanied by Fitzgerald article. See C 135.

I 11
Stratton, Florence, ed. *Favorite Recipes of Famous Women.* New York and London: Harper & Brothers, 1925.

"Breakfast," p. 98. Humorous recipe.

I 12
"Our Own Movie Queen," *Chicago Sunday Tribune* (7 June 1925), magazine section, 1–4.

Fiction. Partly by Fitzgerald (Ledger, p. 143, notes "half mine"). Published under his name only. See C 152.

I 13
"What Became of Our Flappers and Sheiks?" *McCall's*, LIII (October 1925), 12, 30, 42, 66, 69.

Article accompanied by Fitzgerald article. See C 156.

I 14
"The Changing Beauty of Park Avenue," *Harper's Bazar*, LXII (January 1928), 61–63.

Article. By-lined "Zelda and F. Scott Fitzgerald," but credited to Zelda in Ledger (p. 143). See C 170.

I 15
"Looking Back Eight Years," *College Humor*, XIV (June 1928), 36–37.

Article. By-lined "F. Scott and Zelda Fitzgerald," but credited to Zelda in Ledger (p. 143). See C 175.

I 16
"Who Can Fall in Love After Thirty?" *College Humor*, XV (October 1928), 9, 92.

Article. By-lined "F. Scott and Zelda Fitzgerald," but credited to Zelda in Ledger (p. 143). See C 179.

I 17
"Editorial on Youth," written for *Photoplay* in 1927. Published as "Paint and Powder," *The Smart Set*, LXXXIV (May 1929), 68.

Article. By-lined "F. Scott Fitzgerald" only, but credited to Zelda in Ledger (p. 143). See C 187.

I 18
"The Original Follies Girl," *College Humor*, XVII (July 1929), 40–41, 110.

Fiction. By-lined "Zelda and F. Scott Fitzgerald," but credited to Zelda in Ledger (p. 143). See C 191.

I 19
"Southern Girl," *College Humor*, XVIII (October 1929), 27–28, 94, 96.

Fiction. By-lined "F. Scott and Zelda Fitzgerald," but credited to Zelda in Ledger (p. 143). See C 194.

I 20
"The Girl the Prince Liked," *College Humor*, no. 74 (February 1930), 46–48, 121–122.

Fiction. By-lined "F. Scott and Zelda Fitzgerald," but credited to Zelda in Ledger (p. 143). See C 197.

I 21
"The Girl with Talent," *College Humor*, no. 76 (April 1930), 50–52, 125–127.

Fiction. By-lined "F. Scott and Zelda Fitzgerald," but credited to Zelda in Ledger (p. 143). See C 201.

I 22
"A Millionaire's Girl," *The Saturday Evening Post,* CCII (17 May 1930), 8–9, 118, 121.

Fiction. By-lined "F. Scott Fitzgerald" only, but credited to Zelda in Ledger (p. 143). See B 39, C 204.

I 23
"Poor Working Girl," *College Humor,* no. 85 (January 1931), 72–73, 122.

Fiction. By-lined "F. Scott and Zelda Fitzgerald," but credited to Zelda in Ledger (p. 143). See C 210.

I 24
"Miss Ella," *Scribner's Magazine,* XC (December 1931), 661–665.

Fiction. Originally titled "Miss Bessie."

I 25
"The Continental Angle," *The New Yorker,* VIII (4 June 1932), 25.

Article.

I 26
"A Couple of Nuts," *Scribner's Magazine,* XCII (August 1932), 80–84.

Fiction.

I 27
" 'Show Mr. and Mrs. F. to Number ———,' " *Esquire,* I–II (May and June 1934), 19, 154B; 23, 120.

Autobiographical article. By-lined "F. Scott and Zelda Fitzgerald," but credited to Zelda in Ledger (p. 143). In *CU.* See C 236.

I 28
"Auction—Model 1934," *Esquire,* II (July 1934), 20, 153, 155.

Autobiographical article. By-lined "F. Scott and Zelda Fitzgerald," but credited to Zelda in Ledger (p. 143). In *CU*. Occ C 239.

I 29
Colum, Padraic, and Cabell, Margaret Freeman, eds. *Between Friends*. New York: Harcourt, Brace & World, [1962].

Quotes from letters and papers. See B 54.

I 30
Milford, Nancy. *Zelda*. New York, Evanston, and London: Harper & Row, [1970].

Quotes from letters and papers. See B 75.

I 31
Mayfield, Sara. *Exiles from Paradise*. New York: Delacorte [1971].

Quotes from letters and papers. See B 78.

* * *

Note

Zelda Fitzgerald's play, *Scandalabra*, was performed by the Junior Vagabonds, Baltimore, 26 June–1 July 1933. Unpublished.

Appendices / Index

Appendix 1

English-Language Editions of Story Collections Published in Japan

This appendix is restricted to books made up entirely of stories by Fitzgerald; contributions to anthologies have been omitted.

1.1
[gothic] Kenkyusha Pocket English Series | [rule] | BABYLON REVISITED | AND | WINTER DREAMS | BY | F. SCOTT FITZGERALD | *Introduction & Notes by* | IKUO UEMURA | [seal] | TOKYO | KENKYUSHA

1955.

1.2
[gothic] Nan'un-do's Modern Readings | [rule] | F. SCOTT FITZGERALD | THE CRACK-UP | *Hitoshi Miyata* | NAN'UN-DO | TOKYO

1958.

"Sleeping and Waking," "The Crack-Up," "Handle With Care," "Pasting It Together."

1.3
[gothic] Nan'un-do's Contemporary Library | [rule] | F. SCOTT FITZGERALD | MAY DAY | *Edited with Notes* | *by* | Toshisaburō Koyama | Ken-ichi Haya | [seal] | TOKYO | NAN'UN-DO

1958. Reprinted 1959.

1.4
[gothic] Nan'un-do's Modern Readings | [rule] | F. S. FITZGERALD | BABYLON REVISITED | Notes by | *Yoshitaka Sakai* | NAN'UN-DO | TOKYO

1959. Reprinted 1960.

313

1.5
TWO SHORT STORIES | OF | F. S. FITZGERALD | *EDITED
WITH NOTES* | BY | MITSUO YOSHIDA | [seal] SHOHAKUSHA
| TOKYO

1960.

"The Last of the Belles" and "The Rich Boy."

1.6
TODAY LIBRARY 56 | [rule] | F. Scott Fitzgerald | A NIGHT
AT THE FAIR | AND | FORGING AHEAD | WITH INTRODUC-
TION AND NOTES | by YOSHIHIDE UEKI | YAMAGUCHI
SHOTEN

1961.

1.7
THE BABY PARTY & | GRETCHEN'S FORTY WINKS | BY |
F. SCOTT FITZGERALD | EDITED WITH NOTES BY | HIRO-
SHI YAMAMOTO | [seal] | GAKUSEISHA | ATOM MODERN
SERIES | BY READY VOCABULARY METHOD

1962.

1.8
TODAY LIBRARY 58 | [rule] | F. Scott Fitzgerald | THE DIA-
MOND | AS BIG AS THE RITZ | WITH INTRODUCTION AND
NOTES | by TOSHISABURO KOYAMA | YAMAGUCHI SHOTEN

1962.

1.9
[gothic] Kenkyusha Pocket English Series | [rule] | THREE
"BASIL" STORIES | BY | F. SCOTT FITZGERALD | *Annotated,
with an Introduction, by* | AKIO ATSUMI |[seal] | TOKYO |
KENKYUSHA

1964.

"The Scandal Detectives," "The Freshest Boy," and "The Captured Shadow."

1.10
FRANCIS SCOTT FITZGERALD | [tapered rule] | THE SHORT
STORIES OF | F. SCOTT FITZGERALD | *Edited with Notes* |
by | TAMOTSU NISHIYAMA | YASUTAKA AWA | [seal] |
EICHOSHA'S NEW CURRENT BOOKS

1968

" 'The Sensible Thing' " and "The Rough Crossing."

1.11
FRANCIS SCOTT FITZGERALD | [tapered rule] | THE ICE
PALACE | AND | MAGNETISM | *Edited with Notes* | *by* |
SHUICHI MOTODA | AKIRA KATAOKA | [seal] | EICHOSHA'S
NEW CURRENT BOOKS

1968.

1.12
F. SCOTT FITZGERALD | THE ICE PALACE | AND | ABSOLU-
TION | *Edited with Notes* | *by* | M. KASHAHARA | T. TASAKA |
KŌBUNSHA

1969.

Appendix 2

Unlocated Clippings

These clippings from newspapers and magazines were preserved by F. Scott Fitzgerald in his scrapbooks.

2.1
"American Writer Finds a Home in Rome."

Based on interview with Fitzgerald. Datelined Rome. Winter 1924–25.

2.2
Untitled clipping, beginning "And whom did we see in New York? Well, there was F. Scott Fitzgerald, for one. . . ."

Based on interview with Fitzgerald.

2.3
"Author Asks Author How to Write Story."

Includes Fitzgerald's letter to Robert L. Terry. Probably in Atlanta, Ga., paper.

2.4
"The Author of *This Side of Paradise* reviews a new novel for us. . . ."

Fitzgerald's comment on Cummings's *The Enormous Room*. Possibly from a Boni & Liveright dust jacket.

2.5
"Fitzgerald and Flappers."

Interview with Fitzgerald.

2.6
"Fitzgerald Finds He Has Outgrown Jazz Age Novel."

Interview with Fitzgerald, c. 1929 (?).

2.7
Fulton, "Bart." "Fitzgerald, Flapperdom's Fiction Ace, Qualifies as Most Brilliant Author, But Needs Press Agent, Says Scribe."

Interview with Fitzgerald in Montgomery, Ala.

2.8
Babcock, Muriel. "Flaming Youth Called Feeble."

Based on interview with Fitzgerald in Los Angeles. Reprinted in A 32.

2.9
Rennels, Mary. "Frankness Often Wins A Husband!"

Quotes Fitzgerald conversation. Possibly in Cleveland paper.

2.10
"F. Scott Fitzgerald Is Hunting Trouble."

Quotes Fitzgerald. Probably in Baltimore, Md., paper, c. 1931.

2.11
" 'Gatsby's' Author Boasts His Child, Not His Novel."

Based on interview. Possibly in *New York Herald*, 1925.

2.12
"His Fame Arrived Early."

Quotes Fitzgerald, 1920.

2.13
"Horace B. Liveright, Gelett Burgess, F. Scott Fitzgerald And Others of Authors' League Fellowship Help Along 'Friendly Discourse'."

Quotes Fitzgerald.

2.14
"In Literary New York."

Letter to Bernard. (Fall-Winter 1923). See A 32.

2.15
"Painted St. Paul's Name on Literary Signboard."

Based on interview with Fitzgerald.

2.*16*
"Popular Writer Leaves For Pau."

Quotes Fitzgerald. Possibly in *Paris Herald* or *Paris Tribune*, c. January 1926.

2.*17*
"Ruggiero Auto and Cycle Co. Donate this space to the Girl Scouts this week . . ."

Includes tribute by Fitzgerald. In *Fitzgerald/Hemingway Annual 1971*.

2.*18*
Millen, Gilmore. "Scott Fitzgerald Lays Success to Reading."

Interview, Los Angeles, c. 1927.

2.*19*
"There Are Super-Flappers in Addition to Flippant Ones, St. Paul Author Opines."

Quotes Fitzgerald's statements at St. Paul Women's City Club. Probably in St. Paul, Minn., paper, December 1921.

2.20
"The Virtue of Persistence."

Based on interview with Fitzgerald.

2.2*1*
Fulton, Bart. "Was This Author Merely Teasing at Woman's College or Did He Forget?"

Quotes Fitzgerald. Probably in Montgomery, Ala., paper.

2.22
Untitled clipping.

Interview with Fitzgerald about movie version of *TSOP*, "Grit," and *VEG*.

2.23
Untitled clipping.

Interview with Fitzgerald and Cornelius Vanderbilt, Jr., about beauty contest. See note following C 183.

Appendix 3

Published Plays Based on Stories

3.1
The Young and Beautiful | A PLAY IN THREE ACTS | *by Sally
Benson* | Based on *The Saturday Evening Post* "Josephine" |
short stories by F. Scott Fitzgerald. | [device] | SAMUEL
FRENCH, Inc. | 25 West 45th Street NEW YORK 36 |
7623 Sunset Boulevard HOLLYWOOD 46 | *LONDON TO-
RONTO*

1956.

The play opened at the Longacre Theatre in New York, 1 October 1955.

3.2
Three Hours Between | *Planes* | A PLAY IN ONE ACT | *by
Elihu Winer* | Based on the short story | *by F. Scott Fitzgerald* |
[device] | SAMUEL FRENCH, INC. | 25 West 45th Street
NEW YORK 36 | 7623 Sunset Boulevard HOLLYWOOD 46 |
LONDON TORONTO

1958.

Appendix 4

Unpublished Plays Produced in St. Paul, Minn.

None of the acting scripts for these plays has been located.

4.1
The Girl from Lazy J, August 1911.

4.2
The Captured Shadow, August 1912.

4.3
"*The Coward*," 29 August 1913.

4.4
Assorted Spirits, August 1914.

4.5
Fitzgerald worked on *Midnight Flappers*, produced by the St. Paul Junior Frolic, 17 April 1922.

Appendix 5

Mimeographed Film Scripts

This list includes only those film scripts seen by the compiler.

5.1
"The Red-Headed Woman." MGM. Dialogue continuity by Bess Meredyth and C. Gardner Sullivan. Version with cuts and amendments by F. Scott Fitzgerald. 3 December 1931.†

5.2
"A Yank at Oxford," Notes. MGM. 13 July 1937.*

"A Yank at Oxford," Outline with Dialogue (Corrected Version). MGM. 19 July 1937.*

"A Yank at Oxford" (by Commander Frank Wead and F. Scott Fitzgerald). MGM. 26 July 1937.*

5.3
"Three Comrades." MGM. 1 September 1937.*

"Three Comrades" (by F. Scott Fitzgerald and E. E. Paramore). MGM. 5 November 1937.*

"Three Comrades" (by F. Scott Fitzgerald and E. E. Paramore). MGM. 7 December 1937.*

"Three Comrades," Fitzgerald-Paramore First Revise. MGM. 13 December 1937.*

"Three Comrades" (by F. Scott Fitzgerald and E. E. Paramore), 2nd Revised. MGM. 21 December 1937.*

"Three Comrades" (by F. Scott Fitzgerald and E. E. Paramore), 3rd Revised. MGM. 21 January 1938.*

---

† Fitzgerald Papers, Princeton University Library, Princeton, N.J.
* MGM archives, Culver City, Calif.

"Three Comrades" (by F. Scott Fitzgerald and E. E. Paramore—Script okayed by Joseph Mankiewicz). MGM. 1 February 1938.*

5.4
"Infidelity," Miscellaneous Notes. MGM. 3 February–3 May 1938.*

"Infidelity," Theme and Characters. MGM. 23 February 1938.*

"Infidelity." MGM. 7–8 March 1938.*

"Infidelity." MGM. 9 March 1938.*

"Infidelity," Script to page 75 with servant situation changed. MGM. 23 April 1938.*

"Infidelity," First Revision. MGM. 26 April 1938.*

"Infidelity," New Treatment for the End. MGM. 10 May 1938.*

5.5
"The Women," Complete Outline. MGM. 31 May 1938.*

"The Women," Complete Outline. MGM. 3 June 1938.*

"The Women," General Outline & Breakdown. MGM. 6 June 1938.*

"The Women," Addenda to Outline. MGM. 9 June 1938.*

The Women. MGM. 9 July 1938.*

"The Women," Temporary Incomplete (85 pages). MGM. 15 August 1938.*

The Women, First Revise—Temporary Incomplete (84 pages). MGM. 15 August 1938.*

"The Women" (by Donald Ogden Stewart and F. Scott Fitzgerald). MGM. 20 September 1938.*

5.6
"Madame Curie," Sequence Outlines. MGM. 21 November 1938.*

"Madame Curie" (Incomplete Scripts—66 pp.). MGM. 28 November 1938.*

"Madame Curie." MGM. 17 December 1938.*

"Madame Curie," First Revise. MGM. 27 December 1938.*

"Madame Curie," Second Revise. MGM. 3 January 1939.*

5.7
"Honoria," A Screenplay by F. Scott Fitzgerald. 29 May 1940.
Lester Cowan.†

"Babylon Revisited," A Screenplay by F. Scott Fitzgerald. Revised 30 July 1940. Lester Cowan.†

"Cosmopolitan," A screenplay by F. Scott Fitzgerald. Second
draft revised. 12–13 August 1940. Lester Cowan.†

"Babylon Revisited." 1940. Lester Cowan.†

5.8
The Light of Heart. 20th Century-Fox. 11 October 1940.†

Appendix 6

Movie-Writing Assignments

6.1

Titles for *Glimpses of the Moon* (adapted by L. Sheldon). Famous Players, 1923.

6.2

Grit (screenplay credited to Fitzgerald). Film Guild, 1924.

6.3

"Lipstick" (unproduced). United Artists, 1927.

6.4

Red-Headed Woman. MGM, 3 December 1931.

6.5

A Yank at Oxford. MGM, 7 July–26 July 1937[1] (three weeks).

6.6

Three Comrades. MGM, 4 August, 1 September, 1 December 1937–1 February 1938 (six months).

6.7

"Infidelity" (unproduced). MGM, 3 February, 9 and 19 March 1938 (four months).

6.8

Marie Antoinette. MGM (Hunt Stromberg), 16 May 1938.

6.9

The Women (with Donald Ogden Stewart). MGM, 27 May–8 October 1938 (six months).

---

1. These dates are taken from scripts in the MGM archives, Culver City, Calif., or the Fitzgerald Papers at Princeton University Library, Princeton, N.J.

6.10
Madame Curie. MGM, 7 November 1938–3 January 1939 (three months).

6.11
Gone With the Wind. David O. Selznick (on loan from MGM), 11–24 January 1939.

6.12
Winter Carnival. United Artists (Walter Wanger), 1–11 February 1939.

6.13
"Air Raid" (with Donald Ogden Stewart). Paramount, 14–31 March 1939 (one month).

6.14
"Open That Door" (based on the novel *Bull by the Horns*). Universal, 16–22 August 1939 (one week).

6.15
Everything Happens at Night. 20th Century-Fox, September 1939 (one day).

6.16
Raffles. Goldwyn, 6–12 September 1939 (one week).

6.17
"Cosmopolitan" ("Babylon Revisited"). Columbia (Lester Cowan), March–August 1940.

6.18
"Brooklyn Bridge" (unproduced; what Fitzgerald did on this script is not known). 20th Century-Fox, 12 August 1940.

6.19
Emlyn William's play *The Light of Heart* (produced as *Life Begins at Eight-Thirty* by Nunnally Johnson, 1942). 20th Century-Fox, 11 October 1940.

Appendix 7

Movies Made from Fitzgerald's Work

7.1
"Head and Shoulders" (retitled *The Chorus Girl's Romance*).
Metro, 1920. Scenario by Percy Heath; directed by William C.
Dowlan.

7.2
"Myra Meets his Family" (retitled *The Husband Hunter*). Fox,
1920. Directed by Howard M. Mitchell.

7.3
"The Offshore Pirate." Metro, 1921. Directed by Dallas M. Fitzgerald.

7.4
The Beautiful and Damned. Warner Brothers, 1922. Adapted by
Olga Printzlau; directed by William Seiter.

7.5
Grit (from an original story by Fitzgerald). Film Guild, 1924.
Directed by Frank Tuttle.

7.6
The Great Gatsby (from the Owen Davis play). Famous Players,
1926. Script by Becky Gardiner; adaptation by Elizabeth Me-
chan; directed by Herbert Brenon.

7.7
"The Pusher-in-the Face." Paramount-Famous-Lasky, 1929.

7.8
The Great Gatsby. Paramount, 1949. Screenplay by Cyril Hume
and Richard Maibaum; directed by Elliott Nugent.

7.9
"Babylon Revisited" (retitled *The Last Time I Saw Paris*). MGM,
1954. Screenplay by Philip G. Epstein, Julius J. Epstein, and
Richard Brooks; directed by Richard Brooks.

7.10
Tender is the Night. 20th Century-Fox, 1962. Screenplay by
Ivan Moffat; directed by Henry King.

* * *

Note 1
Fitzgerald's Ledger lists for "The Camel's Back": 'Sold to Warner
Bros. "Conductor 1492" '. No trace of this movie has been found.

Note 2
This Side of Paradise was sold to Famous Players in 1923 but
was not made.

Appendix 8

Publications in Braille

8.1
Babylon Revisited and Other Stories. 6 vols. 1965(?) Transcribed by the Red Cross. Distributed by the Division for the Blind and Physically Handicapped, Library of Congress, Washington, D.C.

8.2
Babylon Revisited and Other Stories. 6 vols. 1967. Hand-copied by Sylvia Woll for Westside Transcribers for the Blind, West Los Angeles, Calif. Distributed by the Student Braille Library of the Foundation for the Blind, Los Angeles, Calif.

8.3
The Beautiful and Damned. 8 vols. 1965. Hand-copied by Mrs. James Pennington. Distributed by the Iowa Commission for the Blind, Des Moines, Iowa, and by the Division for the Blind and Physically Handicapped, Library of Congress, Washington, D.C.

8.4
Flappers and Philosophers. 4 vols. 1962. Transcribed by the Red Cross. Distributed by the Division for the Blind and Physically Handicapped, Library of Congress, Washington, D.C.

8.5
The Great Gatsby. 2 vols. 1966. Printed by the American Printing House for the Blind, Louisville, Ky. Distributed by the Braille Institute Library, Los Angeles, Calif.

8.6
The Pat Hobby Stories. 3 vols. 1969. Hand-copied by Edith Penman for the Sisterhood Central Synagogue, Rockville Centre, N.Y. Distributed by the Jewish Guild for the Blind, New York, N.Y.

8.7
The Stories of F. Scott Fitzgerald. 14 vols. 1965. Transcribed by the Iowa Commission for the Blind. Distributed by the Division

for the Blind and Physically Handicapped, Library of Congress, Washington, D.C.

8.8
Tender is the Night. 7 vols. 1961. Transcribed by the New York Sisters. Distributed by the Division for the Blind and Physically Handicapped, Library of Congress, Washington, D.C.

Appendix 9

Contracts

An author's contracts are a crucial part of the record of his career. Professional writers write for money, and F. Scott Fitzgerald was a professional. Indeed, it is impossible to understand Fitzgerald's career without realizing that he could not live on his book royalties.[1] His books—with the exception of *This Side of Paradise*—did not sell well; and for this title the 49,075 copies sold in 1920–1921 brought the author $12,445. Even a thrifty man would have been hard put to live on Fitzgerald's book royalties. At thirty cents per copy, the income from the 23,870 copies of *The Great Gatsby* printed in 1925 would have been $7,161.

Contracts for all of the books F. Scott Fitzgerald published during his lifetime survive: those for *Flappers and Philosophers* at the Princeton University Library and others in Fitzgerald's scrapbooks. The contract for *F&P* (11 May 1920) stipulates a straight 15 percent royalty on the retail price, with $500 advance. The contracts for the three other story collections (*Tales of the Jazz Age*—12 April 1922; *All the Sad Young Men*—27 July 1925; *Taps at Reveille*—12 June 1934), as well as the contract for *The Vegetable* (21 March 1923), have the same escalated royalty: 15 percent of list price on the first 20,000 copies, 17½ percent on the next 20,000, and 20 percent over 40,000. In point of fact, the escalator provision was meaningless for these volumes because none reached 20,000 copies.

The most interesting stipulation in the contracts is the advance of $6,600 for *Tender is the Night*, the largest advance Fitzgerald received. The finances for this novel are complicated, and certain parts are still obscure; but it is clear that part of the $6,600 had been already loaned to Fitzgerald by Scribners and that the balance was a true advance to support Fitzgerald while the book was in press.[2]

---

1. For Fitzgerald's own year-by-year accounts of his earnings, see "Fitzgerald's Ledger," *Fitzgerald/Hemingway Annual 1971*, pp. 3–31. The economics of Fitzgerald's career are greatly misunderstood. He did not earn a fortune: before going to Hollywood, he never earned as much as $40,000 in one year.

2. See Matthew J. Bruccoli and Jennifer Atkinson, eds., *As Ever, Scott Fitz—* (Philadelphia and New York: Lippincott, 1972), pp. 239–240.

Memorandum of Agreement, *made this* **twenty-third** *Day of* **September** *19* **19**

between **F. SCOTT FITZGERALD**

of **St. Louis, Missouri,** — — — — *hereinafter called "the* AUTHOR,*"* and CHARLES SCRIBNER'S SONS, *of New York City, N. Y., hereinafter called "the* PUBLISHERS.*" Said* — — **F. Scott Fitzgerald** — — — *being the* AUTHOR *and* PROPRIETOR *of a work entitled :*

——————— **THIS SIDE OF PARADISE** ———————

in consideration of the covenants and stipulations hereinafter contained, and agreed to be performed by the PUBLISHERS, *grants and guarantees to said* PUBLISHERS *and their successors the exclusive right to publish the said work in all forms during the terms of copyright and renewals thereof, hereby covenanting with said* PUBLISHERS *that he is the sole* AUTHOR *and* PROPRIETOR *of said work.*

Said AUTHOR *hereby authorizes said* PUBLISHERS *to take out the copyright on said work, and further guarantees to said* PUBLISHERS *that the said work is in no way whatever a violation of any copyright belonging to any other party, and that it contains nothing of a scandalous or libelous character ; and that he and* **his** *legal representatives shall and will hold harmless the said* PUBLISHERS *from all suits, and all manner of claims and proceedings which may be taken on the ground that said work is such violation or contains anything scandalous or libelous ; and he further hereby authorizes said* PUBLISHERS *to defend at law any and all suits and proceedings which may be taken or had against them for infringement of any other copyright or for libel, scandal, or any other injurious or hurtful matter or thing contained in or alleged or claimed to be contained in or caused by said work, and pay to said* PUBLISHERS *such reasonable costs, disbursements, expenses, and counsel fees as they may incur in such defense.*

Said PUBLISHERS, *in consideration of the right herein granted and of the guarantees aforesaid, agree to publish said work at their own expense, in such style and manner as they shall deem most expedient, and to pay said* AUTHOR, *or* — **his** — *legal representatives,* **TEN (10)** ——————— *per cent. on their Trade-List (retail) price, cloth style, for* **the first five thousand (5000) copies of said work sold by them in the United States and FIFTEEN (15) per cent. for all copies sold thereafter in the United States.** *Provided, nevertheless, that one-half the above named royalty shall be paid on all copies sold outside the United States ; and provided that no percentage whatever shall be paid on any copies destroyed by fire or water, or sold at or below cost, or given away for the purpose of aiding the sale of said work.*

It is further agreed that the profits arising from any publication of said work, during the period covered by this agreement, in other than book form shall be divided equally between said PUBLISHERS *and said* AUTHOR.

Page 1 of contract for *TSOP*

Expenses incurred for alterations in type or plates, exceeding twenty per cent. of the cost of composition and electrotyping said work, are to be charged to the AUTHOR's *account.*

The first statement shall not be rendered until six months after date of publication; and thereafter statements shall be rendered semi-annually, on the AUTHOR's *application therefor, in the months of February and August; settlements to be made in cash, four months after date of statement.*

If, on the expiration of **five** *years from date of publication, or at any time thereafter, the demand for said work should not, in the opinion of said* PUBLISHERS, *be sufficient to render its publication profitable, then, upon written notice by said* PUBLISHERS *to said* AUTHOR, *this contract shall cease and determine; and thereupon said* AUTHOR *shall have the right, at* **his** *option, to take from said* PUBLISHERS, *at cost, whatever copies of said work they may then have on hand; or, failing to take said copies at cost, then said* PUBLISHERS *shall have the right to dispose of the copies on hand as they may see fit, free from any percentage or royalty, and to cancel this contract.*

Provided, also, that if, at any time during the continuance of this agreement, said work shall become unsalable in the ordinary channels of trade, said PUBLISHERS, *shall have the right to dispose of any copies on hand, paying to said* AUTHOR — **fifteen (15)** — *per cent. of the net amount received therefrom, in lieu of the percentage hereinbefore prescribed.*

In consideration of the mutuality of this contract, the aforesaid parties agree to all its provisions, and in testimony thereof affix their signatures and seals.

Witness to signature of
   F. Scott Fitzgerald

Witness to signature of
   Charles Scribner's Sons

Page 2 of contract for *TSOP*

Memorandum of Agreement, *made this* **second** *Day of* **May** *19* **21**

between **F. SCOTT FITZGERALD** _____

of **St. Louis, Missouri,** – – – – *hereinafter called the* "AUTHOR," *and* CHARLES SCRIBNER'S SONS, ~~INCORPORATED~~, *of New York City, N. Y., hereinafter called "the* PUBLISHERS." *Said* – **F. Scott Fitzgerald** – – *being the* AUTHOR *and* PROPRIETOR *of a work entitled:*

_____ **THE BEAUTIFUL AND DAMNED** _____

in consideration of the covenants and stipulations hereinafter contained, and agreed to be performed by the PUBLISHERS, *grants and guarantees to said* PUBLISHERS *and their successors the exclusive right to publish the said work in all forms during the terms of copyright and renewals thereof, hereby covenanting with said* PUBLISHERS *that he is the sole* AUTHOR *and* PROPRIETOR *of said work.*

Said AUTHOR *hereby authorizes said* PUBLISHERS *to take out the copyright on said work, and further guarantees to said* PUBLISHERS *that the said work is in no way whatever a violation of any copyright belonging to any other party, and that it contains nothing of a scandalous or libelous character; and that he and* **his** *legal representatives shall and will hold harmless the said* PUBLISHERS *from all suits, and all manner of claims and proceedings which may be taken on the ground that said work is such violation or contains anything scandalous or libelous; and he further hereby authorizes said* PUBLISHERS *to defend at law any and all suits and proceedings which may be taken or had against them for infringement of any other copyright or for libel, scandal, or any other injurious or hurtful matter or thing contained in or alleged or claimed to be contained in or caused by said work, and pay to said* PUBLISHERS *such reasonable costs, disbursements, expenses, and counsel fees as they may incur in such defense.*

Said PUBLISHERS, *in consideration of the right herein granted and of the guarantees aforesaid, agree to publish said work at their own expense, in such style and manner as they shall deem most expedient, and to pay said* AUTHOR, *or* – **his** – *legal representatives,* **FIFTEEN (15)** –––––––––––*per cent. on their Trade-List (retail) price, cloth style, for all copies of said work sold by them* ~~after the sale of~~ _____ ~~copies in the United States.~~ *Provided, nevertheless, that one-half the above named royalty shall be paid on all copies sold outside the United States; and provided that no percentage whatever shall be paid on any copies destroyed by fire or water, or sold at or below cost, or given away for the purpose of aiding the sale of said work.*

It is further agreed that the profits arising from any publication of said work, during the period covered by this agreement, in other than book form shall be divided equally between said PUBLISHERS *and said* AUTHOR.

Page 1 of contract for *B&D*

Expenses incurred for alterations in type or plates, exceeding twenty per cent. of the cost of composition and electrotyping said work, are to be charged to the AUTHOR's account.

The first statement shall not be rendered until six months after date of publication; and thereafter statements shall be rendered semi-annually, on the AUTHOR's application therefor, in the months of February and August; settlements to be made in cash, four months after date of statement.

If, on the expiration of **five** *years from date of publication, or at any time thereafter, the demand for said work should not, in the opinion of said PUBLISHERS, be sufficient to render its publication profitable, then, upon written notice by said PUBLISHERS to said AUTHOR, this contract shall cease and determine; and thereupon said AUTHOR shall have the right, at* **his** *option, to take from said PUBLISHERS, at cost, whatever copies of said work they may then have on hand; or, failing to take said copies at cost, then said PUBLISHERS shall have the right to dispose of the copies on hand as they may see fit, free from any percentage or royalty, and to cancel this contract.*

Provided, also, that if, at any time during the continuance of this agreement, said work shall become unsalable in the ordinary channels of trade, said PUBLISHERS shall have the right to dispose of any copies on hand, paying to said AUTHOR **– fifteen (15) –** *per cent. of the net amount received therefor, in lieu of the percentage hereinbefore prescribed.*

In consideration of the mutuality of this contract, the aforesaid parties agree to all its provisions, and in testimony thereof affix their signatures and seals.

Witness to signature of
Charles Scribner's Sons

[signature]

{ L. S. }

[signature]

Witness to signature of
F. Scott Fitzgerald

[signature]

[signature: F. Scott Fitzgerald]   *[seal]*

Page 2 of contract for *B&D*

Memorandum of Agreement, *made this* **twenty-second** *day of* **December** 19**24**

between **F. SCOTT FITZGERALD**

of   *hereinafter called "the* AUTHOR,*"*

and CHARLES SCRIBNER'S SONS, *of New York City, N. Y., hereinafter called "the*
PUBLISHERS." *Said* – – **F. Scott Fitzgerald** – – *being the* AUTHOR
and PROPRIETOR *of a work entitled:*

THE GREAT GATSBY

*in consideration of the covenants and stipulations hereinafter contained, and agreed to be per-
formed by the* PUBLISHERS, *grants and guarantees to said* PUBLISHERS *and their successors the
exclusive right to publish the said work in all forms during the terms of copyright and renewals
thereof, hereby covenanting with said* PUBLISHERS *that he is the sole* AUTHOR *and*
PROPRIETOR *of said work.*

Said AUTHOR *hereby authorizes said* PUBLISHERS *to take out the copyright on said
work, and further guarantees to said* PUBLISHERS *that the said work is in no way whatever a
violation of any copyright belonging to any other party, and that it contains nothing of a scandalous or libelous character; and that he and* **his** *legal representatives shall and will hold
harmless the said* PUBLISHERS *from all suits, and all manner of claims and proceedings which
may be taken on the ground that said work is such violation or contains anything scandalous or
libelous; and he further hereby authorizes said* PUBLISHERS *to defend at law any and all
suits and proceedings which may be taken or had against them for infringement of any other copyright or for libel, scandal, or any other injurious or hurtful matter or thing contained in or
alleged or claimed to be contained in or caused by said work, and pay to said* PUBLISHERS *such
reasonable costs, disbursements, expenses, and counsel fees as they may incur in such defense.*

Said PUBLISHERS, *in consideration of the right herein granted and of the guarantees
aforesaid, agree to publish said work at their own expense, in such style and manner as they
shall deem most expedient, and to pay said* AUTHOR, *or* – **his** – *legal representatives,*
FIFTEEN (15) —————————— *per cent. on their Trade-List (retail) price, cloth style, for*
**the first forty thousand (40,000) copies of said work sold by them in the United
States and TWENTY (20) per cent. for all copies sold thereafter.** ————
*Provided, nevertheless, that one-half the above named royalty shall be paid on all copies sold out-
side the United States; and provided that no percentage whatever shall be paid on any copies
destroyed by fire or water, or sold at or below cost, or given away for the purpose of aiding the
sale of said work.*

*It is further agreed that the profits arising from any publication of said work, during
the period covered by this agreement, in other than book form shall be divided equally between
said* PUBLISHERS *and said* AUTHOR.

Page 1 of contract for *GG*

Expenses incurred for alterations in type or plates, exceeding twenty per cent. of the cost of composition and electrotyping said work, are to be charged to the AUTHOR'S account.

The first statement shall not be rendered until six months after date of publication; and thereafter statements shall be rendered semi-annually, on the AUTHOR'S application therefor, in the months of February and August; settlements to be made in cash, four months after date of statement.

If, on the expiration of **five** *years from date of publication, or at any time thereafter, the demand for said work should not, in the opinion of said PUBLISHERS, be sufficient to render its publication profitable, then, upon written notice by said PUBLISHERS to said AUTHOR, this contract shall cease and determine; and thereupon said AUTHOR shall have the right, at* **his** *option, to take from said PUBLISHERS, at cost, whatever copies of said work they may then have on hand; or, failing to take said copies at cost, then said PUBLISHERS shall have the right to dispose of the copies on hand as they may see fit, free from any percentage or royalty, and to cancel this contract.*

Provided, also, that if, at any time during the continuance of this agreement, said work shall become unsalable in the ordinary channels of trade, said PUBLISHERS shall have the right to dispose of any copies on hand, paying to said AUTHOR **fifteen (15)** *per cent. of the net amount received therefor, in lieu of the percentage hereinbefore prescribed.*

In consideration of the mutuality of this contract, the aforesaid parties agree to all its provisions, and in testimony thereof affix their signatures and seals.

Witness to signature of
F. Scott Fitzgerald

Witness to signature of
Charles Scribner's Sons

{ L. S. }

Page 2 of contract for *GG*

Memorandum of Agreement, *made this* eighth *day of* February 1934

between F. SCOTT FITZGERALD

of Baltimore, Maryland, - - - - *hereinafter called "the* AUTHOR," *and* CHARLES SCRIBNER'S SONS, *of New York City, N. Y., hereinafter called "the* PUBLISHERS." *Said* - - F. Scott Fitzgerald - - *being the* AUTHOR *and* PROPRIETOR *of a work entitled:*

TENDER IS THE NIGHT

in consideration of the covenants and stipulations hereinafter contained, and agreed to be performed by the PUBLISHERS, *grants and guarantees to said* PUBLISHERS *and their successors the exclusive right to publish the said work in all forms during the terms of copyright and renewals thereof, hereby covenanting with said* PUBLISHERS *that he is the sole* AUTHOR *and* PROPRIETOR *of said work.*

Said AUTHOR *hereby authorizes said* PUBLISHERS *to take out the copyright on said work, and further guarantees to said* PUBLISHERS *that the said work is in no way whatever a violation of any copyright belonging to any other party, and that it contains nothing of a scandalous or libelous character; and that* he *and* his *legal representatives shall and will hold harmless the said* PUBLISHERS *from all suits, and all manner of claims and proceedings which may be taken on the ground that said work is such violation or contains anything scandalous or libelous; and* he *further hereby authorizes said* PUBLISHERS *to defend at law any and all suits and proceedings which may be taken or had against them for infringement of any other copyright or for libel, scandal, or any other injurious or hurtful matter or thing contained in or alleged or claimed to be contained in or caused by said work, and pay to said* PUBLISHERS *such reasonable costs, disbursements, expenses, and counsel fees as they may incur in such defense.*

Said PUBLISHERS, *in consideration of the right herein granted and of the guarantees aforesaid, agree to publish said work at their own expense, in such style and manner as they shall deem most expedient, and to pay said* AUTHOR, *or* - his - *legal representatives,* FIFTEEN (15) ------------------- *per cent. on their Trade-List (retail) price, cloth style, for* the first twenty thousand (20,000) copies of said work sold by them in the United States, SEVENTEEN & ONE-HALF (17½) per cent.for all copies sold thereafter up to forty thousand (40,000),and TWENTY(20)per cent.for all copies sold beyond forty thousand.

Provided, nevertheless, that one-half the above named royalty shall be paid on all copies sold outside the United States; and provided that no percentage whatever shall be paid on any copies destroyed by fire or water, or sold at or below cost, or given away for the purpose of aiding the sale of said work.

It is further agreed that the profits arising from any publication of said work, during the period covered by this agreement, in other than book form shall be divided equally between said PUBLISHERS *and said* AUTHOR.

Page 1 of contract for *TITN*

Expenses incurred for alterations in type or plates, exceeding twenty per cent. of the cost of composition and electrotyping said work, are to be charged to the AUTHOR'S account.

The first statement shall not be rendered until six months after date of publication; and thereafter statements shall be rendered semi-annually, on the AUTHOR'S application therefor, in the months of February and August, settlements to be made in cash, four months after date of statement.

If, on the expiration of **five** *years from date of publication, or at any time thereafter, the demand for said work should not, in the opinion of said PUBLISHERS, be sufficient to render its publication profitable, then, upon written notice by said PUBLISHERS to said AUTHOR, this contract shall cease and determine; and thereupon said AUTHOR shall have the right, at* **his** *option, to take from said PUBLISHERS, at cost, whatever copies of said work they may then have on hand; or, failing to take said copies at cost, then said PUBLISHERS shall have the right to dispose of the copies on hand as they may see fit, free from any percentage or royalty, and to cancel this contract.*

Provided, also, that if, at any time during the continuance of this agreement, said work shall become unsalable in the ordinary channels of trade, said PUBLISHERS shall have the right to dispose of any copies on hand paying to said AUTHOR **twenty (20)** *per cent. of the net amount received therefor, in lieu of the percentage hereinbefore prescribed.*

Said Publishers shall pay to said Author the sum of Sixty-six Hundred Dollars ($6,600.00), the receipt of which is hereby acknowledged, as an advance payment on royalty account, said amount to be reimbursed to said Publishers from the first moneys accruing under said royalties.

~~All moneys due under this contract shall be paid to Harold Ober, 40 East 49th Street, New York City, as representative of said author, and his receipt shall be a valid discharge for all said moneys.~~

In consideration of the mutuality of this contract, the aforesaid parties agree to all its provisions, and in testimony thereof affix their signatures and seals.

Witness to signature of
F.Scott Fitzgerald

Witness to signature of
Charles Scribner's Sons

Page 2 of contract for *TITN*

Appendix 10

Principal Works About Fitzgerald

Bruccoli, Matthew J. *The Composition of Tender is the Night.* Pittsburgh: University of Pittsburgh Press, 1963.

————. *F. Scott Fitzgerald Collector's Handlist.* Columbus, Ohio: Fitzgerald Newsletter, 1964.

————. *Checklist of F. Scott Fitzgerald.* Columbus, Ohio: Merrill, 1970.

————, ed. *Profile of F. Scott Fitzgerald.* Columbus, Ohio: Merrill, 1971. Collection.

Bryer, Jackson R. *The Critical Reputation of F. Scott Fitzgerald.* Hamden, Conn.: Archon, 1967.

Callaghan, Morley. *That Summer in Paris.* New York: Coward-McCann, 1963.

Cowley, Malcolm and Robert, eds. *Fitzgerald and the Jazz Age.* New York: Scribners, 1966. Collection.

Cross, K. G. W. *Scott Fitzgerald.* Edinburgh and London: Oliver & Boyd, 1964; New York: Barnes & Noble, 1966.

Eble, Kenneth. *F. Scott Fitzgerald.* New York: Twayne, 1963.

Fitzgerald/Hemingway Annual. Edited by Matthew J. Bruccoli and C. E. Frazer Clark, Jr. Washington: NCR Microcard Editions, 1969–.

Fitzgerald Newsletter (1958–1968). Edited by Matthew J. Bruccoli. Washington: NCR Microcard Editions, 1969.

Goldhurst, William. *F. Scott Fitzgerald and His Contemporaries.* Cleveland and New York: World, 1963.

Graham, Sheilah. *College of One.* New York: Viking, 1967.

————. *The Rest of the Story.* New York: Coward-McCann, 1964.

Graham, Sheilah, and Frank Gerold. *Beloved Infidel.* New York: Holt, Rinehart & Winston, 1958.

Hemingway, Ernest. *A Moveable Feast.* New York: Scribners, 1964.

Higgins, John A. *F. Scott Fitzgerald: A Study of the Stories.* Jamaica, N.Y.: St. John's University Press, 1971.

Hindus, Milton. *F. Scott Fitzgerald: An Introduction and Interpretation.* New York: Holt, Rinehart & Winston, 1968.

Hoffman, Frederick J., ed. *The Great Gatsby: A Study.* New York: Scribners, 1962. Collection.

Kazin, Alfred, ed. *F. Scott Fitzgerald: The Man and His Work.* Cleveland and New York: World, 1951. Collection.

La Hood, Marvin J., ed. *Tender is the Night: Essays in Criticism.* Bloomington: Indiana University Press, 1969. Collection.

Latham, John Aaron. *Crazy Sundays: F. Scott Fitzgerald in Hollywood.* New York: Viking, 1971.

Lehan, Richard D. *F. Scott Fitzgerald and the Craft of Fiction.* Carbondale: Southern Illinois University Press, 1966.

Lockridge, Ernest, ed. *Twentieth Century Interpretations of The Great Gatsby.* Englewood Cliffs, N.J.: Prentice-Hall, 1968. Collection.

Mayfield, Sara. *Exiles from Paradise.* New York: Delacorte Press, 1971.

Milford, Nancy. *Zelda.* New York: Harper and Row, 1970.

Miller, James E., Jr. *The Fictional Technique of F. Scott Fitzgerald.* The Hague: Nijhoff, 1957. Enlarged edition: *F. Scott Fitzgerald: His Art and His Technique.* New York: New York University Press, 1964.

Mizener, Arthur. *The Far Side of Paradise.* Boston: Houghton Mifflin, 1951. Revised edition, 1965.

———. *F. Scott Fitzgerald: A Collection of Critical Essays.* Englewood Cliffs, N.J.: Prentice-Hall, 1963. Collection.

Moseley, Edwin M. *F. Scott Fitzgerald—A Critical Essay.* Grand Rapids, Mich.: Eerdmans, 1967.

Perosa, Sergio. *The Art of F. Scott Fitzgerald.* Ann Arbor: University of Michigan Press, 1965.

Piper, Henry Dan, ed. *Fitzgerald's The Great Gatsby: The Novel, The Critics, The Background.* New York: Scribners, 1970. Collection.

———. "F. Scott Fitzgerald: A Check List," *The Princeton University Library Chronicle,* XII (Summer 1951), 196–208.

———. *F. Scott Fitzgerald: A Critical Portrait.* New York: Holt, Rinehart & Winston, 1965.

———. "Scott Fitzgerald's Prep-School Writings," *The Princeton University Library Chronicle,* XVII (Autumn 1955), 1–10.

———. "Zelda Sayre Fitzgerald: A Check List," *The Princeton University Library Chronicle,* XII (Summer 1951), 209–210.

Shain, Charles E. *F. Scott Fitzgerald.* Minneapolis: University of Minnesota Press, 1961.

Sklar, Robert. *F. Scott Fitzgerald: The Last Laocoön.* New York: Oxford University Press, 1967.

Stern, Milton R. *The Golden Moment: The Novels of F. Scott Fitzgerald.* Urbana: University of Illinois Press, 1970.

Turnbull, Andrew. *Scott Fitzgerald.* New York: Scribners, 1962.

Index

343

DATE DUE			
GAYLORD			PRINTED IN U.S.A